MICHIGAN'S WAR

T0307873

THE CIVIL WAR IN THE GREAT INTERIOR

Series Editors
Martin J. Hershock and Christine Dee

The Civil War in the Great Interior is a series of short documentary histories on the Civil War in the midwestern states. Each volume presents fresh primary sources that will aid professors and students, as well as the informed general reader, in exploring the social, political, and military impact of the Civil War.

Ohio's War: The Civil War in Documents, edited by Christine Dee
Missouri's War: The Civil War in Documents, edited by Silvana R. Siddali
Indiana's War: The Civil War in Documents, edited by Richard F. Nation and Stephen E. Towne
Kansas's War: The Civil War in Documents, edited by Pearl T. Ponce
Illinois's War: The Civil War in Documents, edited by Mark Hubbard
Michigan's War: The Civil War in Documents, edited by John W. Quist

FORTHCOMING:

Wisconsin's War: The Civil War in Documents, edited by Chandra Manning

MICHIGAN'S WAR

The Civil War in Documents

~

EDITED BY JOHN W. QUIST

Ohio University Press

Athens

Ohio University Press, Athens, Ohio 45701
ohioswallow.com
© 2019 by Ohio University Press
All rights reserved

Cover illustration: Annie Etheridge (Lorinda Anna Blair Etheridge).
Source: L. P. Brockett and Mary C. Bellows, *Woman's Work in the Civil War: A Record
of Heroism, Patriotism and Patience* (Philadelphia: Zeigler, McCurdy, 1867), 747

Printed in the United States of America
Ohio University Press books are printed on acid-free paper ∞ ™

29 28 27 26 25 24 23 22 21 20 19   5 4 3 2 1

Library of Congress Cataloging-in-Publication Data
Names: Quist, John W., 1960- author.
Title: Michigan's War : The Civil War in Documents / John W. Quist.
Description: Athens, Ohio : Ohio University Press, 2018. | Series: Civil War
in the Great Interior | Includes bibliographical references and index.
Identifiers: LCCN 2018025985 | ISBN 9780821423127 (paperback) | ISBN
9780821446287 (pdf)
Subjects: LCSH: Michigan--History--Civil War, 1861-1865. |
Michigan--History--Civil War, 1861-1865--Sources. | BISAC: HISTORY /
United States / Civil War Period (1850-1877). | HISTORY / United States /
State & Local / Midwest (IA, IL, IN, KS, MI, MN, MO, ND, NE, OH, SD, WI).
Classification: LCC F566 .Q85 2018 | DDC 977.4/03--dc23
LC record available at https://lccn.loc.gov/2018025985

For Johanna and Arbor (aka Lauren)

Contents

One

Michigan, Slavery, and the Coming of the Civil War   5

Two

The Secession Crisis   26

Three

Shifting Michigan to a War Footing 38

Four

The Soldier's Life 52

Five

Conscription, Commutation, and Dissent   84

Six

Civilians Confront the War   97

Seven

Michigan's Wartime Politics   122

Eight

The Civil War Changes Michiganians' Relationship to Slavery 143

Nine

The Civil War's End and Reconstruction 160

Illustrations

Series Editors' Preface

The Civil War in the Great Interior series focuses on the Middle West, as the complex region has come to be known, during the most critical era of American history. In his Annual Message to Congress in December 1862, Abraham Lincoln identified "the great interior region" as the area between the Alleghenies and the Rocky Mountains, south of Canada and north of the "culture of cotton." Lincoln included in this region the states of Ohio, Indiana, Michigan, Wisconsin, Illinois, Missouri, Kansas, Iowa, Minnesota, and Kentucky; the area that would become West Virginia; and parts of Tennessee and the Dakota, Nebraska, and Colorado territories. This area, Lincoln maintained, was critical to the "great body of the republic" not only because it bound together the North, South, and West but also because its people would not assent to the division of the Union.

This series examines what was, to Lincoln and other Americans in the mid-nineteenth century, the most powerful, influential, and critical area of the country. It considers how the people of the Middle West experienced the Civil War and the role they played in preserving and redefining the nation. These collections of historical sources—many of which have never been published—explore significant issues raised by the sectional conflict, the Civil War, and Reconstruction. The series underscores what was unique to particular states and their residents while recognizing the values and experiences that individuals in the Middle West shared with other Northerners and, in some cases, with Southerners.

Within these volumes are the voices of a diverse cross-section of nineteenth-century Americans. These include African Americans, European immigrants, Native Americans, and women. Editors have gathered evidence from farms and factories, rural and urban areas, and communities throughout each state to examine the relationships of individuals, their communities, the political culture, and events on the battlefields. The volumes present readers with layers of evidence that can be combined in a multitude of patterns to yield new conclusions and raise questions about prevailing interpretations of the past.

The editor of each volume provides a narrative framework through brief chapter introductions and background information for each document, as well as a timeline. As these volumes cannot address all aspects of the Civil War experience for each state, they include selected bibliographies to guide readers in further research. Documents were chosen for what they reveal about the past, but each also speaks to the subjective nature of history and the decisions that historians face when weighing the merits and limits of each piece of evidence they uncover. The diverse documents included in these volumes also expose readers to the craft of history and to the variety of source materials historians utilize as they explore the past.

Much of the material in these works will raise questions, spark debates, and generate discussion. Whether read with an eye toward the history of the Union war effort, a particular state or region, or the Civil War's implications for race, class, and gender in America, the volumes in The Civil War in the Great Interior help us consider—and reconsider—the evidence from the past.

Martin J. Hershock
Christine Dee

Preface

The military contest commonly known as the American Civil War lasted four years. Historians view this war as part of a broader nineteenth-century sectional conflict between nonslave states and slave states—states often rendered geographically as the North and the South. This lengthy struggle involved the Civil War's context, coming, consequences, and attempted resolution—an epoch historians often term the Civil War Era. While many people are familiar with the broad narrative of these years, many contemporaries knew this period from the perspective of their state and community. *Michigan's War* tells how residents of the Wolverine State confronted the Civil War Era—a time characterized both by national conflict and by conflict within Michigan. Despite Michigan's relatively small and largely white population, state residents, during these years, never spoke with one voice.

Conflict defined Michigan's politics from its territorial beginnings. Notwithstanding the strong majorities that the territory, and later state, displayed for Democrats in the decades preceding 1854, Antimasons, and after 1834, Whigs, combated Democrats on economic development and morality's role in politics. During the 1850s, prohibitionists won a series of political victories that temporarily halted the sale of liquor in Michigan. Prohibition often overlapped with nativism, both being fueled by Protestants fearful of immigrants who were mostly Catholic. Detroit, Michigan's largest city and the state's first capital, often found itself at odds with an otherwise rural state and lost its capital status to an unsettled township in 1847. And conflict over the role of railroads in Michigan remained a contentious issue before and after the Civil War.[1]

Slavery and race proved to be especially divisive. Michigan's small yet significant African American population stood resolutely against slavery and racial discrimination even as law and custom restricted African Americans' access to the public sphere. Abolitionists, both white and black, were always a minority in Michigan and elsewhere across the antebellum North. Their small numbers notwithstanding, abolitionists aroused Michiganians' deep misgivings regarding slavery. Few white Michiganians thought slavery to be good, but most could not agree why it was bad. Some thought slavery the most immoral institution created by humans—the "sum of all villainies," as John Wesley and some abolitionists put it.[2] Others agreed that slavery was wrong, but retorted that abolitionists' emphasizing slavery's immorality only served to threaten the national Union, the disruption of which, this group believed, would be far worse than the immoralities stemming from slavery. Large segments saw slavery either as economically inefficient or as a threat to white wage laborers, or both. Another faction believed slave owners' political and economic power undermined representative government. And many white Michiganians nodded their heads at all these points and ultimately regarded slavery as somebody else's problem.

Upon its formation in Michigan in 1854, the Republican Party succeeded in bringing together many who opposed slavery regardless of their reasons, as well as others who ranked slavery as a low political priority. Republicans also adopted much of the Whigs' economic agenda, and for decades thereafter commanded the support of a significant, if not overwhelming, majority of the state's voters. Following its creation, nearly half of Michigan's voters rejected the Republican Party by voting Democratic, with many Democrats hopeful that the new party would implode and that Democrats would again control the state.

After Confederate forces fired on Fort Sumter in April 1861, the divisiveness that had defined the state since its beginning temporarily disappeared as people in both parties joined to preserve the Union and to wage war on the Confederacy. In the end, slavery proved decisive in ending that temporary unity. When Republicans advanced emancipation as a necessary war objective, or simply embraced it because they had long desired slavery's end, most Democrats balked, even as they continued to support national reunification. Although the ensuing conflict in Michigan over the Civil War's conduct—exacerbated by conscription and the hardships wrought by a protracted military struggle—was a far cry from war itself, some wondered whether the state's tensions might overwhelm the war against the Confederacy. The Civil War's conclusion failed to resolve Michiganians' divided mindset as residents continued to contest Reconstruction, racial equality, and the war's meaning.

Michigan's War narrates this broader story through voices of the Wolverine State's women and men. Many of these documents are unpublished or otherwise obscure, but all have an editorial introduction that provides context to each document. In preparing these documents for this volume, I have aimed to retain as many features of the contemporary vernacular as practical while also making them accessible to the modern reader. At the same time, modern readers often find the vernacular of nineteenth-century Americans excessively verbose. With this in mind I have eliminated some passages from the documents—eliminations identified with ellipses—without changing the original author's intent. I often identified obvious misspellings with [*sic*], while in other instances I have silently modernized spelling, corrected obvious typographical errors, and added commas and other punctuation for clarity. In many documents I have inserted additional words within brackets to make the documents more easily understood. Typesetting emphases, such as italics and words spelled entirely with capital letters, appear as they did in the original documents.

Acknowledgments

Longer ago than we would care to acknowledge, Martin Hershock and Christine Dee asked to me to write for their series, The Civil War in the Great Interior. My thanks go to Marty and to Chris for their encouragement, their valuable suggestions, and their patience. Gillian Berchowitz, the director at Ohio University Press, kindly offered support along the way and maintained a strong interest in the series and in *Michigan's War*. Nancy Basmajian, the Press's managing editor, used her impressive eye for detail to copyedit and greatly improve the manuscript. Others at Ohio University Press—Beth Pratt, Samara Rafert, and Sally Welch—shepherded this volume through production, and I owe them gratitude for their fine work. Brian Edward Balsley, GISP, expertly designed and drew the book's map.

Numerous librarians and archivists have provided assistance along the way and made it easier for me to track down sources. They include the staffs at the Archives and Regional History Collections, Western Michigan University; the Burton Historical Collection, Detroit Public Library; the Clarke Historical Library, Central Michigan University; the Library of Michigan in Lansing; the Huntington Library, San Marino, California; and the Special Collections Library, University of California, Santa Barbara. I am especially grateful to Diane Kalathas, who so capably directed Shippensburg University's Interlibrary Loan.

One of the great pleasures of working on *Michigan's War* is the opportunity it afforded me to work at the University of Michigan's Bentley Historical Library, which holds the Michigan Historical Collections. My thanks to everyone at the Bentley—especially its former director, Francis X. Blouin; its current director, Terrence McDonald; and especially to Bill Wallach, who directed the Mark C. Stevens Researcher Travel Fellowship that the Bentley Library awarded me.

I remain appreciative of Shippensburg University History / Philosophy Department and its graduate assistants—Ashley Abruzzo, Jamie Bollinger, Janetmarie Bowen, Charles Evans, Michael Fauser, Ashley Sewell, and Alan Schulze—who patiently transcribed documents from original, and sometimes nearly illegible, sources. James H. Mike, Dean of the College of Arts and Sciences, generously funded the creation of the book's map.

My thanks also go to numerous friends and colleagues who asked how this project was progressing. Mark and Linda Johnson subsidized this volume by kindly allowing me to stay with them during several research trips and always made those trips more enjoyable. I am especially grateful to Anne for tolerating me as I while away my life studying history.

Introduction

*W*HEN THE CIVIL WAR began in 1861, Michigan had been a state for less than a quarter century. The frontier was still either a recent memory or a current reality for much of the state's white, black, and native population. The preceding year's census enumerated 749,113 residents, ranking Michigan sixteenth among the Union's thirty-four states. Nine-tenths of the state's population lay within the southern four tiers of counties. Detroit, with 45,619 residents, ranked only nineteenth among American cities. Michigan's next-largest cities in 1860—Grand Rapids, Adrian, Kalamazoo, and Ann Arbor—had only between 5,000 and 8,000 residents apiece, marking them more as towns than cities by modern standards. The region north of Saginaw remained largely isolated (particularly during the winter after the Great Lakes froze), unsettled, and defined by forests, lakes, and the Upper Peninsula's copper and iron mines. The 1860 federal census reported eleven of the state's seventy-three counties as being unpopulated (though in many cases populated by indigenous peoples) and another thirteen counties as having fewer than one thousand residents (see map). Given the frontier conditions throughout much of the state, it should come as no surprise that American Indians constituted almost 2 percent of the state's population, the highest proportion of any state east of the Mississippi River.[1]

Completion of the Erie Canal in 1825 connected Michigan to the Northeastern United States and broader Atlantic world and fueled Michigan's settlement, bringing statehood in 1837. During the thirty years following 1820, Michigan's population grew almost forty-five-fold, and it nearly doubled again in the decade following 1850. Even with this growth, in 1860 Michigan had the smallest population of any state contained entirely within the Northwest Territory, including Wisconsin, which became a state in 1848, eleven years after Michigan. Michigan's small urban population underlined the state's dominant rural character. In 1860, 84.2 percent of Michigan's population lived in the countryside or in towns with fewer than 2,500 residents, making Michigan's population more rural than both the national and the free-state figures.[2] And although railroad mileage more than doubled in Michigan during the 1850s, it grew at a slower rate than in any other state in the Old Northwest and at half the national rate. Railroad mileage in Michigan also grew at a slower rate during the 1850s than in all but two states of the future Confederacy—and six future Confederate states had more railroad mileage in 1860 than did Michigan.[3] Michigan's concentration of population and economic activity in its four southern tiers of counties made the state smaller, in many ways, than its geographic size might have suggested.

As in most of the United States during the mid-nineteenth century, agriculture defined Michigan's economy, and those employed in agriculture constituted the majority of the state's workforce. While some Michiganians farmed at the subsistence level, many farmers specialized their production and sold their crops—chiefly wheat, corn, and oats—or their animal products, primarily butter, cheese, and wool. The cash value of Michigan's farmland, farm equipment, and livestock exceeded the capital invested in manufacturing by a factor of eight. The state's modest manufacturing sector was largely extractive or connected to agriculture, with half of the state's manufactured products' value coming from flour or lumber mills and another eighth drawn from iron and copper mining.

Michigan's initial white settlers overwhelmingly came from the northeastern United States, being either New Englanders or New Yorkers—with most of the New Yorkers being a generation removed from New England.[4] Not many white southerners settled as far north as Michigan, and consequently few of the state's white residents had observed slavery or had family or financial ties to the peculiar institution. Nonetheless, slavery loomed large in the early years of the territory and state, even though there were few slaves in Michigan. In 1787 the Confederation Congress passed the Northwest Ordinance—a law that claimed federal authority over those lands then held by the United States that lay west of Pennsylvania and north of the Ohio River. Article VI of the Ordinance provided, "There shall be neither slavery nor involuntary servitude in the said territory, otherwise than in the punishment of crimes whereof the party shall have been duly convicted."

Despite this language's clarity, small numbers of slaves resided in Michigan and throughout the Old Northwest for several decades thereafter, as courts and legislatures bestowed exceptions for slaves who lived in the region when the law was passed, permitted the migration of African American "indentured servants" into their states or territories, or granted temporary residence to enslaved visitors. When the British finally vacated their forts in the Old Northwest following the Jay Treaty of 1796, British citizens who remained in Michigan continued to hold slaves.[5] The 1810 US census listed twenty-four slaves in a territorial population of 4,762; by 1830, only one slave still lived within the boundaries of what became the state of Michigan in 1837. Michigan's 1835 Constitution unconditionally ended slavery when Article XI incorporated language taken from the Northwest Ordinance's slavery prohibition.[6]

Only 6,799 African Americans lived in Michigan in 1860—less than 1 percent of the state's population. As in other states across the antebellum North, however, blacks in Michigan confronted widespread racial discrimination and inequality. Generally, black men could neither serve on juries nor vote; in a statewide referendum in 1850, only 28.5 percent of Michigan voters supported black-male suffrage. And whenever activists demanded that blacks' suffrage rights be recognized, opponents of black suffrage, who were generally Democrats, heaped racially charged ridicule on the idea.[7] Besides being denied the full rights of citizenship, Michigan's African Americans generally held low-skill jobs and were disproportionately poor.[8]

Within the larger Atlantic world, organized opposition to slavery emerged in the eighteenth century, propelled by ideals from the European Enlightenment and the American, French, and Haitian revolutions. African Americans had long mobilized against slavery, but the growth of antebellum revivalism increasingly led some white Northerners to embrace immediatist abolitionism. Abolitionists hoped to end slavery by launching a moral revolution. They placed the ending of slavery at the top of their moral and political agenda, joined abolitionist societies, formed churches that deemed slavery a sin, and voted for abolitionist political parties. Abolitionists differed from those who thought slavery to be wrong but believed that Northerners should nonetheless respect the property rights of Southern slaveholders.

Abolitionist activity in Michigan commenced among Lenawee County Hicksite Quakers, led by Elizabeth Chandler, in 1832, and in 1836 abolitionists convened in Ann Arbor to form the Michigan State Anti-Slavery Society. Throughout the 1830s Michigan abolitionists generally aligned with the American Anti-Slavery Society. After 1840, most Michigan abolitionists, male and female, embraced electoral politics and eventually sided with the Liberty Party and its female auxiliaries. The Liberty Party captured almost 8 percent of statewide ballots in 1845, a figure that made Michigan the state with the strongest Liberty Party—and abolitionist—support outside of New England.[9] And beyond the Liberty Party, whose members regarded the ending of slavery as their primary political and moral objective, many of Michigan's Whigs and Democrats held a deeper antipathy to slavery than did their counterparts in other Northern states. Yet whatever misgivings white Michiganians felt toward slavery before the Civil War, most placed a higher value on maintaining a strong federal union. Nonetheless, slavery's shadow grew during the increasingly sectionalized politics that preceded the war, and further increased during the war itself.

Michigan Counties, 1860, by population. Sources: 1860 County boundaries based on *Johnson's new illustrated (steel plate) family atlas, with descriptions, geographical, statistical, and historical* (New York: Johnson and Ward, 1862), image 43. County population figures taken from *Population of the United States in 1860; Compiled from the Original Returns of the Eighth Census* (Washington, DC: Government Printing Office, 1864), 236. Map by Brian Edward Balsley, GISP.

ONE

~

Michigan, Slavery, and the
Coming of the Civil War

$\mathcal{T}$HROUGHOUT THE 1830S and 1840s, politics in Michigan, and in the rest of the country, focused mostly on economic issues—protective tariffs, government aid to transportation projects, and banking—and, in the North, on ethnic and cultural issues that divided white Americans. Nationwide, the Whigs and Democrats were evenly balanced, with the parties alternating control of the US presidency between the mid-1830s and the mid-1850s. But aside from victories Michigan Whigs enjoyed in 1839 and 1840, Democrats dominated state politics before 1854. The abolitionist Liberty Party contributed to the Democrats' domination of the state because most Liberty voters came from the ranks of the Whigs. Undaunted, by the mid-1840s the Whigs tried to win back Liberty defectors by speaking more harshly against slavery.

Michigan's Democrats did not regard themselves as favoring slavery or as belonging to a proslavery party. They believed, however, that a strong federal union, even one that included slaveholders, should be the nation's political bedrock. And because state Democrats belonged to a national party that depended on slaveholders for its political success, Democrats often attacked slaveholders' Northern adversaries and minimized the moral shortcomings of slavery. Additionally, many Democrats disliked the moral reform impulse that characterized abolitionists and many Whigs.

In 1844, Michigan Whigs made a frantic attempt to convince Liberty voters that Henry Clay's election as president would keep Texas from being annexed and thus prevent the expansion of slave territory. Clay's loss, and Democrat James K. Polk's victory, in 1844 ultimately led to annexation of Texas, war with Mexico, and a fervent debate over the status of slavery in lands that the United States would acquire from Mexico.

Many Michigan Whigs joined with the Liberty Party in opposing the Mexican-American War, and even more Whigs opposed the expansion of slavery into territory acquired from Mexico. While most Northern Democrats strongly supported the war with Mexico and territorial expansion generally, slavery proved to be a divisive issue for Northern Democrats as well. Within weeks of the US Congress declaring war on Mexico on May 13, 1846, David Wilmot, a Pennsylvania Democrat in the US House of Representatives, introduced an amendment to a bill that would have provided for the prohibition of slavery in any territory acquired from Mexico. Although the Senate never passed the Wilmot Proviso, the status of slavery in the federal territories, an issue that most Americans believed to have been settled by the Missouri Compromise of 1820, became a divisive matter that, in a number of ways, occupied Americans' attention until the Civil War.

Once the Mexican-American War started, many Northern Democrats worried that they would lose votes to the Whigs unless they opposed the expansion of slavery. At the same time, Northern Democrats also wanted to maintain their strong ties with the Southern wing of their party and to embrace a position on slave-state expansion that would unite all Democrats. (The national Whig Party, in contrast, avoided taking a stance on slave expansion.) The Democratic Party built its consensus on nonintervention, popularized by Senator Lewis Cass of Michigan in his 1848 presidential campaign and later called popular sovereignty by Senator Stephen A. Douglas of Illinois in 1854. Cass regarded "merely sectional" questions, such as whether slavery should exist in federal territories, as threatening the continued existence of the Union. Arguing that white inhabitants of federal territories should "regulate their internal concerns in their own way," Cass held that Congress should surrender its constitutional power to govern federal territories and allow the white residents there to do it themselves.

Cass's position united the national Democratic Party for a few years. Believing slavery to be immoral and inefficient, however, caused some Northern Democrats, including US Representative Kinsley Bingham of Michigan, to differ with Cass and their party's orthodoxy from the start. (At the same time, some Southern Democrats had misgivings about nonintervention because it failed to recognize the right to own human property in federal territory.) Some of these Northern Democrats remained within their party, but considerable numbers joined with antislavery Whigs and most Libertyites to form the Free Soil Party (later called the Free Democratic Party) in 1848. The Free Soil Party insisted that all federal territory be closed to slavery and as the party's state convention declared in 1848, "free labor and slave labor cannot exist upon the same soil."[1]

But when Stephen Douglas introduced the Kansas-Nebraska Bill in January 1854, which became law in May, the national Democratic consensus on slavery fragmented. In organizing the Kansas and Nebraska Territories, Douglas provided that these lands, from which slavery had previously been excluded through the Missouri Compromise, would now be open to slavery. In response to the passage of this bill, Whigs, Free Democrats, and antislavery Democrats joined together in several Northern states to form the Republican Party, a party that recognized the rights of states to regulate slavery however they wished but one that steadfastly opposed slavery in any federally owned lands. The party's foundation rested on its success in arguing, as the Free Soil Party did before, that the Northern system of "free labor" offered ordinary workers economic opportunities that Southern slave labor denied them. Republicans further argued that the federal territories represented their country's future and that those territories would be effectively closed to Northern workers if Congress permitted slavery to expand there. In July 1854, the first Republican Party state convention met in Jackson, Michigan. By 1856 conflict over slavery in the Kansas Territory resulted in Republican parties forming in states across the North. And by this time Michiganians' opposition to slavery in the federal territories led one Democratic editor to declare—disingenuously— "the Democratic party is no more in favor of slavery or slave extension than is the Republican party."[2]

Because the Liberty Party rank and file generally aligned themselves with the Free Soilers and the Republicans, the 1850s witnessed something of an anomaly: as slavery opposition grew stronger, abolitionism, as a movement separate from the major political parties, grew weaker. By the late 1850s, the only organized abolitionists in Michigan were the Garrisonians, who formed the small Michigan Anti-Slavery Society in 1853, and a remnant of the Liberty Party, also known as the Liberty League and later as the Radical Abolition Party.[3] Nonetheless, Michigan's Republicans attempted to undermine slavery where they could; their successes included the state legislature's passage of a personal liberty law in 1855 and an 1859 law that prohibited slaveholders from bringing slaves into Michigan.[4] And unless goaded by the Democrats, Michigan's Republicans also generally avoided the blatant expressions of white racism that their political opponents commonly expressed.

HENRY BIBB WRITES FROM DETROIT TO HIS FORMER OWNER IN KENTUCKY

Born as a slave in Kentucky, Henry Bibb first escaped from slavery in 1837 by crossing the Ohio River to Indiana. After traveling to Detroit, Bibb returned to Kentucky to retrieve his wife and daughter with the goal of escaping with them to Canada. Following his capture and reenslavement, Bibb and his family were sold and transported to Louisiana. There, Bibb lost contact with his family when his new owner sold him but refused to sell his wife and daughter. After escaping, again, from slavery, Bibb reached Detroit, where he became active in the state's abolitionist movement. In May 1844, Bibb began telling Michigan audiences about his former life as a slave; in 1845, Michigan's abolitionist Liberty Party employed Bibb as an itinerant lecturer. Thereafter Bibb spoke before more Michigan audiences than any other former slave. Bibb left Michigan in 1846 and eventually immigrated to Canada, where he edited the first Afro-Canadian newspaper, the Voice of the Fugitive, *in Sandwich, Canada West (now Ontario).*

In this excerpt from his memoir, Bibb reproduces a letter he wrote to his former owner, revealing the nature of slavery and his reasons for escape.

The first direct information that I received concerning any of my relations, after my last escape from slavery, was communicated in a letter from Wm. H. Gatewood, my former owner. . . .

Never was I more surprised than at the reception of this letter, it came so unexpected to me. There had just been a State Convention held in Detroit, by the free people of color, the proceedings of which were published in pamphlet form. I forwarded several of them to distinguished slaveholders in Kentucky—one among others was Mr. Gatewood, and gave him to understand who sent it. After showing this letter to several of my anti-slavery friends, and asking their opinions about the propriety of my answering it, I was advised to do it, as Mr. Gatewood had no claim on me as a slave, for he had sold and got the money for me and my family. So I wrote him an answer, as near as I can recollect, in the following language:

DEAR SIR:—I am happy to inform you that you are not mistaken in the man whom you sold as property, and received pay for as such. But I thank God that I am not property now, but am regarded as a man like yourself, and although I live far north, I am enjoying a comfortable living by my own industry. If you should ever chance to be traveling this way, and will call on me, I will use you better than you did me while you held me as a slave. Think not that I have any malice against you, for the cruel treatment which you inflicted on me while I was in your power. As it was the custom of your country, to treat your fellow men as you did me and my little family, I can freely forgive you.

I wish to be remembered in love to my aged mother, and friends; please tell her that if we should never meet again in this life, my prayer shall be to God that we may meet in Heaven, where parting shall be no more.

You wish to be remembered to King and Jack [two former slaves from Kentucky]. I am pleased, sir, to inform you that they are both here, well, and doing well. They are both living in Canada West. They are now the owners of better farms than the men are who once owned them.

You may perhaps think hard of us for running away from slavery, but as to myself, I have but one apology to make for it, which is this: I have only to regret that I did not start at an earlier period. I might have been free long before I was. But you had it in your power to have kept me there much longer than you did. I think it is very probable that I should have been a toiling slave on your plantation to-day, if you had treated me differently.

To be compelled to stand by and see you whip and slash my wife without mercy, when I could afford her no protection, not even by offering myself to suffer the lash in her place, was more than I felt it to be the duty of a slave husband to endure, while the way was open to Canada. My infant child was also frequently flogged by Mrs. Gatewood, for crying, until its skin was bruised literally purple. This kind of treatment was what drove me from home and family, to seek a better home for them. But I am willing to forget the past. I should be pleased to hear from you again, on the reception of this, and should also be very happy to correspond with you often, if it should be agreeable to yourself. I subscribe myself a friend to the oppressed, and Liberty forever.

HENRY BIBB. . . .

Detroit, March 23d, 1844.

Narrative of the Life and Adventures of Henry Bibb, an American Slave (New York, 1849), 175–78.

Henry Bibb, 1815–1854. Source: *Narrative of the Life and Adventures of Henry Bibb, An American Slave,* Third Stereotype Edition (New York, 1849), frontispiece

NORTHERNERS ARE SLAVES TO THE SLAVEHOLDERS

Dedicated to ending slavery, the Liberty Party mostly polled in the low single digits across the North during its eight-year existence. While the overwhelming major- ity of religiously active Northerners saw no need to confront slavery, Liberty Party members often viewed their hostility to slavery as stemming from their religious faith, with many devoting their energies to having their churches declare slavery a sin. Michigan abolitionist Seymour B. Treadwell privately complained in 1841, though, that abolitionists focused too much on the immorality of slavery while neglecting the "political and financial power of slavery." He further argued that Americans "must be made to see clearly and forcibly that Slavery in all its bearings is not only immoral and outraging all their rights of human nature but that it is the OVERWHELMING political and financial power in the nation which has in truth already subverted AMERICAN LIBERTIES."[5] Two years later Ann Arbor resident George W. Jewett, speaking at a local meeting of the Liberty Party, expressed similar views.

Col. G. W. JEWETT having been called on, addressed the meeting at considerable length. He said he had always been a Democrat, and contended for the largest liberty of the largest number.—He had uniformly sustained the Democratic prin- ciples of our fathers through life, and expected to maintain them the remainder of his days. In this respect he was unchanged. But of late years he had received new light on the subject of slavery. He had ever abhorred it; but he had ascertained that the people of the North were in a sense slaves to the slaveholders. They were not, indeed, subject to the lash, but their purses were heavily drained, the honors and emoluments of office were largely monopolized by these few slaveholders, and our national policy controlled by them. Every thinking person could easily satisfy himself by a little reflection, that a slaveholding community, where only half the people are laborers, cannot support itself. But the slaveholders live, and live in the greatest splendor too, and it comes out of Northern laborers. They trade largely with the North, and every few years, by a Bankrupt act or otherwise, wipe out their indebtedness of two or three hundred millions.

Signal of Liberty (Ann Arbor), November 6, 1843.

LEWIS CASS FAVORS NONINTERVENTION IN THE TERRITORIES

Immediately after the United States declared war on Mexico in 1846, American politicians debated whether any territory seized from Mexico should be open to slav- ery. David Wilmot, a Democratic congressional representative from Pennsylvania, favored keeping slavery out of those territories. In 1846 and 1847, the majority of Northern senators and house members supported Wilmot's position, which came to be known as the Wilmot Proviso. While the US Constitution gives states considerable latitude in governing their affairs, Article IV, Section 3 of the Constitution gives Congress power to "make all needful Rules and Regulations respecting the Territory or other Property belonging to the United States."

Lewis Cass stood among those Northerners opposed to the Wilmot Proviso, and eventually many Northern Democrats embraced the Cass doctrine of nonintervention—one that fellow Northerner Stephen Douglas later called popular sovereignty. Michigan's preeminent antebellum politician, Cass served as territorial governor, US senator, and a cabinet officer in two presidential administrations. While seeking the 1848 Democratic presidential nomination, Cass explained to Alfred O. P. Nicholson of Tennessee his opposition to the Wilmot Proviso. Cass later secured the nomination but lost the 1848 election to Zachary Taylor.

The Wilmot Proviso has been before the country some time. It has been repeatedly discussed in congress, and by the public press. I am strongly impressed with the opinion . . . that the principle it involves should be kept out of the national legislature, and left to the people of the confederacy in their respective local governments. . . .

We may well regret the existence of slavery in southern states, and wish they had been saved from its introduction. But there it is, and not by the act of the present generation, and we must deal with it as a great practical question, involving the most momentous consequences. We have neither the right nor the power to touch it where it exists. . . .

The theory of our government presupposes, that its various members have reserved to themselves the regulation of all subjects relating to what may be termed their internal police. . . . Local institutions . . . whether they have reference to slavery or to any other relations, domestic or public, are left to local authority. . . . Congress has no right to say, that there shall be slavery in New York, or that there shall be no slavery in Georgia. . . .

[P]eople inhabiting [the territories should] regulate their internal concerns in their own way. They are just as capable of doing so, as the people of the states; and they can do so, at any rate, as soon as their political independence is recognized by admission into the union. . . . For, if the relation of master and servant may be regulated or annihilated by its legislation, so may the relation of husband and wife, of parent and child, and of any other condition which our institutions and the habits of our society recognize. . . .

Of all the questions that can agitate us, those which are merely sectional in their character, are the most dangerous and the most to be deprecated. . . . I am satisfied, from all I have seen and heard here, that a successful attempt to engraft the principles of the Wilmot proviso upon the legislation of this government, and to apply them to new territory, should new territory be acquired, would seriously affect our tranquility. . . .

Briefly, then, I am opposed to the exercise of any jurisdiction by congress over this matter; and I am in favor of leaving to the people of any territory, which may be hereafter acquired, the right to regulate it themselves, under the general principles of the constitution. . . .

I say this is the event of the extension of slavery over any new acquisition. But can it go there? This may well be doubted. All the descriptions which reach us of the condition of the Californias and of New Mexico . . . unite in representing those countries as . . . generally unfit for the production of the great staples, which can alone render slave labor valuable. . . . [T]he inhabitants of those regions, whether they depend upon their ploughs or their herds, cannot be slaveholders. . . .

The question, it will be therefore seen, on examination, does not regard the exclusion of slavery from a region where it now exists, but a prohibition against its introduction where it does not exist. . . .

The Wilmot proviso seeks to take from its legitimate tribunal a question of domestic policy, having no relation to the Union, as such, and to transfer it to another created by the subject matter involved in this issue. By going back to our true principles, we go back to the road of peace and safety. Leave to the people, who will be affected by this question, to adjust it upon their own responsibility, and in their own manner, and we shall render another tribute to the original principles of our government, and furnish another guaranty for its permanence and prosperity.

Lewis Cass to A. O. P. Nicholson, December 24, 1847, *Niles National Register* 73 (January 8, 1848): 293–94.

A DEMOCRAT OPPOSES LEWIS CASS ON SLAVERY

Lewis Cass's position on slavery in the federal territories became the Democratic Party's stance in 1848. Some Northern Democrats, however, opposed the Cass Doctrine, or popular sovereignty, as it was later called. Democrat Kinsley Bingham, a member of the US House of Representatives from Livingston County, supported Cass in 1848 but differed from his party on slavery in the territories. In this speech, delivered in Congress on August 7, 1848, Bingham embraced the Wilmot Proviso, argued for the economic advantages of the North's free labor system over Southern slavery, and implicitly demonstrated that the positions of the antislavery Free Soil Party extended beyond the membership of that party. Even though Bingham's speech ignores slavery's effects on the slaves themselves, his moderate antislavery stance still led the Democrats to oust him from their party in 1850. Bingham then joined the Free Soilers, and afterward the Republicans, who elected him the governor of Michigan in 1854.

I am anxious that my constituents should understand the reasons which will govern my action on the organization of Territories. . . .

Meantime the attention of the country was awakened to the subject, and the Legislatures of a large majority of the free States, my own among the number, gave utterance to the nearly unanimous sentiment of the people, by the passage of resolutions, calling upon Congress to *prohibit* the extension of slavery over territory to be acquired from Mexico where it had never existed. . . .

Shall the wise, beneficent, and human provisions of the ordinance of 1787 be extended over it, or shall it be doomed to the blighting influences of slavery?. . . .

The founders of the Republic, and the framers of the Constitution, spared no efforts to *prevent* the *increase* of slavery by importation, and its spread into territories which it had not yet reached. . . . [G]reat as the evil is acknowledged to be, disgraceful as would be the stigma which would attach to our Government were we to conquer and acquire *free* territory that slavery might be extended over it, we should yet hesitate, if the powers were not conferred upon us, and if we had not clearly the right to prohibit its introduction. . . .

Regarding slavery as a political evil; as a hinderance [*sic*] to the growth and prosperity of a State; as an element of weakness wherever it exists; as wholly incompatible with that degree of intelligence which makes labor either respectable or profitable,—I insist that we should fail to discharge our duty were we to tolerate its introduction and spread over this vast extent of country which has just come into our possession *free*. . . .

[A]side from the impolicy and injustice of permitting slavery to enter this new acquisition, an *equitable* division would seem to demand, that every inch of this new territory should be reserved for the emigrant and the free laborer. . . . [T]he iron heel of oppression has been crushing for centuries millions of our fellow men in Europe, of our own race and color. If we were to turn a listening ear to their prayer, we should hear them cry, "Save, oh! save this land for us and for our children." One after another, as the downtrodden race escapes from the exactions of their cruel taskmasters, they are fleeing to this land of promise, this asylum for the oppressed, as fast as the ships of the sea can bear them. This tremendous current of immigration *naturally* flows to the free States. . . .

[I]f the bitter fruits of experience have proved that slavery is an evil—are we not called upon, by all the prompting of duty and patriotism, to inhibit its introduction over the wide plains of California, so recently come into our possession, and whose destiny for ages and generations to come seems so dependent on our action?

Congressional Globe, 30th Congress, 1st sess., 1108–10 (1848).

MICHIGAN REPUBLICAN PLATFORM, 1854

Democrats overwhelmingly dominated Michigan politics from 1841 to 1854, largely because the Liberty and Free Soil Parties drew their ranks disproportionately from the Whigs. Whigs and Free Soilers attempted to join forces in the late 1840s and early 1850s, but none of these efforts resulted in a permanent coalition. The political dynamic changed, though, once Congress passed the Kansas-Nebraska Act in 1854, permitting slavery in federal territories where it had been previously prohibited. The anger toward this bill's passage, more pronounced in Michigan than in most other states, brought Michigan's Free Soilers and antislavery Whigs and Democrats together in Jackson, Michigan, on July 6, 1854. Their resolutions vigorously denounced slavery, embraced the economic advantages of "free labor" (as opposed to slave labor), adopted the name "Republican" for their new party, discounted old partisan divisions as being irrelevant to the crisis at hand, and called for a national convention to adopt "other more effectual measures" to resist slavery. Michigan Republicans took this platform—which barely and vaguely addressed the state's domestic affairs—to the voters and easily won control of the governorship and legislature. Two years later, at its first national convention in Philadelphia, the new party parroted one of the Jackson resolutions by calling slavery a "relic of barbarism." The Philadelphia delegates generally used tamer language, though, than Michigan Republicans did at their first state convention in Jackson. This 1854 platform also contributed to Michigan's reputation as a bastion of party radicals who favored an aggressive stand against the "slave power." Radicals also generally favored a stronger commitment to African Americans rights, even though this platform failed to address the topic.

The Freemen of Michigan, assembled in Convention in pursuance of a spontaneous call emanating from various parts of the state, to consider the measures which duty demands of us, as citizens of a free state to take, in reference to the late acts of Congress on the subject of Slavery and its anticipated further extension,

Resolved, That the institution of Slavery, except in punishment of crime, is a great moral, social and intellectual evil; that it was regarded by the Fathers of the Republic . . . who contemplated and intended its gradual and peaceful extinction, as an element hostile to the liberties for which they toiled. . . .

Resolved, That Slavery is a violation of the rights of man as a man; that the law of nature, which is a law of liberty, gives to no man, right[s] superior to those of another; that God and nature have secured to each individual this inalienable right of equality, any violation of which must be the result of superior force: and that slavery is therefore a perpetual war upon its victims. . . . [W]e find [slavery] to be like imprisonment for debt, but a relic of barbarism, as well as an element of weakness in the midst of the State, inviting the attacks of external enemies, and a ceaseless cause of internal apprehension and alarm. Such are the lessons taught us not only by the histories of other commonwealths, but by that of our own beloved country.

Resolved, That the history of the formation of the Constitution . . . abundantly shows it to have been the purpose of our fathers not to promote, but to prevent the spread of slavery. And we . . . oppose . . . all attempts, direct or indirect, to extend slavery in this country, or to permit it to be extended into any region or locality in which it does not now exist by positive law, or to admit new slave States into the Union.

Resolved, That the Constitution of the United States gives to Congress full and complete power for the municipal government of the Territories thereof. . . .

Resolved, That the repeal of the "Missouri Compromise," contained in the recent act of Congress, for the creation of the Territories of Nebraska and Kansas, thus admitting slavery into a region until then sealed by law, equal in extent to the thirteen old States, is an act unprecedented in the history of the country, and one which must engage the earnest and serious attention of every Northern man. And as Northern freemen, independent of all party ties, we here hold this measure up to the public execration for the following reasons:

That it is a plain departure from the policy of the fathers of the Republic, in regard to slavery, and a wanton and dangerous frustration of their purposes and their hopes.

That it actually admits, and *was intended to admit,* slavery into said territories!. . . .

That it was sprung upon the country stealthily and by surprise, without necessity, without petition and without previous discussion, thus violating the cardinal principles of republican government, which requires all legislation to accord with opinions and sentiments of the people.

That on the part of the South it is an open and undisguised breach of faith, as contracted between the North and South in the settlement of the Missouri question in 1820, by which the two sections was restored!. . . .

That it is also an open violation of the compromise of 1850, by which, for the sake of peace, and to calm the distempered impulse of certain enemies of the union at the South, the North accepted and acquiesced in the odious "fugitive slave law" of that year:—

That it is also an undisguised and unmanly contempt of the pledge given to the country by the present dominant party at their national convention in 1852, not to *"agitate the subject of slavery either in or out of Congress"*—being the same convention which nominated Franklin Pierce to the presidency:—

That it is greatly injurious to the free States and to the territories themselves, tending to retard their settlement, and to prevent the improvement of the country by means of *free labor;* and to discourage foreign emigrants from resorting thither for homes.

That one of its principal aims is to give to the Slave States such a decided and practical preponderance in all the measures of government as shall reduce the North with all her industry, wealth and enterprise to be the mere provinces of a few slaveholding oligarchs of the South!—to a position too shameful to be contemplated:—

Because as is openly avowed by its southern friends it is intended as an entering wedge to the still further augmentation of the slave power by the acquisition of other territories cursed with the same "leprosy."

Resolved, That the obnoxious measures to which we have alluded, ought to be *repealed,* and a provision substituted for it, prohibiting slavery in said territories and each of them.

Resolved, That after this gross breach of faith and wanton affront to us as Northern men, we hold ourselves absolved from all *"compromises,"* except those expressed in the Constitution for protection of slavery and slave owners; that we now demand measures of protection and immunity for ourselves, and among them we demand the REPEAL OF THE FUGITIVE SLAVE LAW; and an act to abolish slavery in the District of Columbia.

Resolved, That we notice without dismay certain popular indications of slaveholders on the frontier of said territories, of a purpose on their part to prevent by violence the settlement of the country by non-slaveholding men. To the latter, we say, be of good cheer; persevere in the right; THE NORTH WILL DEFEND YOU. . . .

Resolved, That in view of the necessity of battleing [*sic*] for the first principles of Republican Government and against the schemes of aristocracy, the most revolting and oppressive with which the earth was ever cursed or man debased, we will cooperate and be known as REPUBLICANS until the contest be terminated.

Resolved, That we earnestly recommend the calling of a general convention of the free states, and such of the slaveholding states or portions thereof as may desire to be there represented, with a view to the adoption of other more extended and effectual measures in resistance of the encroachments of slavery.

Washtenaw Whig, July 12, 1854.

MICHIGAN'S PERSONAL LIBERTY LAWS

Among the earliest acts passed by the Michigan legislature, following the Republican victories in the 1854 election, were two personal liberty laws—statutes designed to prevent the capture and rendition of fugitive slaves. The first Fugitive Slave Act, passed by the US Congress in 1793, proved ineffectual, as Northern states—Michigan not being among them—increasingly placed legal barriers in the way of fugitive rendition. These laws infuriated slaveholders, who argued that the

Constitution required Northerners to cooperate with slave catchers. Congress responded to slaveholders' concerns by passing a Fugitive Slave Act in 1850 designed to prevent states from hindering slave owners' pursuit of their escaped property. Most Northern states maintained their personal liberty laws, some of which provided that all accused of being escaped slaves have their cases decided by a jury trial— a position that stood contrary to the 1850 Fugitive Slave Act. In passing its first personal liberty laws, the Michigan legislature in 1855 asserted the primacy of state authority over federal authority—a position more often assumed by Southern politicians during these years. Six years later, during the secession crisis, when Southern Unionists called for Northern states to rescind their personal liberty laws as a way of easing sectional tensions, the Michigan legislature refused to do so.[6]

AN ACT TO PROTECT THE RIGHTS AND LIBERTIES OF THE INHABITANTS OF THIS STATE.

SECTION 1. *The People of the State of Michigan enact,* That it shall be the duty of the prosecuting attorneys within their respective counties, whenever any inhabitant of this State is arrested or claimed as a fugitive slave . . . to use all lawful means to protect and defend every such person so arrested or claimed as a fugitive slave.

Sec. 2. All persons so arrested and claimed as fugitive slaves, shall be entitled to all the benefits of the writ of habeas corpus and of trial by jury. . . .

Sec. 5. No person arrested and claimed as a fugitive slave shall be imprisoned in any jail or other prison in this State; and any person having the care or control of any jail or prison, and knowingly permitting the imprisonment of such alleged fugitive slave therein, shall be subjected to the payment of a fine of not less than five hundred nor more than one thousand dollars.

Sec. 6. Every person who shall falsely declare, represent or pretend, that any free person entitled to freedom is a slave, or owes service or labor to any person or persons, with intent to procure, or aid or assist in procuring the forcible removal of such free person from this State as a slave, shall be imprisoned not less than three nor more than five years in the State Prison.

Sec. 7. Every person who shall wrongfully and maliciously seize, or procure to be seized, any free person entitled to freedom, with intent to have such person held in slavery, shall pay a fine of not less than five hundred nor more than one thousand dollars, and be imprisoned five years in the State Prison. . . .

Sec. 10. All acts or parts of acts conflicting with the provisions of this act are hereby repealed.

Approved February 13, 1855.

Acts of the Legislature of the State of Michigan Passed at the Regular Session of 1855 (Lansing: George W. Peck, 1855), 413–15.

ABRAHAM LINCOLN CAMPAIGNS IN KALAMAZOO

After serving eight years in the Illinois legislature and two years in the US House of Representatives as a Whig, Abraham Lincoln retired from politics in 1849 and devoted himself to his law practice. With the passage of the Kansas-Nebraska Act in 1854, though, Lincoln reentered politics and became a leading figure in the Illinois Republican Party. After placing second in the vice-presidential balloting at the 1856 Republican national convention, Lincoln spent the summer and fall of 1856 campaigning for the Republican presidential nominee, John C. Frémont, in Illinois. Although he was invited to speak in several states, Lincoln's only out-of-state speech was one he gave in Kalamazoo on August 27. Stenographically transcribed by a reporter, it is the most completely recorded speech Lincoln gave that year—not surprising, given his modest political stature at the time. While denunciatory of slavery, Lincoln underlined the importance of "free labor"—as opposed to slave labor—as a key to economic mobility. He also placed greater emphasis on keeping the federal territories free of slavery, so that they might serve as future homes of free white Americans. Lincoln's moderation may be best appreciated by comparing his remarks with the Jackson resolutions of 1854.

Fellow countrymen:—Under the Constitution of the U.S. another Presidential contest approaches us. . . . The question of slavery, at the present day, should be not only the greatest question, but very nearly the sole question. Our opponents, however, prefer that this should not be the case. To get at this question, I will occupy your attention but a single moment. The question is simply this:—Shall slavery be spread into the new Territories, or not?. . . .

We have been in the habit of deploring the fact that slavery exists amongst us. We have ever deplored it. Our forefathers did, and they declared, as we have done in later years, the blame rested on the mother Government of Great Britain. . . .

Have we no interest in the free Territories of the United States—that they should be kept open for the homes of free white people? As our Northern States are growing more and more in wealth and population, we are continually in want of an outlet, through which it may pass out to enrich our country. In this we have an interest—a deep and abiding interest. . . .

I have noticed in Southern newspapers, particularly the Richmond Enquirer, the Southern view of the Free States. They insist that slavery has a right to spread. They defend it upon principle. They insist that their slaves are far better off than Northern freemen. What a mistaken view do these men have of Northern laborers! They think that men are always to remain laborers here—but there is no such class. The man who labored for another last year, this year labors for himself, and next year he will hire others to labor for him. These men don't understand when they think in this manner of Northern free labor. When these reasons can be introduced, tell me not that we have no interest in keeping the Territories free for the settlement of free laborers. . . .

Our adversaries charge Fremont with being an abolitionist. When pressed to show proof, they frankly confess that they can show no such thing. They then run off upon the assertion that his supporters are abolitionists. But this they have never attempted to prove. . . .

They tell us that we are in company with men who have long been known as abolitionists. What care we how many may feel disposed to labor for our cause? Why do not you, Buchanan men, come in and use your influence to make our party respectable? (Laughter.) How is the dissolution of the Union to be consummated? They tell us that the Union is in danger. Who will divide it? Is it those who make the charge? Are they themselves the persons who wish to see this result? A majority will never dissolve the Union. Can a minority do it?

Detroit Daily Advertiser, August 29, 1856.

JOHN BROWN AND FREDERICK DOUGLASS
DEBATE SLAVE INSURRECTION IN DETROIT

On October 16, 1859, John Brown and a biracial group of twenty-one male accomplices attacked the federal armory at Harpers Ferry, Virginia (now West Virginia), with the goal of launching an insurrection to end slavery. Within thirty-six hours, federal troops and local militia had captured or killed all but seven of Brown's raiders, with two others being captured in southern Pennsylvania within nine days. After a brief trial, the state of Virginia executed Brown less than seven weeks later.

Brown revealed an early version of his plan, which had already evolved through several years of preparation, to a small group of African American sympathizers in Detroit on March 12, 1859. At the time, Brown was on his way to Canada, leading a group that he and others had recently liberated from slavery in Missouri. Detroit historians have long heralded this meeting, which included Frederick Douglass, who happened to be in Detroit that evening delivering a public address. In 1962 Michigan erected a state historical marker to commemorate this event. Meanwhile most biographers of Brown and Douglass have ignored it.[7]

Based on reminiscences of those present, this document probably constitutes the earliest published account of this important meeting.

Brown and five of his men arrived in Detroit with 14 slaves from Missouri in the summer of 1859.[8] One of the slaves gave birth to a male child on the way. The boy was named John Brown, and now lives in Windsor.[9] By a strange coincidence Fred Douglass happened to be lecturing in this city the same evening that

Brown arrived.[10] After the lecture the leaders of the insurrectionary movement got together in the house of Wm Webb, on Congress Street, near Antoine street, and arranged the plan for the raid on the South, which broke out prematurely at Harper's [sic] Ferry. Mr. Webb was for years the manager of the plug tobacco factory on Jefferson avenue, and was a highly respected man. He is now dead. The leading colored people of Detroit and Chatham [Ontario] were also present at the meeting.

Douglass objected to Brown's plan, which originally was to make raids on single plantations until he had collected a force of about 1,000 slaves, and then swoop down on the large towns and cities, collecting force and material as he progressed. Brown grew wrathy, and asked Douglass if he was a coward, and referred to his successes in Kansas as an augury of the Virginia campaign. Douglass replied that he was not a coward, and would give material aid to the plan if he did not approve of it, or did not go himself.[11]

Geo. De Baptiste[12] also disapproved of the plan, but proposed a gunpowder plot, by which some 15 of the largest churches in the South would be blown up on a fixed Sunday. Brown objected to that plan on the score of humanity, asserting that by his plan not a hundred lives would be lost, his intention being not to shed blood unless it became absolutely necessary. De Baptiste still urged radical measures, declaring that Brown's plan would fail, and perhaps cause the loss of a million lives before the troubles likely to ensure would be ended. He cited in support of his position the fact that the Nat Turner insurrection, in 1831, by which 53 white lives were lost, had had the effect of causing the next Virginia Legislature to consider a bill for the gradual emancipation of the slaves, which bill was lost by only two votes.

Osawatomie's [John Brown's sobriquet] counsel finally prevailed, and the only favor, beside money and advice, that he asked of his Detroit friends,[13] was to furnish him one man, which they did, a Chathamite.[14] The news of the disturbance at Harper's Ferry, which took the Nation with so much surprise, was perfectly well understood by the colored people of this city. They were anticipating the event, since one Foster had divulged in Washington the plans of Brown, who, in consequence, was obliged either to abandon his enterprise or precipitate matters, even if at fearful odds.[15] He chose the latter alternative. The sequel is sufficiently well known. These facts, however, have been kept with sworn secrecy, until lately, by the colored men of Detroit. The particulars have never been published. It may be only necessary to add that subsequent to the meeting at Webb's house, on Congress street, a meeting was held in Chatham, at which the "cap sheaf" was put on the plan. Now that Negroes are equal, politically, before the law, they have no fear in letting their connection with this affair be known. They glory in it.

A NONPARTISAN NEWSPAPER BOLTS FOR THE REPUBLICANS

Most nineteenth-century American newspapers aligned with a political party, but occasionally one took a nonpartisan stance. That the Ingham County News *switched from being neutral to Republican in 1860 points to the ways that sectionalism increased political polarization on the state and local levels across the North. This announcement also suggests how Northern Democrats paid a steep political price for the pro-Southern policies of the Pierce and Buchanan administrations, underlines how Northerners' hostility to the "slave power" exceeded their humanitarian concerns for the slaves' plight, and demonstrates how antebellum Republicans broadened their appeal beyond a hostility to slavery.*

As will be seen we have this week placed at the head of our column our political Banner, upon which is inscribed the names of Lincoln and Ham[b]lin, the candidates of our choice to support, during the coming campaign.

In making this change it is due to our subscribers, that we should state to them frankly our reasons for the course we have taken. . . .

In regard to our political views—everybody knows and feels that our National Administrations have for the last few years been a disgrace to the country. It is needless to recount the reasons that induced the Detroit *Free Press*, and other Democratic papers to "thank God that the administration of Franklin Pierce had drawn to a close." Neither is it necessary to attempt to show why it is that the administration of James Buchanan has sunk so low that no Democratic convention can be prevailed upon to endorse it. It is only necessary to point to the repeal of the Missouri Compromise, and to the infamous Lecompton Constitution and the untiring efforts of the Democratic party, to fasten upon the Territory of Kansas, as witnesses against them. . . .

No democrat can deny that his party has departed, step by step, from the principles of Jeffersonian democracy. Neither can he dispute that this has been done through concessions to the southern wing of the party. To satisfy the demands of the Slave power, and to gain its support, one democratic principle after another has been abandoned, until scarce one can be said to remain.—And now, because still farther concessions cannot be obtained, we see it divided and broken to pieces!

The great and noble purpose of the Republican party is to restore the general government to the principles upon which it was established by the Father of the Republic.

While it has no design to meddle with the institutions or the rights of the South, it believes Slavery and Poligamy [*sic*] to be abominations, and that all constitutional means should be employed to prevent the Territories of the United States from being cursed with this poisonous miasmatic influence.

But this is not all. The Republican party are thoroughly identified with the free labor interests of the country.

They would foster and protect the commerce of our rivers and lakes.

They would give homes to the landless, upon the unsettled lands of the west. They are pledged to the speedy construction of a Rail Road to the Pacific, which would give employment to thousands of our citizens, and would bind the Union together with a band of iron. . . .

A great contest is near at hand, and the question is to be settled whether Freedom or Slavery shall mould the future destinies of our beloved country. In this contest we cannot be an idle and indifferent spectator. . . .

In conclusion, we take pleasure in presenting the names of ABRAM [sic] LINCOLN and HANNIBL [sic] HAMLIN [sic], as candidates for President and Vice-President—two men, worthy in every respect, of your confidence and suffrages—men whom the people have tried and found them true to the interests of the country, and who to-day stand upon a platform of principles, of justice, and humanity, pledged to its support if elected.

Ingham County News, May 24, 1860.

STEPHEN A. DOUGLAS, "THE CONFLICT AND THE CAUSE"

In 1860, the Democratic Party split, with the Southern-dominated faction nominating Vice President John C. Breckinridge of Kentucky for president and the Northern-dominated faction nominating Senator Stephen A. Douglas of Illinois. Douglas broke with tradition and aggressively campaigned in the North and South for the presidency. On October 15, 1860, Douglas spoke before a large Detroit audience that he declared to be "one of the monster meetings of the season. I am not certain that I have addressed a larger one anywhere." In that speech he defended the policy of popular sovereignty—or nonintervention—and attacked Republicans for fomenting sectional discord and for being too favorable to African Americans.

So long as this country shall be divided into geographical parties, and all the Northern people shall be rallied under one banner, and all the southern people under another banner, and the two engaged in fierce conflict with each other, there never can be peace. . . .

When this government was formed the Union consisted of thirteen States, twelve of which were slaveholding and one only a free State. Suppose that when the convention assembled which formed the constitution, the doctrine which we are now taught by the republican party had prevailed. Suppose that Gen Washington, when he took his seat as President of the convention had declared, as Lincoln did in his Springfield speech, "that this Union cannot endure half free and half

slave; that this government cannot exist divided into free and slave States; that
these States must all be free or be slave, otherwise the Union must be dissolved."
("Never," Never") I say, suppose, if there be not sacrilege and treason in the sup-
position, that George Washington had avowed those principles which Mr. Lincoln
now holds. ("George Washington knew better."). . . .

It is evident that if the doctrine now advocated by the republicans had prevailed when the government was made, the States would have been slave States
forever, beyond the right of the people to control the subject. All that the friends
of free institutions desired at that day was, that the Federal government should
not be permitted to interfere with the question of slavery.—("That's it."); that
non-intervention by the Federal government should be the invariable rule; and
that the people should be permitted to have slavery or not, as they preferred. . . .

This sectional strife has alienated one-half of this Union from the other.
("Right.") It has separated father from son, mother from daughter, and brother
from sister. It has entered our legislative bodies, and produced discord and corruption. It has entered Congress, and brought one-half of the Senators and Representatives in hostile collision with the other. It has entered the house of God,
and separated men of the same faith around the holy communion table. . . . How
long do you think political ties will last when religious ones are severed? How long
do you think that politicians are going to sit together in peace in the same Senate
chamber when Christians cannot sit around the communion table in the house of
God without grumbling?. . . .

[T]he republicans of the North, under Mr. Lincoln, and the secessionists of the
South, under Mr. Breckinridge, agree in principle. . . . Agreeing thus far, they differ
only as to which way Congress shall exercise this power. The republicans desire to
have Congress exercise the power in all cases against the South and in favor of the
North, and the southern fire eaters desire it to exercise the power always against
the North and in favor of the South. (Laughter.). . . . Having thus arrayed one
section against the other, Mr. Lincoln is then to come forward with all the power
of the Federal government and enforce the doctrine that these States must all be
free or all be slave, otherwise this Union cannot endure. Do not you see this Union
cannot exist under the lead of either of the sectional parties? ("That's so.") There
is no salvation for the country; there is no peace for the people, except to the doctrine of non-interference by Congress with the whole subject of slavery. ("Amen,"
and cheers.) We must . . . return to those great principles of self-government upon
which the constitution rests. The constitution, as our fathers made it, is good
enough for me. ("It is good enough for us all," and cheers.). . . .

According to the doctrine of the democratic party, this government was made
for white men, for the benefit of white men, to be administered by white men
and nobody else. (Cheers.) Mr. Seward and his followers think it was made by

white men and negroes, for the benefit of white men and negroes, forever on terms of equality and universal suffrage. (Cheers.)—It is on this very point that our republican friends feel so savage toward the Supreme Court for its decisions in the Dred Scott case. In that case the courts decided that Dred Scott, being a Negro, descended of African parents, was not a citizen of the United States. (Cries of "Right," "Good," "Correct.") The republicans think that it is unjust, cruel, barbarous, monstrous, not to allow a negro to be a citizen. And they say, because we are opposed to making negroes citizens, therefore we are in favor of making them slaves. That does not follow by any means. On the contrary, the democratic party hold that the negro race everywhere ought to be permitted to enjoy all the rights, all the privileges, and all the immunities that can be safely extended to them with the safety of society. (Cheers.). . . .

It may be entirely safe and prudent to extend to the negroes in Michigan, where you have very few, rights and privileges which would be unsafe and dangerous to give them in South Carolina, where the slaves outnumber the whites two to one. That being the case, you must take care of your own negroes, make your own laws, establish your own institutions, mind your own business, and let South Carolina alone. (Immense applause.) In return, South Carolina must make her own laws, establish her own institutions, regulate her own affairs, take care of her own negroes, and let us alone. (Cheers.) Apply that principle to every other State and every Territory in this Union, and there will be peace on the slavery question. (Cries of "Good," "That's so," and applause.) You cannot have peace on any other principle. You must come back to the old doctrine of non-intervention by Congress . . . or you are bound to have sectional strife in Congress until this Union is broken up. (Cheers.). . . .

Our material interests are not attended to. Why not? The slavery question stands in the way. . . .

The democratic party desires to get the negro question out of Congress in order that white men can have a little time for their business. (Cheers.). . . . I tell you that, so long as that exciting question is kept there, it will absorb all others. It diverts public attention from the financial interests, State and National, and makes elections turn solely on the negro question, instead upon others affecting the material interest in which we all have so much at stake.

Michigan Argus (Ann Arbor), October 26, 1860.

STEPHEN A. DOUGLAS RESPONDS TO HECKLERS IN DOWAGIAC

After speaking in Detroit, Stephen A. Douglas traveled by train across southern Michigan, making speeches along the way. Never willing to shun a political fight, Douglas here contends with a hostile Republican crowd in Dowagiac. Reproving his detractors for their rudeness, Douglas hints at the nature of his quarter-century rivalry with fellow Springfield resident, Lincoln, whom Douglas identifies as his "friend."

[Stephen A. Douglas] took the cars of the Michigan Central [in Kalamazoo] for Chicago. At every station along the road crowds of people are assembled to catch a glimpse of the distinguished Senator, but so fatigued was the Judge,[16] having been compelled to make his appearance at every station from Detroit to Kalamazoo, and had delivered some eight speeches, that he kept his car until he arrived at Dowagiac, 14 miles east.[17]

At Dowagiac about 50 wide awakes[18] made their appearance and paraded by the side of the car in which was Juge [*sic*] Douglas. From their dress, it was supposed, at first, they were his friends who had come to greet him. The Judge made his appearance upon the platform of the car, and after taking several gentlemen by the hand proceeded to say that he thanked them for this manifestation of their kindness, when the wide awakes sent up three cheers for Lincoln followed by three groans for Stephen A. Douglas. The Judge was perfectly calm and composed, and proceeded to address them in substance as follows: This is the first time in my travels through the Union that I have been compelled to submit to an insult so base. I am a stranger among you, but I do not believe you would of yourselves so insult any stranger. I cannot blame the gentlemen I see before me, for no doubt they are obeying the orders of their leaders, and came here to offer me this gross insult.

Three cheers again went up for Lincoln and three groans for Douglas. Judge Douglas continued:—"I have perhaps mistaken you for gentlemen. I hope and trust no democrat insulted Mr. Seward[19] as he passed through the country. In fact in one place in Illinois, democrats and republicans united in giving him a reception. Yes, notwithstanding democrats differed with him in opinion, they paid him the respect due to him as the distinguished leader of the republican party. I came here not to insult, or say ought against any man. Mr. Lincoln is my personal friend, and I am his. I am opposed to his political principles, believing them to be in direct conflict with the letter and spirit of the constitution, and [*three cheers for Lincoln and three groans for Douglas*] at war with the peace and harmony of the Union." The Judge now aimed some pointed arrows at the gang of brutish beasts that stood before him, that would have caused less baser wretches to sink down in shame, and retired to his car, leaving the disgraced gang to parade in front of him until the cars left.

Niles Republican, October 20, 1860.

TWO

~

The Secession Crisis

*D*ESPITE STEPHEN A. DOUGLAS'S campaign tour through southern Michigan in October 1860, voters in the Wolverine State decidedly favored Abraham Lincoln the following month, 57 to 42 percent—almost identical to John C. Frémont's margin over James Buchanan in the state four years earlier. Lincoln did better across the North than Frémont did in 1856, though, with Lincoln winning almost 54 percent of the votes in the free states. More importantly, Lincoln's 180 electoral votes—59 percent of the total—secured the presidency. But since he won virtually no votes in the slaveholding states, Lincoln received less than 40 percent of the national vote.

Michiganians, and Americans generally, wondered what would happen next. Southern rights proponents had proclaimed that Frémont's election in 1856 would result in slave states' leaving the union. Buchanan's victory that year averted a secession crisis, but voices warning of the consequences stemming from a Republican victory were even louder in 1860.

Although he would not be sworn into office for nearly four months, events moved quickly following Lincoln's victory. South Carolina acted first. On December 6, voters there selected delegates to a state secession convention, which on December 20 unanimously voted for South Carolina's separation from the Union. By early February, Mississippi, Florida, Alabama, Georgia, Louisiana, and Texas followed suit, with delegates from these states (save Texas, whose delegates arrived late) forming the provisional government of the Confederate States of America in Montgomery, Alabama, on February 4, 1861. After declaring themselves independent of the United States, secessionists claimed possession of federal property within their borders, including customs offices, mints, and military bases.

In Michigan, Republicans and most Democrats rejected secession but responded differently to the crisis. Recognizing that secession resulted from the election of their party's nominee, Michigan's leading Republicans, such as Governor Austin Blair and Senator Zachariah Chandler, rejected compromise with secessionists and insisted that federal laws be upheld. Michigan Democrats, in contrast, blamed Republicans' antislavery rhetoric for driving the South from the Union and urged compromise measures that might retain peace. Republicans regarded Democrats' compromise proposals as ploys to change the results of the recently completed election.

After the seizure of federal property across the seven seceded states during the winter of 1860–61, only four military installations in the region remained in federal control. The most significant of these installations, Fort Sumter, guarded the entrance to Charleston Harbor. An uneasy peace prevailed in Charleston during the three months after South Carolina seceded in December 1860, with the Stars and Stripes still flying within sight of this secessionist hotbed. Talk of war spread throughout both the North and the South, and some prepared for the likelihood of conflict. In March, the Republican-dominated Michigan legislature criticized "Certain states" that had "resolved to secede from the federal Union," "forcibly seized" federal property, and "willfully fired upon and insulted the flag of the United States." Recognizing these states as being in "open rebellion," the legislature effectively declared that "a state of war actually exists" and prepared to "meet this public emergency" by authorizing the governor to muster two regiments of Michigan's state militia into federal service, should they be needed, and to purchase provisions to keep these prospective regiments outfitted.[1]

As the Michigan legislature issued this declaration, authorities in Washington still hoped to defuse the secession crisis. Meanwhile, supplies for US troops at Fort Sumter ran low. After President Abraham Lincoln informed South Carolina governor Francis Pickens that federal ships planned to resupply Fort Sumter with food only, but not military supplies, Confederate artillery began bombarding Sumter. Designed to protect Charleston from an oceanic naval assault, Sumter proved to be an easy target for mainland batteries. Thirty-one hours after the cannon began firing, Sumter's seventy-seven federal troops surrendered on April 13, 1861.

Following this attack on Sumter, Lincoln called on the twenty-seven states remaining in the Union, both slave and free, for troops to suppress the rebellion, "to cause the laws to be duly executed," and to maintain "the perpetuity of popular government." That Lincoln summoned only 75,000 troops to serve for merely ninety days—with Michigan's quota being 780—indicates that he, and many people across the North, initially expected the struggle to be brief.[2] Confederates likewise believed that Unionists would soon recognize the permanency of their newly declared nation. Both sides' optimism proved misplaced, as eventually some 2 million men fought for the Union, while 750,000 fought for the Confederacy.[3] Lincoln's call for troops, though, led four additional slave states—Arkansas, North Carolina, Tennessee, and Virginia—to secede and join the Confederacy.

GOVERNOR AUSTIN BLAIR DECLARES "SECESSION IS REVOLUTION"

Elected Michigan's governor the same day that Abraham Lincoln won the presidency, Austin Blair represented the views of the Republicans' radical wing. By the time of Blair's inauguration on January 2, 1861, South Carolina had seceded, and six other states would do so within five weeks. The nation's increasingly rancorous dispute over slavery thus shifted to one over disunion—whether the United States would remain one nation or become two. Like other radicals, Blair proved to be uncompromising on secession, and his remarks were far less conciliatory than Lincoln's inaugural had been two months later. Reelected to a second term in 1862, Blair played a vital role in the recruitment of Michigan's soldiers until 1865.

While we are citizens of the State of Michigan, and as such deeply devoted to her interests and honor, we have a still prouder title. We are also citizens of the United States of America. . . . The people of Michigan are loyal to that government—faithful to its Constitution and its laws. Under it they have had peace and prosperity; and under it they mean to abide to the end. . . .

The existence of the government is threatened, not by enemies from without, but by traitors from within. The State of South Carolina, possessing a free white population of less than three hundred thousand, of all ages and sexes, has assumed to dissolve the national government. . . .

We are one nation, and our people indivisible, with a common government, and common interests. South Carolina is still a State of the Union in spite of her ordinance, and her people cannot be absolved from their obligation to obey the Constitution and laws of our common country. . . .

It is not concession that is needed now: it is patriotic firmness and decision. All the present evils either arise from, or are greatly aggravated, by the weak and compromising policy of timid men, in the past. Treason has been abetted and encouraged by humiliating expedients, until the mal-contents of the present, feel secure in the temporizing precedents of the past. Let us have an end of compromises, and appeal only for constitutional rights. Besides it is not claimed or even pretended that the Personal Liberty laws have in fact had the effect to prevent the execution of the Fugitive Slave law in a single instance. They have stood as a mere protest on the statute book. . . .

It is not at the personal liberty laws that the secessionists aim. They openly scout at the notion that their repeal will satisfy them. Their war is upon the Constitution of the United States. That instrument does not answer their purposes, and they demand its amendment or its overthrow. Its great doctrine of government by majorities stands in the way of the establishment of the great slave Empire which they have set themselves to erect, with the infamous African slave trade for one of its pillars, and one way or another it must be destroyed. . . . That is the real question, and the only one. Shall the Government continue as our fathers made it? Shall it be administered by majorities or shall a new one be constructed to be ruled by minorities[?]. The people have, in a constitutional and legal manner, chosen an eminent citizen of the State of Illinois, President of the United States, and the South demand that we shall repent of it. . . .

Secession is revolution, and revolution, in the overt act, is treason, and must be treated as such. The Federal Government has the power to defend itself and I do not doubt that that power will be exercised to the utmost. It is a question of war that the seceding States have to look in the face. They who think that this powerful government can be disrupted peacefully, have read history to no purpose. The sons of the men who carried arms in [the American Revolution against] the most powerful nation in the world, to establish this government, will not hesitate to make equal sacrifices to maintain it. . . . On the heads of the traitors who provoke it, must rest the responsibility. In such a contest the God of battles has no attribute that can take sides with the revolutionists of the Slave States. . . .

Oh, for the firm, steady hand of a Washington, or a Jackson, to guide the Ship of State in this perilous storm. Let us hope that we shall find him on the 4th of March. Meantime, let us abide in the faith of our fathers—"Liberty and Union, one and inseparable, now and forever."

"Governor's Inaugural Message," Document #2, *Joint Documents of the State of Michigan for the Year 1860* (Lansing: Hosmer and Kerr, 1861), 17–24.

Austin Blair (1818–1894), Michigan governor, 1861–65. Source: Library of Congress

SECESSION RESULTED FROM REPUBLICANS' AGITATION ON SLAVERY

Michigan's Republicans blamed the secession crisis on the secessionists' refusal to accept Abraham Lincoln's election. Meanwhile, Michigan Democrats blamed the crisis on Republicans and abolitionists—two distinct groups, with some overlap, that Democratic rhetoric frequently conflated—rather than on their political allies in the South. While many Northern Democrats personally opposed slavery, they thought a strong national union was more important than attacking slavery and thus tolerated slavery to secure a lasting Union. Consequently, Democrats depicted slavery's vocal opponents as fanatics intent on ending slavery by destroying society's cherished foundations.

Its title notwithstanding, the Niles Republican *was an unwavering Democratic newspaper.*

We contend that nothing but evil has been the offspring of this slavery agitation. It has been productive of more mischief than a century can wipe out, and perhaps a thousand years. It may change the whole tide of the nation. It may wipe out a large portion of the present generation of men by war, civil war.

Men claim to have a conscience so pure that they cannot sanction slavery. So pure that they cannot sanction a constitution that recognizes slavery—that restores servants to their masters. Yet, these same men have consciences that can look upon the dead bodies of their fellow countrymen, upon their burning dwellings, and say it is God's work to rid the nation of slavery.—This is their conscience. They had rather see war, pestilence and famine, than slavery. They had rather see the best government the sun shone upon broken up than yield up to the South their constitutional rights.

Such consciences will ruin a great people bound together by every sacred tie.

The agitation has now reached a crisis. It has assumed a most alarming attitude. One star has dropped off the American flag. Others will soon follow. The great and happy Union is broken up. . . .

Yet the [R]epublican leaders tell us all is safe. Republicans tell us there is no danger, and they scoff at all who assure them otherwise.

Their cry is, stick to the platform and sacrifice the country, when they know positively it will lead to civil war and destruction of every thing dear to Americans. It will deprive the people of liberty. A military despotism will reign over us. We shall become a prey to the monarchies of the earth, a by-word among the nations. . . .

This is the spectacle before us. This is the sad sight presented to our view as we enter upon 1861. How can we avoid it?. . . .

Will not the [R]epublican [P]arty abandon their unjust position? Will they not for the sake of peace, for the sake of their own liberty, and for the perpetuity of the happiness and prosperity of thirty-one millions of people, abandon their position? Will they not make the sacrifice for their country? Is there not patriotism enough among the people to save the nation?

Will not Christian Ministers, for the sake of peace, for the sake of civilization and Christianity, abandon their preaching against an institution which has been handed down to us by our fathers, and sanctioned by them? Or, must we fall, through our own folly[?]

The people must preserve the Union, if it is preserved at all—politicians will never do it.

Niles Republican, January 5, 1861.

"THE BLOOD OF SOUTHERN MEN ENRICHED THE SOIL OF MICHIGAN"

As both Michigan and national Republicans rejected Democrats' compromise proposals during the secession crisis, an Adrian Democratic editor asked Michiganians to recall the white Southerners who died during the War of 1812 at the Battle of Frenchtown, fought in neighboring Monroe County.

Having done all that was in our power, before the election, to avoid the threatened danger to the Union, we have had very little to say or advise, as to the course which the people of this State should pursue to bring about a favorable result in this crisis, because we felt that any proceeding, with such an object in view, would obtain little countenance, unless it originated with members of the dominant party. We . . . hope that conservative republicans will not be intimidated by the threats of the leaders to excommunicate them, if they dare to express any willingness to compromise. We . . . hope that all of the members of the republican party are not as eager to imbue their hands in the blood of their fellow countrymen of the South, as indicated by the savage tone of the leaders and press of the party; and we shall trust that a large portion of our opponents will be found willing to make any sacrifice, rather than see brothers arrayed against brothers in deadly strife.

We can scarcely believe that those who show so much eagerness to go to war against the South, have any realizing sense of the fact that they are fellow countrymen whom they desire to slay. Do they realize that the blood of southern men enriched the soil of Michigan to rescue the Territory from the dominion of foreign foes? Do they realize that in an adjoining county the bones of Kentuckians lie mingled with the earth, where the gallant soldiers were slain while they came to drive the enemy out? If the South owes the North many obligations, surely we owe the South as much. Let it not be said that we are ambitious to cut the throats of those who have shared dangers with us, for the good of all; and this upon a mere abstraction, for all the difference between the North and the South, is not more, so far at least as the North is concerned. . . . With childish vindictiveness, Gov. Blair in his message, intimates when the South cease to do wrong then Michigan "will be willing to do towards the South, not only what is just, but all that is generous." That is the spirit of childishness, though coming from the Governor.—In that spirit there will be no adjustment, but that is not the spirit of the people of Michigan, who are not merely political partisans.

Adrian Daily Watchtower, January 17, 1861.

AN ANTI-ABOLITION RIOT DURING THE SECESSION CRISIS

As the site of Michigan's first statewide abolitionist gathering in 1836, and as the home of the state's most successful abolitionist newspaper, the Signal of Liberty *(1841–48), by 1861 Ann Arbor had a strong antislavery tradition. Yet a January 1861 meeting of the Friends of Freedom in Michigan met with strong opposition from some Ann Arbor residents, particularly after Parker Pillsbury called for the creation of a "Free Northern Republic"—one separated from the slave states (abolitionists attending this gathering were primarily Garrisonian abolitionists, who had long rejected the political activity of the Liberty, Free Soil, and Republican parties). Ann Arbor's self-proclaimed Unionists condemned Pillsbury and "fanatical Abolitionists," as well as Southern secessionists, and violently disrupted the meeting. Although Charles M. Hunt, the author of this document and of the accompanying illustration, claimed that "students and their allies" caused the disruption, University of Michigan students countered that "the greater portion of students" condemned the violence and the melee's participants.[4]*

The radical Abolitionists assembled in our city on Saturday [February 16], and attempted to hold a disunion convention, but were prevented from bringing their meeting to a successful termination by a band or mob of citizens, and students belonging to the University.

We have in our institution over 650 young men, and when about noon it was rumored around that Parker Pillsbury was to speak, and that some strong disunion resolutions were to be passed, the boys went en masse to the meeting, in sufficient numbers to out-vote the Abolitionists, voted down all radical anti-Union motions, and succeeded in carrying a series of strong Union measures over the heads of the convention.

Among the sentiments contained therein, the resolutions recommended the "preservation of the Union at any cost," and "the hanging of disunion traitors, whether Secessionists in the South or fanatical Abolitionists North." Of course this took the members of the Convention by surprise, and they dispersed in dismay, vainly hoping to meet again in the evening, and listen to Mr. Pillsbury, and Mrs. [Josephine] Griffin[g] (the celebrated Ohio strong minded woman, and champion of woman's rights).

Fearing a disturbance, the proprietors of the several public halls in town refused to admit them to their respective halls; a futile application was made for the Court-House, and at last they were obliged to assemble in a little chapel or church on State street, owned or occupied under the name of the "Free Church" by the Spiritualists or Free Thinkers.

Here again they were overrun by the students and their allies. One of their own number was duly elected chairman, and on attempting to take the chair was driven from the stand by the Abolitionists. A student from the Law Department rising to make a motion, was seized by one of the city marshals and an attempt made to take him to jail; he was, however, rescued by his companions, and a general row commenced.

The lights were extinguished, the seats and furniture kicked and broken to pieces, and arming themselves with the fragments, they broke the windows, knocked down the stovepipe, and pushing, swaying and striking in all directions, drove the Abolitionists out through the windows, including the speakers and ladies.

The affair has caused the most intense excitement here, and although the Mayor and his whole police force were on hand at the time, they confessed themselves utterly unable to help the matter.

New York Illustrated News, February 16, 1861.

"Breaking Up of An Abolition Meeting in Michigan." Sketched by Charles J. Hunt, University of Michigan. Source: *New York Illustrated News*, February 16, 1861

THE MICHIGAN LEGISLATURE OPPOSES
COMPROMISE WITH SECESSIONISTS

In the month following Governor Austin Blair's inauguration, six other states followed South Carolina's lead and in early February formed the Confederate States of America. As the Virginia legislature debated secession, on January 19, 1861, it called for a national convention to find compromises that might keep the country intact. Most of the states remaining in the Union—including seven slave states—sent delegates to this convention, dubbed the Washington Peace Conference, which met in Washington, DC, from February 4 to February 27. Michigan, however, did not. After spending several weeks deadlocked on competing resolutions that condemned secession, news of Virginia's call for a compromise-driven conference spurred the Michigan legislature into action. In addition to passing resolutions that barred concession or compromise with "traitors," the legislature refused to send delegates to the Washington Peace Conference.[5]

JOINT RESOLUTIONS ON THE STATE OF THE UNION.

Whereas, Certain citizens of the United States are at this time in open rebellion against the government, and by overt acts threaten its peace and harmony, and to compass its final overthrow; therefore

Resolved, That the government of the United States is supreme, with full inherent powers of self-protection and defense.

Resolved, That Michigan adheres to the government, as ordained by the constitution, and for sustaining it intact hereby pledges and tenders to the general government all its military power and material resoures.

Resolved, That concession and compromise are not to be entertained or offered to traitors, while the rights and interests of Union-loving citizens should be regarded and respected in every place and under all circumstances.

Resolved, That His Excellency, the Governor, be requested to forward a copy of these resolutions to our Senators and Representatives in Congress, and to the Governors of our sister States.

Approved February 2, 1861.

Acts of the Legislature of the State of Michigan, Passed at the Regular and Extra Sessions of 1861 (Lansing: John A. Kerr, 1861), 579.

ZACHARIAH CHANDLER'S "BLOOD-LETTING" LETTER

After the Michigan legislature refused to send delegates to the Washington Peace Conference, some Republicans worried that conservative members of their party would agree to a compromise on slavery in the federal territories. Reflecting these fears, Senator Zachariah Chandler of Michigan urged Governor Blair to send delegates to the Washington Peace Conference who would resist compromise. After

Governor Blair showed Chandler's letter to several legislators in the hope of per-suading them to send delegates to the conference (which the legislature refused to do), a copy of Chandler's letter leaked to Democrats, who in turn shared it with the Detroit Free Press, *which immediately published it.[6] In the US Senate, Kentucky's Lazarus Whitehead Powell read Chandler's letter into the record and used it to argue that Republicans cared more about the fortunes of their party than they did about the fate of the nation. Others used Chandler's postscript to maintain that the Michigan senator welcomed bloodshed.*

Washington, February 11, 1861.

MY DEAR GOVERNOR: Governor BINGHAM[7] and myself telegraphed you on Saturday, at the request of Massachusetts and New York, to send delegates to the peace or compromise Congress. They admit that we were right and that they were wrong; that no Republican State should have sent delegates; but they are here and cannot get away. Ohio, Indiana, and Rhode Island are caving in, and there is danger of Illinois; and now they beg us, for God's sake, to come to their rescue, and save the Republican party from rupture. I hope you will send *stiff-backed* men or none. The whole thing was gotten up against my judgment and advice, and will end in thin smoke. Still, I hope as a matter of courtesy to some of our erring brethren, that you will send the delegates.

Truly your friend,
Z. CHANDLER.
His Excellency AUSTIN BLAIR.

P. S. Some of the manufacturing States think that a fight would be awful. Without a little blood-letting this Union will not, in my estimation, be worth a rush.

Congressional Globe, 36th Congress, 2nd sess., 1247 (1861).

Zachariah Chandler (1813–1879), US senator from Michigan, 1857–75, 1879. Source: Library of Congress

A DEMOCRAT'S PESSIMISTIC RESPONSE TO
LINCOLN'S INAUGURAL: "WE SHALL HAVE WAR"

Many Michigan Democrats looked to the Detroit Free Press, *the party's largest-circulation newspaper in the state, for political direction. In this excerpt,* Free Press *editor Wilbur Storey criticizes Lincoln's first inaugural address for rejecting conciliation. Storey afterward left the* Free Press *for the* Chicago Times *and became a leading Copperhead—a contemporary term for Democrats who harshly opposed Lincoln, Republicans, and the federal war effort.*

We shall have the secession of the border slave states and war. This is our fear, from the temper of Mr. LINCOLN's Inaugural Address and the construction of his Cabinet. The border slave States have been held in the Union thus far only by the hope that some terms of adjustment would be conceded by the incoming administration satisfactory to their people and which would revive the Union sentiment in the seceded States. This hope has been wholly disappointed. Mr. LINCOLN countenances no such terms. He turns his back upon such terms. He does not even recommend a convention to amend the constitution "one, two, or three years hence," as Mr. SEWARD, in one of his recent speeches, suggested would be eminently proper. In view of the fact that "many worthy and patriotic citizens are desirous of having the constitution amended," he "fully recognizes the full authority of the people over the whole subject," and he would, "under existing circumstances, favor rather than oppose a fair opportunity being afforded to act upon it." This is all. This is the extent of his idea of adjustment. Meanwhile, *he avows his purpose to use the power confided to him "to hold, occupy and possess the property and places belonging to the government, and to collect duties on imports*; but BEYOND WHAT MAY BE NECESSARY FOR THESE OBJECTS, there will be no invasion—no using of force against or among people anywhere." For what other objects could he use force in the seceded States? For these objects *he will use force*; and this is what the whole South regards as COERCION; and against coercion the whole South is committed, and coercion the whole South will resist.

Detroit Free Press, March 5, 1861.

NORTHERN MICHIGAN LEARNS OF THE WAR

Michiganians who lived in towns connected to the telegraph—all of which were located in the southern part of the state—learned of the Confederate attack on Fort Sumter within a day of its occurrence. Residents in Traverse City, isolated in the Northern Lower Peninsula, read of the start of the Civil War in their town's newspaper two weeks after it began—and of both Fort Sumter's surrender and the North's reaction in the same editorial.

A Civil War has been inaugurated by the South, and hostillities [*sic*] have commenced! The contest is between the Slave Power and the Government of the United States—between Despotic Rule and the Freedom of the People to govern themselves.

The news which we publish to-day will arouse the nation from centre to circumference. Mr. Lincoln, for refusing to surrender Fort Sumter to the Southern traitors and robbers, without an effort to re-inforce and provision it, will receive the plaudits of every true friend of Constitutional Freedom, North and South, and they will sustain him to the end. The South has forced this unnatural drama upon us, and there can be no more hesitation in the mind of any Patriot as to the duty which the emergency imposes. The Stars and Stripes must be sustained at all hazards and at every sacrifice. The man is a traitor who shrinks now from rendering loyal service to the authorities which are entrusted with the honor and integrity of the nation.

Pennsylvania has already been placed on a war footing. The Legislature has passed, and the Governor has signed, a bill appropriating half a million dollars for this purpose. Every Northern State will doubtless follow the example set by Pennsylvania, and furnish its quota of men and money to aid the Government in defence of its established rights. We presume that Gov. BLAIR will call an Extra Session of the Legislature of this State, forthwith; at all events we think he should do so. There should be no flinching now. Michigan must not be behind her sister States in rendering efficient aid to the General Government in this great struggle for Freedom, and the right to sustain itself on the principles upon which it was founded.

Grand Traverse Herald, April 26, 1861.

University of Michigan president Henry Tappan speaking in the Ann Arbor Courthouse Square after the attack at Fort Sumter, April 15, 1861. Source: Bentley Historical Library, University of Michigan

THREE

~

Shifting Michigan to a War Footing

$\mathcal{T}$HE CONFEDERATE ATTACK on Fort Sumter and Lincoln's call for troops galvanized Unionists and Michiganians in unprecedented ways. Michigan's intense political partisanship, characteristic of the state since its days as a territory, briefly disappeared. In these early days of the war, Democrats and Republicans put aside their ideological differences in an effort to preserve the Union. Typical was a resolution passed at an "immense meeting" at Detroit's Fireman's Hall "of all parties" on April 15, 1861: "We hereby pledge our undivided loyalty to the maintenance of the Government and its laws and in the present crisis we avow our united purpose, if need be, to devote our lives, our fortunes, and our sacred honor to the support of the integrity of that Government and the honor of its flag." Across the state in St. Joseph, patriotic fervor caused locals to conjoin the Democratic and Republican flagpoles from the recent election, each of which had waved partisan flags, and have "the Flag of the Union be supported by both in common."[1]

On the eve of the Civil War, the United States Army numbered 16,402 professional soldiers.[2] When Lincoln called for 75,000 troops on April 15, he looked to the states' militias. Militias operated under their respective state laws and the authority of their governors, unless (as provided by the US Constitution) called into federal service. During the Civil War, this process of converting state militias into federal forces, as well as the subsequent recruitment of volunteers—distinct from the militia—occurred through the auspices of state governors. Congress asserted its power to support armies throughout the war but rendered to governors the power to raise them.[3]

Following Lincoln's call for troops on April 15, and the same-day instructions telegraphed by Secretary of War Simon Cameron that set Michigan's troop quota at 780, Governor Austin Blair issued a proclamation of his own. The preceding month the Michigan legislature had authorized Blair to muster as many as two regiments of the state militia into federal service "whenever required by the President." Given Michigan's quota, on April 16 Blair directed "ten companies of infantry" be mustered into federal service "for three months (unless sooner disbanded)." Blair authorized John Robertson, the state's adjutant general, to select those companies "for immediate service," while those "not immediately required will be formed into . . . additional regiments, as the exigencies of the service may demand."[4]

At the time of Blair's proclamation, the state militia, from which the first two regiments would be drawn, consisted of 1,241 soldiers in twenty-eight scattered companies. Few militia members possessed practical military experience. With the state having previously allocated merely $3,000 annually for military purposes, Michigan's prospective regiments were unprepared for combat.[5] And notwithstanding the implied optimism of Blair's proclamation that these soldiers might serve less than three months, Michigan officials immediately calculated that the cost of provisioning a single three-month regiment would be $100,000—an amount the state treasury lacked. With the legislature out of session, the state could not furnish the money—through the issuing of bonds—to pay for the soldiers' upkeep (despite previously authorizing Blair to muster state militia into federal service, the legislature did not appropriate the funding to do so). Although an extra session of the legislature would convene on May 7 and authorize the necessary bonds,[6] the urgency of the moment required that troops be mustered and equipped before then.

On the day Blair issued his proclamation, he conferred with state treasurer John Owen and other Detroit leaders on how the state, without money at hand, might supply the regiment. After immediately securing $23,000 from prominent Detroiters and launching a statewide effort that, by July, secured an additional $81,000, Owen then negotiated a loan that proved sufficient for the state to provision the regiment.[7] A few weeks later the extra session of legislature assumed this debt, authorized the state to raise an additional ten regiments, and financed everything with a $1 million bond.[8] By early May, the stark realities of a war hardly begun had diminished Blair's hope for a short contest. As he explained to the legislature on May 7:

> We are just entering upon a war, the exact result of which no man can foresee. The sudden and splendid outburst of popular enthusiasm which has illumined its commencement will shortly, in a great measure, disappear, and must be replaced by calm determination and resolute vigor. There will be calamities and disasters which have not been looked for. He who went forth joyously singing the national anthem, will sometime be brought back in a bloody shroud. The national resources will be rapidly consumed, business will suffer and ordinary avocations be sadly broken up. This is to be no six week's [*sic*] campaign.[9]

Raising these first ten regiments—eight of infantry and one each of artillery and cavalry—proved to be easy. By June, the US War Department reported that it had more than enough soldiers and instructed the state to hold off on further enlistments, a disappointment that caused some prospective Michigan soldiers to

The 3rd Michigan Infantry Regiment marching in front of the Michigan Exchange, Detroit, June 3, 1861. Source: *New York Illustrated News,* July 11, 1861

join out-of-state regiments.[10] Following the Union defeat at the First Battle of Bull Run on July 21, though, the US Congress authorized an additional half-million volunteers and recruitment in Michigan continued. By the end of 1861, some 16,475 soldiers had joined Michigan regiments.[11]

MICHIGAN'S DECEPTIVE SILENCE WHILE WAR FEVER ESCALATES

As the war spirit grew across the North in the weeks after the attack on Fort Sumter, "Mirabeau," a pseudonymous correspondent for the New York Times, *described his travels from Illinois to Detroit along the Michigan Central Railroad and reported that silence prevailed across the Wolverine State.*

"Mirabeau's" letter stirred an angry response from a Detroit resident that the Times *published a week later and that underlines the high degree of state pride and patriotism during the war's early months.*

Detroit. Friday, June 28, 1861.

In traversing Michigan to-day, its rurel [*sic*] quiet aroused my curiosity, if not my skepticism, whilst reading the New-York journals, which all seemed to have been printed with different qualities of gunpowder. I have not seen a uniform or a musket in Michigan. Is she beyond the extreme outer edge of the Cyclone centered in a radius of ten miles around Manassas Junction?. . . .

In Cairo [Illinois] the responsive antistrophe was sweeter, quite as sincere, but far less in volume. In Chicago the echoes were faint, but I thought people were taking breath, or that there was a temporary eddy formed by reëntering and deflecting waves of sound. But when I missed the long familiar canticle in the silence of Michigan, I might have fancied myself in Canada or any where but in the State of Gen. [Lewis] Cass and Senator [Zachariah] Chandler. Not a town, a hamlet, a wayside inn, nor a station in the South, which was not renitent, if not with gold lace, with the gleam of arms and sonorous with the shout of "war to the knife." But the stranger who should land at Detroit this day, more than sixty after the presentation of the bill of exchange drawn by [Confederate General P.G.T.] Beauregard upon the patriotism of the North, and so gallantly accepted by New-York, by the East and by Ohio, Indiana and Illinois, and not deservedly be called prejudiced who should shake his head at the poco-curantism of Michigan.

∽

To the Editor of the New York Times:

In reading the Times of Monday last, I noticed in a communication over the signature of "Mirabeau," certain statements which do the authorities and people of this State great injustice, and which I beg leave to correct. Your correspondent seeks to convey the impression that in this State nothing is being done, and that nothing has been done, to put down the rebellion and war waged by the traitors of the South against the Constitution and the Union. That while New-England, New-York, and the strong young West, have sent forth their thousands of brave and patriotic freemen to the battle, the Peninsula State has remained idle and inactive in the cause. "Mirabeau" has been South, and therefore is not expected to be very well informed in regard to what has been done in this part of the Republic. He must, I think, have come from Chicago in the night, and, slept very soundly at that, in order not to have seen or heard the preparations which are going on to assist the Government in the present crisis.

We of Michigan feel that our State has done her duty thus far, and we *know* that she will persevere to the end. Four regiments have already gone from this State to the seat of war, thoroughly equipped and ready for duty. We believe that our volunteers will compare favorably with those of any other State, both as regards to discipline and character of the men, and the skill and efficiency of their officers. It should be remembered that the first soldiers that arrived in Washington from the West were from Michigan, and that Col. [Orlando] Wil[l]cox, of our First Regiment, received the first sword surrendered by a rebel officer.[12]

There are now organized in this State *three* more regiments, waiting anxiously the call of the Government to take the field. Our Legislature has appropriated a million of dollars to carry on the war, beside nearly an equal amount has been raised by private subscription. But more than this, this State has done what *no other* State has done. A camp of instruction has been established at Fort Wayne, near this City, where are assembled all the officers of the three remaining regiments. . . . The people of Michigan are as patriotic and as truly devoted to the Union as the people of any State, and when we consider her wealth and population we shall all agree that she has done her duty equally well as any other.

AGRICOLA

DETROIT, Tuesday, July 2, 1861.

New York Times, July 1, 1861; July 8, 1861.

A MOTHER TRIES TO CURB HER SON'S DESIRE TO ENLIST

Like thousands of other twenty-two-year-old men in April 1861, Irving Metcalf spoke openly of volunteering. His mother, Jane Betts of Burr Oak, thought her son ill-suited for the army and discouraged him from enlisting. Betts's efforts to keep her son from enlisting failed; by April 23, Metcalfe claimed he had enlisted in a ninety-day regiment. In August 1861 Metcalf enlisted in the 11th Michigan Infantry and served until being "discharged for disability" in 1863.[13]

Dear Irving,

I wrote you quite a long letter and sent it on Monday, from which you will [learn] the state of things here, and my views of the War which is upon [us]. Now, you ask my opinion as to the Expediency of your assisting in this struggle for Freedom. It is no mere, thought to me for ever since the demand has been made, and I see Fathers and Mothers giving up their sons to their Country I have been trying myself to see if I could do the same if necessary. So I am ready to say as Evy did to some one yesterday "He should go if he was called upon[.]" [S]o I say to you that if Our Country ever comes to that straightened point that the needs men of your military abilities, go and do the best you can, for I never want peace again until we are free indeed.

But reason should be exercised in all things. I think that considering your physical weakness and inability to use deadly weapons successfully that you are excusable for the present.

We rejoice that your heart is Loyal and that you are willing to make sacrifices. [W]e can be generous and aid much in word and deed, many rich men have laid their <u>All</u> on their <u>Country's</u> <u>Alter</u> and we can do what we can. . . . I have thought since I commenced that if War continues your present business will not be as good as it has been and perhaps you could get some good situation where some one has left. [I]f Larnard Harkness is still in business in Chicago, perhaps he could get a good place for you if he knew you wished it. . . .

[I]t does not seem to me that this contest can last long but we don't know. . . . We Ladies of Burr Oak met at the Elder's yesterday to scrape lint and make bandages for the Company to take along, so you see how we are doing here, but one feeling seems to prevail, at least but one expressed.

Nothing seems worth talking or writing about but the War so I don't think of any thing else to say at present. . . .

Your loving,
Mother

Jane Betts to Irving Metcalf, undated [April 1861], Doris L. King Family Papers, Clarke Historical Library, Central Michigan University.

THE SOUTH MAY BE CRIMSONED WITH TRAITORS' BLOOD, BUT FREEDOM SHALL BE MAINTAINED

Secession and the Confederate firing on Fort Sumter did not—and could not— immediately lead to battlefield engagements, as both sides first needed to muster troops. By July partisans in both the United States and the Confederacy expected to prevail easily over their antagonists.

Francis G. Russell, a clerk working in the Interior Department and a former resident of Lansing, reflected the martial spirit and optimism that infected the North after the attack on Fort Sumter—and before the Union defeat at First Bull Run. Significantly, Russell, like many other Northerners at this stage of the conflict, had little to say regarding slavery.

Washington, July 3, 1861

The present month is likely to constitute a great history in itself, at least prove the most important and eventful since the organization of our government; this month is to decide whether the honor and integrity of free institutions are to be firmly maintained and absolutely perpetuated or grossly neglected and destroyed; whether this powerful nation must fall, this government be numbered with the follies of the past, or move proudly forward with increased power and prosperity. This month is to introduce the final answer to the great problem, can a people govern themselves?

Through the corruption and baseness of vile unscrupulous politicians, through the internal machinations of scheming despots our great and glorious republic stands trembling on the verge of an awful abyss; the foul dragon, secession, despotism, treason, having enclosed in its loathsome embrace eleven States of our Union, with fiery eyes and hot venomous breath pants for the destruction of the liberties of twenty millions of free northerners. . . .

We know our republic is in a critical condition, but she is about to shake off effectually the deadly coils that have clogged her progress for the last thirty years, she is about to extinguish that vile heresy, that principle of secession, which if established must result in the destruction of every government. The eyes of the world are turned anxiously towards the great Republic of the West; freemen everywhere behold with deep solicitude this great struggle between right and wrong, they expect that the holy cause of liberty, truth and justice will nobly vindicated, that treason and despotism will be wiped out forever. . . .

[T]he day is past when the Representatives of the free North will be bullied and caned by southern chivalry. Then look out for decided and immediate action.—Grand preparation, unparalleled in the history of the world have been made; 250,000 brave men are in the field ready to strike for the stars and stripes, for liberty and right. . . . [T]he honor and integrity of our government will be maintained, even though it cost billions of treasures and hundreds of thousands of lives. Southern hills and vallies may be crimsoned with gore—be whitened with the bones of slain traitors, but freedom shall be maintained, the Constitution and Laws shall be respected and obeyed. "Better die all freemen than live all slaves," "The Union must and shall be preserved" are the mottoes of a great and exerted people in this gigantic effort to crush despotism.

I recently visited the encampments of the Michigan regiments; the men are generally well, but spoiling for a fight. Michigan can well feel proud of her representation.

Lansing State Republican, July 17, 1861.

A VOLUNTEER MEETING

Most Civil War soldiers enlisted in state regiments under the command of their state's governor. And rather than being appointed by political or military authority, most officers obtained their commissions after receiving the votes from the soldiers they would soon lead—just as Company A of the Michigan 3rd Cavalry chose its officers in Allegan.

On Monday Sept. 9th, 1861, at 3 o'clock P.M., the Cavalry Company of Allegan Co[unty]. raised by Hon. G. Moyers, met pursuant to order at the basement of the Court House in the village of Allegan for the election of officers and the transaction of such other business as might properly come before the meeting. . . .

Motion was then made and carried, that the Co[mpany]. proceed to express a choice for Capt. by acclamation, which resulted in the unanimous choice of Hon. Gilbert Moyers, after which three hearty cheers were given for our worthy Capt. Motion was then made, that the Company proceed to the election of 1st Lieutenant, by ballot. It was then moved, that the company form into line passing the Secretary's desk in single file, each man depositing the name of the candidate voted for with the Secretary, which was agreed to. The Company then proceeded to ballot which resulted in a large majority for B.M. Brown. It was then moved and supported that B.M. Brown be declared unanimously elected, which was carried. Motion was then made and carried that the Company proceed by the same method of election to the 2d Lieutenant. The Company then proceeded to ballot and the result showed that Mr. David White had a large majority. A motion was then made that the election of Mr. White be made unanimous, which was carried. A motion was then made that the Capt. appoint the non-commissioned officers, which was amended upon motion, so as to read as follows, to wit: that the Capt. together with the two Lieutenants, appoint the non-commissioned officers, which was to be carried. The Company next proceeded to choose a name by which the Company should be known hereafter in the Regiment, and after a short consultation, (during which several names were proposed, among which were the "Wolverine Rangers," "Allegan Wild Cats," &c.) it was concluded to call the Company by the name of the "Kellogg Guards" in honor of the Colonel Commanding. After which appropriate remarks were made by the officers elect, upon being called out by the Company.—

The Capt. then ordered that every man report himself in person at his office in the village of Allegan on Thursday morning Sept. 12th, at 8 o'clock preparatory to their departure to Grand Rapids, at which place the Regiment is to rendezvous. The meeting then adjourned, *sine die,* after which were given three cheers for the Constitution and the Union, and three groans for Jeff. Davis and his cohorts.

Allegan Journal, September 16, 1861.

RECRUITING A CAVALRY TROOP

Volunteers, abundant at the outbreak of the Civil War, became scarcer with the passage of time. James H. Kidd, a University of Michigan student at the war's outbreak, left the University after his second year to raise a company for the Michigan 6th Cavalry. A brevet brigadier general by the war's end, his reminiscence points to some of the recruitment challenges during the war's second summer.

I finished my sophomore year [at the University of Michigan] in June, 1862, and returned to my home full of military spirit and determined to embrace the first favorable opportunity to enter the volunteer service [in the cavalry]. . . .

I wanted to be a second lieutenant and told my father that I preferred that to higher rank in the infantry. So, the next day, he went down to see the Congressman [Francis William Kellogg]. His application for my appointment was heartily seconded by a number of influential men in the "Valley City," who knew nothing of me, but did it through their friendship for my father, whom they had known for many years as one of the most energetic and honorable business men in the Grand River valley. . . .

Their influence with Mr. Kellogg was potent, and my father obtained more than he asked for. He came home with a conditional appointment which ran thus:
. . .

"Grand Rapids, Aug. 28, 1862
"To Captain James. H. Kidd:
"You are hereby authorized to raise a company of mounted riflemen for this regiment on condition that you raise them within [nineteen] days from this date and report with them at the rendezvous in this city.
                              "F.W. KELLOGG, Colonel Commanding."

My surprise and gratification can better be imagined than described. To say that I was delighted would be putting it mildly.

But the document with the Congressman's signature attached to it was not very much of itself. I was a captain in name only. There was no "company" and would not be unless a minimum of seventy-eight men were recruited, and at the end of [nineteen] days the appointment would expire by limitation. . . .

It was, however, no easy task to get the requisite number of men in the time allowed, after so many men had been recruited for other regiments. The territory which we could draw upon for volunteers had been very thoroughly canvassed, in an effort to fill the quota of the state under Lincoln's last call. But it was less difficult to raise men for cavalry than for infantry and I was hopeful of succeeding. . . .

The method of obtaining enlistments was to hold war meetings in schoolhouses. The recruiting officer accompanied by a good speaker would attend an evening meeting which had been duly advertised. The latter did the talking, the former was ready with blanks to obtain signatures and administer the oath. These meeting were generally well attended but sometimes it was difficult to induce anybody to volunteer. Once, two of us drove sixteen miles and after a fine, patriotic address of an hour, were about to return without results, when one stalwart young man arose and announced his willingness to "jine the cavalry." . . .

The troop . . . was ready on Tuesday, September 16, 1862, to begin its career as a military unit in the great army of union volunteers. It is known in the history of the civil war as Troop E, Sixth Michigan cavalry. . . .

The troop that thus started on its career was a typical organization for that time—that is it had the characteristics common to the volunteers of the early period of the civil war. When mustered into the service it numbered one hundred and five officers and men. Though for the most part older than the men who went out later, the average age was but twenty-eight years. . . . But they were not professional soldiers. At first, they were not soldiers at all. They were farmers, mechanics, merchants, laboring men, students, who enlisted from love of country rather than from love of arms, and were absolutely ignorant of any knowledge of the technical part of a soldier's "business." The militia had been mostly absorbed by the first calls in 1861 and the men of 1862 came from the plow, the shop, the schoolroom, the counting room or the office. With few exceptions, they were not accustomed to the use of arms and had everything to learn. The officers of this particular organization had no advantage over the others in this respect, for, save myself, not one of them knew even the rudiments of tactics. Indeed, at the date of muster, there were but three officers in the entire regiment who had seen service.

J. H. Kidd, *Personal Recollections of a Cavalryman with Custer's Michigan Brigade in the Civil War* (Ionia, MI: Sentinel Press, 1908), 35–45.

LEAVING MICHIGAN FOR THE FRONT

For recruits like Daniel W. De Marbell, joining a regiment and traveling to the front proved to be an exciting adventure. Traveling by train and being treated as heroes along the way, soldiers could leave Michigan and arrive at the front within three days. The first assignment for the Michigan 6th turned out to be guarding a magazine in Baltimore as the regiment prepared for additional drilling. The excitement quickly ended for De Marbell, who soon became disabled and received a discharge in March 1862.

CAMP MCKIM, BALTIMORE, Sept. 4th

We left Kalamazoo and Camp Fremont behind us Friday morning 30th ult., and arrived at Detroit 5:30 P.M., the Detroit Light Guards and Band performed escort duty, and the Michigan 6th Regiment Inf. paraded one hour, and then embarked for Cleveland, Ohio, on board the two post steamers, Ocean Wave and Mayflower made Cleveland Saturday 31st, 9 P.M. At 9:30 P.M., we were all on board of the cars en route for Pittsburgh, the best of good cheer was ours the band playing at every station, was answered by shouts of welcome by hundreds, and sometimes a thousand throats. The ladies of Ravenna [Ohio] brought us a good dinner of pies, cakes, peaches, apples, bread and butter, ham, beef, &c., and when you consider that they fed a thousand soldiers at twenty minutes notice, I think you will give them credit for alacrity. Their smiling faces and silvery voices are fresh in our memory, and they may rest assured the Michigan 6th will not forget them so long as memory has a name. At Rochester, on the banks of the Ohio, we viewed the time-honored banner of the Union.—Roaming over the hills of western Virginia, a large cask of ice water furnished by the ladies of Rochester was welcomed by us all and fully discussed to the satisfaction of the ladies and soldiers. I must not forget to mention that we received plenty of bouquets and kisses in abundance. . . . We reached Pittsburg[h] at 8 o'clock, and were provided with a good breakfast and more kisses; women waving handkerchiefs and men shouting for the Union and on we go, made Harrisburgh at 6 o'clock P.M.; got hot coffee, and took cars for Baltimore at 10:30; made Baltimore at 6 P.M. Monday 2d, were kindly received; took cars for Washington at 12 M. and did'nt [sic] go. We were ordered to remain and guard a magazine containing ninety tons of powder taken from rebels here. The aforesaid magazine is about 30 feet from where I sit writing.

Everything is quiet here; too many soldiers and Union men here for rebels; they look severe but *mum*. . . . We have got arms and the men are drilling, busily learning the art of war.—The hundreds of orders given in less time than I am writing about them, the ring of the ramrods in the bright barrels, the clicking of the lock as the hammers are raised, all give dreadful note of preparation. This morning we had some target practice. About 150 guns were discharged at a small target, and your humble servant got the credit of making two of the best shots. . . . Some sesechers looked on but did'nt [sic] like to see good shooting, it was too ominous of what might befall them in case the *bloody* 6th got a poke at them; they did not say a word about it, but looked awful severe.

Allegan Journal, September 16, 1861.

ORLANDO BOLIVAR WILLCOX SPEAKS IN DETROIT
AFTER HIS RELEASE AS A PRISONER OF WAR

An 1847 West Point graduate, Willcox afterward served in the United States Army for ten years before returning to Detroit to practice law. After Lincoln's call for troops in April 1861, Willcox became the colonel of the Michigan 1st Regiment. Wounded and captured by the Confederates at the First Battle of Bull Run in July 1861, Willcox remained a prisoner for over a year until his exchange on August 19, 1862. By then Willcox had become a national hero. Speaking publicly in Detroit shortly after his release, Willcox, a Democrat, shared his views regarding emancipation in the weeks preceding Lincoln's issuing of the Preliminary Emancipation Proclamation on September 22, 1862. Meanwhile, Willcox's position regarding Northern dissent echoes the most strident Republicans.

This Government must rise and put down all encroachments upon it at whatever cost.

Freedom of speech is not allowed in the South. The questions of the day are not allowed to be discussed in the Press. Now, the ignorant and oppressed hate not only the North but all of her institutions. They hate her schools, colleges, manufactories, and the enterprize [sic] which has given to the country so much success, which has aided to give us the North as well as the South, a nationality. If they succeed in their rebellion, it is the intention of these men to fight eternally against our institutions.

Now, I have nothing to say with regard to the politics of the question, as far as Slavery is concerned. I see this scaly monster which has risen up in our midst, and with his terrible gripe [*sic*] intends to crush us out, and that monster is Slavery. I was a Democrat and I am a Democrat still. I say that this monster is Slavery at the bottom, with that scum of all the earth, Southern chivalry, at the top. We, Democrats and Abolitionists, can shake hands on that subject. This war, with its thunder and its revolution, is crushing out Slavery. Mr. DAVIS and his compeers . . . wish you to . . . raise the banner of emancipation. Make this an emancipation war and you unite the South. The President is right, and I stand by him as long as he carries out his policy. [Applause.]. . . .

There is an organization in the South to which I call your particular attention. . . . They know every one, and they overawe thousands who would be for the Union if they dared. Why cannot we assist our Government with a similar association for the purpose of keeping down secession sympathizers and fraudulent contractors? I say, if the Government is not strong enough to organize a sort of despotism in this war, let there be a despotism of the people established. There is nothing we should scruple at to maintain the Government. [Cries of "That's so."]

Let us, fellow-citizens, have in every ward and town an organization similar to those of the South, so that we can spot every man who is an enemy to the Government. Let us not be mealy-mouthed or tender-hearted. There are streams of messages going over Mason and Dixon's line every day from black-hearted traitors in the North. The papers here contain information that if they were published in the South, their editors would be prosecuted according to law. It is our duty to prevent these evils in every way we can. We should refuse to take papers that publish military information. We should do as they do in the South, have a complete surveillance over everything. Our vast superiority is no advantage when the enemy are aware of everything that is transpiring here.

I tell you we are just beginning this contest. . . . We must rouse ourselves to the necessity of making every exertion to crush the rebellion. Until you make up your mind that you are willing to give the last dollar, as well as the last drop of blood, you cannot conquer. Is your property of more value to you than my life is to me? [Cries of "No," "No."] I tell you my solemn feelings on this subject. I have a son, the darling of my life. I would rather see him begging from door to door than to see this Union destroyed. Nay, I would sooner follow him to the grave, [applause,] because, after this Government is broken up, there is nothing worth living for.

New York Times, August 30, 1862.

ONE YEAR: REFLECTIONS ON THE WAR IN DECEMBER 1861

Before ratification of the Twentieth Amendment in 1933, the US Congress annu-
ally convened on the first Monday in December. Even as secession was being openly
discussed in December 1860, no one, argued the Detroit Free Press, *could have*
imagined the transformations the following year brought. The Democratic editor
placed some of the blame on Northerners for not listening to the voices of Democrats
they had long trusted to lead the country. The Free Press *editor affirmed the neces-*
sity of suppressing the rebellion but also insisted that the road to reunion could not
include having the federal government interfere with slavery and remained hopeful
that Lincoln would continue to resist the emancipationist calls from his party's
abolitionist wing.

As Congress has again assembled at Washington . . . our thoughts involuntarily
turn back to this point last year to ascertain what changes have occurred in the
short space of twelve months in our country, and what hopes we have of the
future. At that time Congress was about to assemble, and representatives from
all the States were already at the capital to participate in its deliberations, and to
decide upon those questions upon which the destanies [*sic*] of the nation for years,
if not forever, seemed to hang. . . .

But the contest had scarcely passed before the far-seeing men of the nation
discovered the cloud of civil war slowly rising above the southern horizon, and
like faithful sentinels warned the nation of the impending danger. But the mass
of the people in the Northern States would not credit the men whom they had
followed so long and so faithfully. They would not have believed, even though
one had risen from the dead, if he had announced that within the space of one
short year a million of men then engaged in their usual avocations of peaceful
labor would be arrayed in arms against each other, and that our country, so long
the envy of the world, would be torn by internal dissension and civil war to that
extent that it would become a byword and reproach among the nations of the
earth. One year since and there was scarcely a man whose thoughts were occupied with the dangers of war, or who ever expected to be engaged in its exciting
scenes as an occupation or from a sense of duty; while to-day the thoughts of
the nation and each individual thereof are almost solely occupied in contemplat-
ing its horrors and weighing the duties it imposes upon them as citizens and
patriots. . . .

The duty to put down the rebellion no one disputes, and the duty also to leave
the negroes of the South to be disposed of by the States where they exist, would
seem to be almost as self evident. We are battling to sustain the constitution and
laws, to maintain the government in all its original integrity . . . and we look to the

President and Congress to take such steps as will most effectually bring us back to the stand-point where we were one short year since.

There will be those in Congress who will endeavor to chain the nation to the chariot-wheels of the abolition party, and proclaim to the world that the object and end of this war is the liberation of the slaves; but it is evident that these men do not represent the feelings of the great mass of the people. Whatever may be said of the leaders, and especially of those who are the most blood-thirsty, the people have engaged in the war solely for the purpose and with a desire to conquer a peace on the basis of the constitution. . . . The South must see that in war they have everything to lose and nothing to gain. Already ruin and desolation prevails in the land.

Detroit Free Press, as reproduced in *Adrian Daily Watchtower*, December 6, 1861.

FOUR

The Soldier's Life

$\mathcal{M}$ODERN ESTIMATES COUNT around two million men in federal service during the Civil War. The size of the regular (or professional) army remained small, numbering around 67,000. Most Civil War recruits entered federal service through their respective states. Approximately 90,000 servicemen came from Michigan[1]—a figure that stands at about 44 percent of the state's male population between the ages of fifteen and forty-nine in 1860.[2] Among the 90,000, almost 15,000 died before returning home, with more than two-thirds of these deaths stemming from disease.[3] Of those who survived, more than 9,000 saw their service end prematurely from disease or from battlefield injury that often left them permanently disabled.[4]

Between three and four thousand Michiganians were employed in either the regular army, the US Navy,[5] or the units of other states. Thus, over 95 percent of Michiganians who saw federal service during the Civil War did so in Michigan units. The great majority—almost two-thirds of Michigan's Civil War soldiers— enrolled in, or were drafted into, one of the state's thirty-five infantry regiments.[6] Slightly more than a fourth served in one of eleven cavalry regiments. Another 4.5 percent were in the artillery, while Michigan's regiments of engineers and mechanics claimed 3.8 percent and sharpshooters 1.5 percent.

One-sixth of Michigan soldiers died before returning, but the likelihood of survival varied widely among Michigan's Civil War soldiers. With a death rate of 7.5 percent, artillerists were the ones most likely to return home, followed by engineers and mechanics (death rate, 9.9 percent), cavalry (14.0 percent), infantry (16.2 percent), and sharpshooters (17.7 percent). In most Michigan units, deaths from disease surpassed combat-related deaths. Of the regiments that served at least three years, the mechanics and engineers, unsurprisingly, had the fewest combat-related deaths (killed in action, death by battle wounds, or death in a Confederate prison), 8 (or 0.3 percent of the regiment's 2,920 enrollees) dying in this manner.[7] Among infantry and cavalry units that served at least three years, the 9th Michigan Infantry had the fewest combat-related deaths, 25, or 1.3 percent. In contrast, the 27th Michigan Infantry, which was in the field for slightly more than two years, saw 251 of its members die from combat (a death rate of 13.2 percent), while the 17th Michigan Infantry, in the field for two years and nine months, saw the highest death rate of any Michigan regiment from combat, 15.2 percent (a figure boosted by the 54 members of the 17th who died in Confederate prisons).

But the 6th Michigan Infantry had the most deaths and the highest death rate from disease at 432, or 21.7 percent, and also had the highest overall death rate (25.9 percent) of any regiment in the state. Of the regiments serving at least three years, the 1st Michigan Infantry was the healthiest, losing only 76 (4.0 percent) of its members to disease. And though artillerists were more likely to escape battlefield-related deaths than the infantry and cavalry, they were the most likely to see their service end prematurely due to disability (12.0 percent), followed by infantry (11.9 percent) and cavalry (8.7 percent). The 3rd Michigan Infantry had 28.2 percent of its enrollees discharged for sickness or injury. When combining deaths and disability discharges, the 7th Michigan Infantry had the highest permanent casualty rate of 50.3 percent, while the 7th Michigan Cavalry had a permanent casualty rate of 18.1 percent, the lowest of any Michigan regiment serving at least three years. The permanent casualty rate among all the state's Civil War regiments was 26 percent.

Historians have long debated Union soldiers' motivations for enlisting during the Civil War. Some historians have emphasized soldiers' fervent devotion to the Union (often coupled with hostility to slavery and to white Southerners), while others have underlined peer pressure or a desire to escape from the boredom of civilian life to pursue the adventurous life of a soldier.[8] After their mustering, the Civil War took on a life of its own, regardless of the soldiers' motivations for enlistment or views on slavery. Most infantry, cavalry, and artillery recruits joined a regiment from their state that included the state's name and an ordinal number that corresponded with its chronological order of organization. Going into service once they had recruited a thousand or so soldiers, regiments were commanded by a colonel. Regiments contained companies of about a hundred men, each led by a captain. Within a year of their organization, though, sickness, injury, death, capture, and desertion reduced most regiments by half, and by 1863, many regiments' effective strength stood at two or three hundred. Four to seven regiments usually constituted a brigade, commanded by a colonel or a brigadier general; two to four brigades made a division, commanded by a brigadier general or major general; two or three divisions made a corps; and three corps constituted an army, which could number eighty thousand soldiers or more. In 1864, the US Army had seven armies in the field.[9]

Because companies and regiments often came from the same community or county, many soldiers viewed their comrades through the lens of prewar acquaintance and the expectation of being neighbors again once they returned—a dynamic that added another dimension to soldiers' comradeship while limiting the ability of officers to issue unpopular orders. Michigan's forty-nine regiments—thirty-five infantry, eleven cavalry, and one each of sharpshooters, engineers, and artillery (the last of which served in fourteen separate batteries)—were never in the field together and thus have sixty-two distinct histories. Most Michigan regiments served in either the Eastern Theater or the Western Theater. Conflict in the Eastern Theater included battles, skirmishes, and movements primarily in Virginia from the District of Columbia's suburbs to Richmond and Appomattox, but also included Virginia's Shenandoah Valley, Maryland, and south-central Pennsylvania. Michiganians who fought in the Western Theater generally went first to Kentucky before being directed to Tennessee, Mississippi, Alabama, and Georgia; by early 1865 they were part of Sherman's march into the Carolinas. A few regiments saw action in other places. The Michigan Colored Infantry (the state's separate African American regiment, eventually redesignated as the 102nd US Colored Troops) spent part of 1864 in Florida before being transferred to coastal South Carolina, well before other Michigan troops saw that state in early 1865. Battery H of the Michigan Light Artillery, and the 2nd and 3rd regiments of the Michigan cavalry, spent the early part of the war in Missouri. Battery G of the Michigan Light Artillery and the 6th Michigan Infantry regiment served the middle years of the war in Louisiana. The 30th Michigan never left the state and guarded the Canadian border along the Detroit and St. Clair Rivers in early 1865. The 12th Michigan spent two and a half years in Arkansas.

Historians estimate that there were approximately 10,000 battles and skirmishes during the Civil War; one nineteenth-century chronicler counted Michigan units as having participated in more than 800 of them.[10] Most were small and involved few casualties. Approximately twenty battles engaged at least 100,000 soldiers, Union and Confederate (with Fredericksburg, at 193,000, being the largest), while about a dozen battles resulted in at least 10,000 casualties for both sides (with Gettysburg, at 51,000, having the highest losses).

Most Civil War soldiers held romanticized views of combat when they enlisted. War's harsh realities caused many soldiers to reexamine their expectations and to explain combat to their family members and to newspapers back home. Regimental and brigade officers, in contrast, wrote detailed battle reports for their superior officers in a more dispassionate tone that nonetheless revealed war's brutality. Through their experiences on the battlefield, extensive marches, and lengthy encampments, soldiers created intense personal bonds that frequently outlasted the war—and for some veterans, made civilian life boring and unfulfilling. Many veterans, burdened by what later generations called shellshock or post-traumatic stress disorder, confronted a world that would never understand them.[11]

The recruiting of soldiers continued throughout the war, with the reorganized 11th Michigan Infantry being mustered into federal service less than a month before Robert E. Lee's defeat at Appomattox on April 9, 1865. Within weeks of Lee's capitulation, the remaining Confederate armies surrendered and Confederate political leaders either were captured (as was Jefferson Davis by the 4th Michigan Cavalry) or had left the country seeking exile. Beginning in late May 1865, Michigan regiments began to be mustered out of service, and by the end of the summer, most had returned to the state. A few remained in the field to keep the peace where rebellion had recently prevailed, including the 12th Michigan in Arkansas, the 28th Michigan in North Carolina, and the 3rd and 4th Michigan Infantry Regiments and the 3rd Michigan Cavalry, in Texas. The Michigan Cavalry Brigade—consisting of the 1st, 5th, 6th, and 7th regiments—went to Fort Leavenworth, Kansas, and established a stronger federal presence in the Nebraska, Dakota, and Utah Territories, often fighting Native Americans (rather than the Confederates they had enlisted to fight), through March 1866. In June 1866, the 28th Infantry Regiment, after spending over a year in North Carolina, became the last Michigan unit to be discharged from federal service.[12]

Private from the 4th Michigan Infantry (probably Richard L. Cramer from Macomb County; sometimes identified as Emory Eugene Kingin of the 21st Michigan Infantry). Photograph by Mathew Brady, c. 1861. Source: National Archives

THE ROUTINE OF CAMP LIFE

Soldiers looked forward to hearing from friends at home and often expressed their longing for civilian life. James W. King of Three Rivers described the winter routine for the 11th Michigan when the prospect of fighting seemed distant. Later wounded at Missionary Ridge in 1863 and outside Atlanta in 1864, King survived the war and eventually became editor of the Lansing State Republican.[13]

I hope you will pardon me for writing so often but I find the greatest pleasures of camp life is writing to friends if they return answers[,] but I think I do not get answers enough. [For] One to appreciate a letter[,] [he] must be separated from friends and home. They are welcome messengers to me always. I hope Dear Jenny you will write every opportunity you get.

We are still in camp Morton near Bardstown [Kentucky] where we will probably stay until the measles abates. This disease rages considerable in our regiment. . . . The small pox has nearly run out. There being only 3 or four cases and they will be brought to camp as soon as new clothes can be provided. I expect you hear strange stories about us, Captain just received a letter stating that he was dead and both of the Lieut's when in fact he has not been sick a day. Other letters state we are dying of thirty or forty a day when in fact there has been very few deaths. I can not see where such reports originate. . . .

The duties we have to perform each day is as follows[:] at daylight the reveille is sounded when we get up pack our knapsacks and attend roll call. The company is formed by one of the Sergeants and each man answers in person to his own name. When this is through with, an inspection of arms and knapsacks takes place. Then we break ranks and prepare for breakfast. Our cooking is done by 3 men detailed as company cooks. Our breakfast consists of a cup of coffee[,] Either Beef or Bacon with a loaf of bread. We have a bakery established here which furnishes the regiment with bread. When our breakfast is ready each squad takes their amount of provisions carry it into their tents and every man helps himself. Our dishes are one tin plate a knife and fork and tin cup which constitute the dishes of a soldier. At nine oclock Knapsack drill takes place which lasts till nearly noon. In the afternoon we have Battalion drill which is superseded by the Colonel at four oclock dress parade takes place when we are disbanded and return to quarters at 9 oclock in the evening another roll call is made when we are free from the duties of the day. . . .

I would like to have been with you Christmas[.] I know I should have enjoyed the ride and singing school very much. Dear Jenny how often that day did my thoughts go back to scenes and pleasures I had left. It is hard Dear Jenny to be separated from all one holds dear, but tis as you say none can escape the burdens of life. But Dear Jenny I think I can see a brighter day dawning for us. I do not think these troubles can last a great while longer, and then how sweet twill be after the dark day is past to return to home and friends.

James W. King to Jenny, January 17, 1862, James W. King Papers, Local and Regional History Collection, Western Michigan University.

SOLDIERS' DETERIORATING MORALS

After suffering defeat at the Battle of Ball's Bluff in October 1861, soldiers of the 7th Michigan retreated to their quarters at nearby Camp Benton, Maryland. There, while awaiting orders, they settled into their winter camp. The regiment's chaplain, A. K. Strong, wrote to the soldiers' hometown newspaper and complained that the troops' morality had deteriorated less than three months after departing Monroe.

Camp Benton, Nov. 25th 1861

The Seventh Michigan Regiment retains its old position near Edwards Ferry, and is likely to continue in this position so far as the information we now have, is concerned. . . .

My own labors as Chaplain differ, of course, from those of all other persons in the army, as well as from my work at home as Pastor of a Church. There is associated with them much that is discouraging and also much that is hopeful. There are a thousand men, more or less, living closely together in tents, free from all those family and social influences which are so well suited to restrain and refine. Left each for himself to do as seemeth unto him good provided only he conforms to certain military rules.

Under these circumstances there is, I had almost said, of necessity, an inconsiderable amount of incivility and rudeness of manners such as would not be seen in good society at home, with, I am very sorry to add, much profanity and Sabbath desecration. Indeed profanity and Sabbath desecration seem to be necessarily incident to a life in the army. And what seems to be peculiarly strange is the fact that officers and soldiers, amid the sick and the dying in the Hospital and on the eve of a battle, when they known not what a day may bring forth, can talk and act as though they had no reverence for either the name or the authority of Him in whose hands their breath is, and whose are all their ways.

All this is discouraging to one who would gladly see his fellow men fear God and keep his commandments. And yet these same men can be reached and influenced by a kind look and a kind word, an honest appeal to their better feelings, a simple and earnest presentation to them of the truths and motives of the Bible. They listen with a very respectful attention to the preaching of the Gospel. They receive at my hands as I go about from tent to tent and thankfully too, books, tracts and papers—and hundreds of these have been so distributed since I came here—and they read them with evident interest. . . . It is a gratification to me to be able to say that I have less profanity and witness less Sabbath desecration than I heard and saw when I first came into this camp.

Monroe Commercial, December 12, 1861.

PAROLING PRISONERS OF WAR

Since few expected the Civil War to last long, neither the Union nor the Confederacy began the war with plans to build prisoner-of-war camps. During the first two years of the war, both sides exchanged prisoners, a process that the Dix-Hill Cartel formalized in 1862. Rather than house prisoners in POW camps, the Union and the Confederacy paroled captive soldiers—meaning that the prisoner would, on his honor, return to his home, or to an exchange camp—before the completion of an exchange.

Because the Confederacy refused to recognize African American troops as prisoners, the exchange and parole system broke down in mid-1863 after the Union began using black soldiers, and did not resume until late 1864. Daniel W. Dutcher of the 6th Michigan Cavalry, captured during a skirmish with John Mosby's Confederate cavalry near Seneca, Maryland, on June 11, 1863, was one of the last prisoners to be paroled before federal authorities suspended the parole system. Since Dutcher rejoined the 6th Cavalry on November 1, 1863, he was probably never formally exchanged.

On PAROLE.—Our old friend Daniel W. Dutcher has just returned from the Libby Prison, Richmond, Va., where he was confined for six days only, after being taken prisoner in the skirmish which his company had with the rebels near Poolesville, Md., an account of which we published a few weeks since. He gives some interesting accounts of the state of affairs in "Dixie," says that Richmond could have been taken very easily, in his opinion, when he was there, as their fortifications contained no guns of consequence, and scarcely any soldiers were to be seen in the city. His rations while there consisted of two ounces of bread and a small piece of boiled meat for breakfast, and the same quantity of bread with the water in which the meat for breakfast was boiled, for supper; two such meals being thought sufficient in a day, no dinner being furnished. As soon as he is exchanged he will return to his regiment, as he expresses a strong desire to help fight our "Southern brethren" to the bitter end, not yet having been converted into a peace man. He has our hearty wishes for his success and safe return at the close of the war, as well as all those who are periling their lives in defences [sic] of our common country.

Mecosta County Pioneer, July 16, 1863.

NOTIFYING A SOLDIER'S FAMILY REGARDING DEATH

When forty-year-old Abram Conant left Flint to enlist with the Michigan Engineers and Mechanics in 1862, he probably expected to see little in the way of combat. Indeed, the regiment, responsible for constructing bridges and buildings and repairing railroad tracks, had just thirteen of its members die from battlefield wounds during their four years of service—among the lowest of Michigan's forty-five regiments. The Engineers and Mechanics' deaths from disease, however, ranked among the highest of the state's regiments. Conant spent less than six months with his regiment before succumbing to typhoid fever. Within days of receiving this letter, Abram's widow, Catherine Conant, began to gather the paperwork she needed to collect a widow's pension of eight dollars per month plus two dollars for each child under sixteen.

In Camp near Nashville, Feb 26, 1863

Mrs. C. E. Conant

Dear Madam,

It is my painful duty to inform you of the death of your husband, A. F. Conant. He died February 12th 1863 at Gen[era]l Hospital No 10 Nashville[,] Tenn[essee] of Typhoid fever. Yours of the 8th inst[ant] to him is open before me. I have taken the liberty to open it to find your address. Enclosed you will find 75 c[en]ts which I found in your letter. I trust you will pardon this liberty I have taken in opening your letter.

The death of your Husband is deeply felt by both Officers and Men of his company. He was an excellent Soldier, and although a vacancy in the ranks is made, our memory will ever cherish the remembrance of brave, patriotic Soldiers whos[e] face we shall see no more save in memories imagination.

You are entitled to his back pay, one hundred ($100.00) [dollars], his bounty and a pension. Enclosed I send you a letter and certificate of his death. I would recommend you to correspond with D. W. [Howard] of Detroit and send my certificate to him. I believe he will assist you all he can.

If I can assist you in any way to procure the am[oun]t due you from the Government I shall do so with the greatest of pleasure.

I remain, Madam,
Very Respectfully Yours,
Marcus Grant
Capt[ain] Co[mpany]. H 1st M.E.& M.

Captain Marcus Grant to Catherine E. Conant, February 26, 1863, Abram J. Conant Papers, Library of Congress.

A SELF-INFLICTED WOUND?

Andrew Cross, a member of the 5th Michigan Cavalry and a resident of Oshtemo, Kalamazoo County, claimed to have been shot in the knee by an African American man who reacted violently to Cross's open hostility to blacks. Although Sarah Coleman acknowledged that some people thought the wound self-inflicted, she believed Cross and also shared his views regarding African Americans. A few months later Coleman asked her brother to steal a revolver from a Confederate and send it to her so that she might "kill off some of the confounded niggers around here."[14] In November 1863 the army discharged Cross for disability.

Dear Brother. . . .

You wished to know how Andrew Cross was shot. It was before I came home but I got my news from the children. He had started for Detroit to get his discharge—if possible—had got a mile or so from Livonia was on the railroad when he came across a negro—they had a few words & I believe the negro asked him where he was going. Andrew told him he was going to fight for such damned Cusses[,] as he was & Whereupon the negro drew his revolver and shot him and then ran into the woods Andrew came back home and never let anyone know it till morning—it was after dark that he was shot. The ball struck him in his left knee. The Dr probed 8 or 10 inches but could not find the ball. [T]hey have discharged the Dr and old Mr Bushirk is nursing him. [H]e is getting along pretty well. . . . Some people think he shot himself to get rid of going to his Regt again but I don't for he was almost sure before he started, of a discharge.

Sarah Coleman to David Coleman, April 5, 1863, Jack B. and Barbara Riegel Collection, Archives and Regional History Collection, Western Michigan University.

EXECUTION OF A DESERTER

Of the more than two million men who wore the blue uniform during the Civil War, at least two hundred thousand deserted. Some deserters left the army without permission and intended to return, while others were bounty hunters who enlisted to collect money and then deserted to reenlist under a different name and collect another bounty. Punishments for desertion could be severe, but armies on both sides generally refrained from widespread execution of deserters. Abraham Lincoln pardoned many and commuted others to prison. Still, many officers believed that executing deserters discouraged desertion, and government records reveal that the military executed 147 Union soldiers for desertion. Among those executed by a firing squad was Julius Milika of Port Huron, who enlisted in the 10th Michigan in January 1862.

May 15—At his time it became the duty of regiment to execute one of their number. Julius Milika, of Company E, was tried by a general court-martial, and convicted of desertion. The case was an aggravated one, as he had deserted several times and from different regiments. He was found in Louisville, Kentucky, by accident, as it were, arrested, and brought to his regiment in irons, shut up in prison until he had his trial, and was sentenced "to be shot dead." The sentence to be carried out May 15, 1863. The detail of twelve men to perform the execution, was made from our regiment. . . .

Before the regiment moved out to witness this sad scene, and at the time the detail received their guns, which had been loaded by the Adjutant, Col. [Charles M.] Lum addressed the detail in an earnest, feeling manner, explaining the necessity of so painful a duty, and closed by asking them to have mercy enough on their comrade to take cool, deliberate aim at his *heart*.

All the troops in the division off duty were required to be present. At half-past 10 o'clock A.M. the troops began to assemble in a large green field west of the city, which had been selected as the place for execution. Milika's grave was dug by his comrades. The troops were formed in three fronts. . . . At a few minutes before 12 o'clock the ambulance containing Milika and his coffin, drove slowly up the inclosure and up towards the grave. It was strongly guarded by cavalry. When Milika alighted he was recognized by his comrades, and his calmness made our hearts but beat the sadder. He shook hands with the officers and then they all retired, leaving only the Chaplains to talk and pray with him. He sat down on his coffin while prayer was offered, and when these ceremonies were ended, he waved an adieu with his hand to his comrades, and, laying his hand upon his breast, said, "comrades, aim here, farewell." The bandage was then placed over his eyes, and he sat very erect, giving a good chance to the detail to do its duty. Then, as the comrades were given, we saw the guns brought to a shoulder. Ready—aim—then every heart was still, not a breath stirred the silent air, and all at once burst forth the valley. We knew that the men had remembered what the Colonel said to them, for we heard, as it were, but one gun, and Julius Milika was no more. He fell backward over his coffin, and died without a struggle. All six of the balls hit him, five of them in the breast. May we never be called upon to perform another so painful a duty. May Milika's fate be a sufficient warning to save all from that terrible end.

F.W.H. [Fletcher Willis Hewes], *History of the Formation, Movements, Camps, Scouts, and Battles of the Tenth Regiment Michigan Volunteer Infantry* (Detroit: John Slater's Book and Job Printers, 1864), 40–41.

A SOLDIER'S THOUGHTS REGARDING REENLISTMENT

The three-year enlistments of nearly a quarter of a million Union soldiers were scheduled to expire in 1864. Desirous of keeping existing regiments intact, the War

Department encouraged soldiers to reenlist through General Orders 191 and 376, is-
sued in June and November 1863, respectively. These orders offered reenlisting soldiers
bounties of $402. Regiments that succeeded in having three-fourths of the members
reenlist would keep their regiments intact, be recognized as veteran regiments, and be
permitted to have a thirty-day furlough during the winter of 1863–64. These induce-
ments, as well as ideological commitment to the war, camaraderie, and peer pressure,
led many to rejoin the army. The War Department later reported that this veteran
volunteer program secured 136,000 reenlistments. Roughly one hundred thousand
soldiers, though, chose to return home after their three-year enlistments expired.

Obviously pleased that the 2nd Michigan would continue as a veteran regiment,
Lieutenant John C. Joss insisted to his hometown newspaper that the government's
inducements had little to do with his fellow soldiers' decisions to reenlist. Less than
four months later Joss lost a leg at the Battle of the Wilderness.

Camp Strawberry Plaines, Tenn.

January 17, 1864. . . .

You undoubtedly would like to hear how our regiment stands in regard to
reenlisting in the Veteran Corps; this is very simply answered by telling you
that it has been reenlisted. . . . The order by the War Department, authorizing
the enlistment of veteran troops stipulates that the men shall visit their State,
and have a furlough for thirty days, at least 30 days before the expiration of the
original term of enlistment. Regiments are constantly leaving, and we expect to
leave for home in a few days. . . . The rest of the men who have not re-enlisted
are to serve out their time in some other regiment of their own State and of
their own selection: they mostly have chosen the Mich. 17th and 20th.

By papers, which occasionally reach us from the north, I perceive, that most all
old regiments of the Army of the Potomac have re-enlisted, the same case here.
The sacrifice is great, and cannot be too highly estimated. True a large bounty is
given, and seemingly, as a great many would say, the men could not do better than
to re-enlist. But here let me put in a few words. The money is no object, at least
with the majority of them. Whoever knows anything of the character of a soldier
and his life, will know the fact, that money is no object with them. It either goes
home to support a family, or it is spent to make the men comfortable. The soldier
is generous to a fault and as long as he has anything to eat he will share it with
his companion who has nothing. The constant life of danger, and the thought,
that the next day or hour may be his last, has that beneficial influence, which is so
proverbial with the sailors. The main object of most of the soldiers here, is, to see
that infernal rebellion crushed. They were the first to respond to their country's
call, regardless of home comforts and a life of ease they did not stop to enquire,
what their pay would be, in fact, the majority did not know if they ever would get

a single cent of pay, except their board and clothing; they did not wait until large bounties were offered; nor did they seek positions before they saw fit to serve their country. There you have the pure, genuine, patriotism. . . . They rather fight to the bitter end, than see a dishonorable peace. . . .

How insignificant and mean does the behavior of those appear at the north, who do shrink from the draft, bringing up excuses for exemption of which a child of seven years would be ashamed. Contrast the two classes. The old veteran and the citizen at home, who is unwilling to protect the flag, which has protected him, under whose folds he has become rich. In whose veins runs the true and self-sacrificing blood, which should pervade every true American, who has the good and grandeur of his country at heart.

The salvation of our glorious Republican Government depends upon the Army and the Navy, and not on the talk or political discussions at home. Come what may, the army is bound to see the thing out, and if the rebels don't want to be subjugated, they *will* be annihilated, that is the motto of the army now.

Let those beware who try to thwart the efforts of the Government. The army has respect for the rebel, who dares to show himself with gun in hand and fights us, but the cowardly villain and back biter, who grovels in the dark, and is constantly at work to undermine this Republic he despises. . . .

The regiment will soon make its appearance in Michigan, and then you can find out their sentiments, and they perhaps will show their contempt in stronger terms than you imagine.

Constantine Mercury and Advertiser, February 4, 1864.

A SOLDIER DISCOURAGES HIS BROTHER FROM ENLISTING

Sometimes the people most active in discouraging enlistments were soldiers themselves. Delos W. Lake of Adamsville, Cass County, joined the 19th Michigan Infantry in August 1862 and served until being mustered out in June 1865. Enlisting at twenty-two, Lake left behind his mother and a teenage brother, Calvin. Less than eighteen months after his enlistment, Delos repeatedly wrote to his brother from McMinnville, Tennessee, to discourage Calvin from enlisting. Delos described on February 12, 1864, how devout Christians "could not resist the temptations that were set before them. [T]hey use profane language and play cards for money and use intoxicating drinks." He added on February 28 that he had "thought the thing over several times. . . . [Y]ou are not old enough to enlist to be sure you are large enough but your mind and strength is not yet matured yet. [I]t is as much as I can do to get along as healthy and tough as I am. . . . Mother does not want to have both of her boys in the army she has don[e] well enough to send half of her small family."[15] Delos's arguments apparently carried the day, as there is no record of Calvin Lake enlisting in any Michigan regiment.

Dear Brother. . . .

I presume that you are willing to go and fight and die if necessary for your Country. [B]ut see here I want you to take my advise [sic] and stay at home, they cant [sic] draft you until a year from now. [A]nd by then the Rebs will be corners so they can't make a move without being jumped. [B]y the time United States Grant (as he is sometimes called) get[s] a good lick at the Rebs at Atlanta there wont bee much left of them in Georgia[.] [I]f I have as good health the next 18 months as I have so far I will come out all right. I want you to keep away from them war meetings and have nothing to do with them.

Delos Lake to Calvin Lake, January 17, 1864, Huntington Library, San Marino, California.

TWO MICHIGAN SOLDIERS ON OPPOSING SIDES OF THE BATTLEFIELD

This letter, written by an unnamed soldier in the 5th Michigan Infantry to his brother in Detroit, notes how soldiers on both sides sometimes came from very similar backgrounds. Less than a year after this letter's publication, a disability resulted in Caleb W. Gifford's premature discharge from the army.

Hunter's Chapel, Arlington Heights, Va., Tuesday, Sept. 24, 1861. . . .

We now send out daily two full companies for picket duty, and the boys have a great deal of fun out there, notwithstanding that on average there is two a day killed. I will give you an illustration: Saturday, Corporal [Caleb W.] Gifford, a member of my company, went out; the rebel pickets and ours met; says Gifford, "if you will lay down your arms, I will mine, and I will give you a little of the Michigan sharp-shooters' whiskey;" (they call us "the d—d Michigan sharp-shooters.") He came over and took a smile with the Corporal. His name was R. Williams, of the Georgia regulars. Gifford traded canteens with him, and a rebel by the name of Fuller, who formerly lived in Troy and Rochester, Michigan, took a smile with him also. Gifford asked him if he had been impressed? He said no, he was there of his own will; believed he was right, and expected to give us a threshing. Of course, my Corporal differed from him. From friendly talk they came to hard words; they both resumed their arms, and the two Michigan men were again enemies to the death.

Detroit Advertiser, as reproduced in the *Ripley (Ohio) Bee,* October 10, 1861.

A HOSPITAL STEWARD DESCRIBES THE BATTLE OF SHILOH

The Battle of Shiloh, fought on April 6–7, 1862, in south-central Tennessee, was the largest and bloodiest battle in United States history to that point; at the war's end, its casualties remained among the highest. Its brutality surprised the participants, including *General Ulysses S. Grant. After the war, Grant recalled that before "the Battle of Shiloh I, as well as thousands of other citizens, believed that the rebellion against the government would collapse suddenly and soon." The Confederates' effort there, though, caused Grant to relinquish "the idea of saving the Union except by complete conquest."*[16]

Briefly a Confederate prisoner during the battle, Samuel Henry Eells of Detroit, a hospital steward for the 12th Michigan, captures the battle's shifting tides from the perspective of the hospital.

Pittsburgh Landing Tenn.
April 13th 1862

My dear friends . . .

I presume you would like to hear from me and to know that I am alive and uninjured after this great battle. Well I am so. But I got my share of the bad luck of last Sunday for I have been a prisoner among the secesh until last night, and had rather a hard time of it, but have got back safe to our lines. . . .

The papers will give you the details of the battle better than I could do. But I will tell you all I know about it in brief. . . . The rebels greatly outnumbered us for we were in hopes our men could hold them at bay until reinforcements should arrive. None came however and our men were gradually forced back. They retired slowly fighting as they went, and doing splendidly for green troops, until they came to the camp. There the enemy began to come in at the sides as well as in front . . . and our men were forced to run to escape being surrounded.

All this time I was in the hospital tents helping to dress the wounded but I managed to run out once in a while to see the fight. The wounded came in pretty fast and soon filled up the hospital and then they were laid down on the ground outside. We were all hard at work and only just begun at that when the rout began. Everybody else was running off as fast as possible, but the surgeons resolved that they would not leave their wounded and I was not going to go either, when my services were most required.

Most of the hospital attendants ran away but some remained and we continued our work of attending to the wounded though the bullets began to come unpleasantly near and thick. One passed through the tent and within three inches of my head as I was dressing a wounded man, smashing a bottle of Ammonia liniment that stood on a box beside me and sending the fluid right into my face and eyes. Very soon the rebels came pouring in on all sides. We of course made no resistance, and they did not fire upon us though some leveled their guns at us and we rather expected to be shot, than otherwise. I know I expected every moment to get hit, for the balls were flying all around though I do not think they were meant for the hospital or any of us around there.

The ground outside was covered with the wounded all around and the yellow flag was over the tent. I did not know but what I should get frightened in the first battle, but I believe I didn't. I was too busy, and if I had been ever so much scared I don't think I could have run off and left our wounded crying for help. It was a pitiful sight I can tell you, I hope never to see the like again. Such groans and cries for help and especially for "Water!" "Water!" all the time. We could not attend to them half as fast as they needed though we worked as hard as we could.

Soon after the first appearance of the rebels[,] Gen. [Thomas] Hindman of Arkansas rode up and placed a guard over us and assured us we should not be molested though we must consider ourselves prisoners. Two rebel surgeons came up too and established their hospital right by us and made liberal use of our medicines and hospital stoves. There we worked all day upon the rebel wounded as well as our own, for there were a great number of them brought there. . . .

The rebel officers and surgeons treated us very well and we fared on the whole better than I expected. . . .

[The Confederates] got pretty well beaten on Monday [April 7.] We could see and hear them all Monday night retreating over the road to Corinth[,] Miss. [,] which passed close by where we were. The road was jammed full of them all that night, and they left quantities of stores & provisions along the way most of which they had taken from our camps. As they retreated our forces advanced. We fully expected to be sent on further South. Those of our wounded who were able to travel were sent on but the Surgeons & I and some of our hospital attendants were left with those who could not be transported without ambulances which they did not have. Then one of our Surgeons of our side made an arrangement with the Surgeons of the other side by which it was agreed that the wounded should be left where they were until they could be carried away & that they should go each to their own party without hindrance from the troops of either side, & their Surgeons & attendants should go with them. We were at the time in their power but our pickets were coming pretty near and the prospect was that they would be captured by our forces before they could get away. So we came back last night and now are in our old camp again.

Samuel Henry Eells to My Dear Friends, April 13, 1862, Samuel Henry Eells Papers, Library of Congress.

A SOLDIER'S REFLECTIONS ON COMBAT AND MILITARY LIFE

Having made a rapid transition from life as civilians, soldiers frequently commented on the dynamics and ironies of military life. Walter C. White's observations stand as among the most poignant. White, of the 4th Michigan Infantry, died at Fredericksburg four days after writing these observations—and six days before the Adrian Watchtower published them.[17]

NEAR FALMOUTH VA.,
Dec. 9th, 1862.

Nothing new. Fredericksburg is *yet* in our front, and the enemy is beyond. Both armies, apparently, are as quiet as if they never expected to be disturbed.— Neither seems to be troubled because of the vicinity of the other, and although the single crack of a rifle may be the signal of a general engagement, to terminate with the total defeat of one or the other, all sleep as quietly and soundly as if in the quiet chambers of their own peaceful homes.

Really war is a study. Especially is it so in its effects on the habits and modes of those actually engaged in its practices. The toilsome march, makes a *"nest"* in the brush, a feathery couch,—exposure to the chilly blasts and storm, makes the leaky shelter tent, a palace,—hunger and exposure, so sharpens the appetite that hard crackers and pork make a feast.—The camp fire, replaces the home hearthstone, and comrades are brothers. Home is but a dream,—to-day we are in camp with all the comforts of this life,—tomorrow in the field with all the discomforts. The only sure thing with us is that we are sure of nothing. What was once our horror, becomes our pride. The murderer in civil life becomes the hero of the battle field.

I have in my mind just now a boy, belonging to the regiment, who has not yet seen his sixteen summers. When he joined us, in April, as we were going to the Peninsula, he appeared so child-like—so girl-like, as to be a subject of general remark. But eight months of war-life has transformed that child, to the man soldier. Yorktown, and Williamsburg, and Fair Oaks, and the Orchard, and Glen Dale, and Malvern Hill, and Manassas, and Bull Run, and Chantilly, saw him foremost, among the bravest of the brave. Then the boy, to-day the man.—But not so always. By his side is another. He joined us, strong of limb, robust in health, with high hopes of future glory, and fair prospects of success. He stands there now, crippled in limb—broken in health—hopes deferred, and prospects blasted, and a dark future in reserve. Then the man—to-day the boy. Such are war's transformations.

Health, and wealth, and strength, and beauty, and deformity, and weakness, and poverty, disease, and age, all are its ban. Nothing shall escape its ruthless hand.—Nor is it satisfied with the present. Its evils and its sorrow, its poverty and its mutilation shall go down into the future, a witness to the coming generations of the folly of this. The historian wild with its infatuation will tell of its glory, and of its grand achievements, and of its great importance for the maintenance of the National dignity and honor. Commenced, this war must be pushed to a successful termination.

Yesterday the regiment came in from the river and joined the brigade, and to-day we have been busy fixing up as well as possible under the circumstances, to make ourselves comfortable while we stay here. The weather is very cold, and tents pitched on the frozen ground do not promise to be very cheerful or warm for the first few days. With fires in them they become muddy from thawing out, without fires you freeze. Between the two, we are bound to be miserable for a while, but "there are better days coming" and we hope before long. If I can guess anything from what can be seen, an attempt to cross the river will be made soon, I think to-morrow or next day.

Adrian Daily Watchtower, December 19, 1862

THE 24TH MICHIGAN INFANTRY AT GETTYSBURG

Recruited from Detroit and Wayne County in the summer of 1862, the 24th Michigan became part of the famed Iron Brigade, which also consisted of regiments from Indiana and Wisconsin. The brigade faced its fiercest fighting at the three-day Battle of Gettysburg in July 1863. Although by the second day of the battle US troops outnumbered the Confederates, the Confederates held the numerical advantage on the morning of July 1 when the Iron Brigade arrived on the battlefield. There, the brigade faced two Confederate brigades, and soon routed the Confederates' initial assault and captured Confederate General James J. Archer. In the afternoon, though, Confederates overpowered the entire Union line. The 24th Michigan found itself in the thickest part of this fight. When leading his troops into battle on July 1, Colonel Henry A. Morrow, who filed this report, counted nearly 500 officers and soldiers in his regiment. A few hours later more than 80 percent of them were dead, wounded, captured, or missing, giving the 24th, in the words of one historian, "the melancholy honor of the highest loss of any federal regiment for the three days at Gettysburg."[18]

Culpeper, Virginia, February 22, 1864. . . .

I have the honor to submit the following report of the part taken by the Twenty-fourth Michigan Volunteers in the battle of Gettysburg, July 1, 1863. . . .

At an early hour on July 1, we marched in the direction of Gettysburg, distant 6 or 7 miles. The report of artillery was soon heard in the direction of this place, which indicated that our cavalry had already engaged the enemy. Our pace was considerably quickened, and about 9 a.m. we came near the town of Gettysburg, and . . . moved forward into line of battle on the double-quick. The cavalry immediately in our front was hotly engaged with the enemy, and the brigade was ordered to advance at once, no order being given or time allowed for loading our guns. . . . The order to charge was now given, and the brigade dashed up and over the hill and down into the ravine, through which flows Willoughby's Run, where we captured a large number of prisoners, being a part of General Archer's brigade. The cavalry in the meantime had taken position on our left flank. In this affair the Twenty-fourth Michigan occupied the extreme left of the brigade, the Nineteenth Indiana being on our right. . . .

We now received orders to withdraw to the east bank of the stream, which was done. The brigade changed front forward on first battalion, and marched into the woods known as McPherson's woods, and formed in line of battle, the Nineteenth Indiana being on the left of the Twenty-fourth Michigan and the Seventh Wisconsin on its right. In executing this movement, my lieutenant-colonel and adjutant were severely wounded, and did not afterward rejoin the regiment, the former having lost a leg, and the latter being severely wounded in the groin. . . .

The woods were shelled, but I have no casualties to report as occurring at this time. I sent officers several times to the general commanding to report the condition of the line, and suggesting a change of position, as it was, in my judgment, untenable. To these reports of the condition of our line, I received answer that the position was ordered to be held, and must be held at all hazards.

The enemy advanced in two lines of battle, their right extending beyond and overlapping our left. I gave direction to the men to withhold their fire until the enemy should come within short range of our guns. This was done, but the nature of the ground was such that I am inclined to think we inflicted but little injury on the enemy at this time. Their advance was not checked, and they came on with rapid strides, yelling like demons. The Nineteenth Indiana, on our left, fought most gallantly, but was overpowered by superior numbers, the enemy having also the advantage of position, and, after a severe loss, was forced back. The left of my regiment was now exposed to an enfilading fire, and orders were given for this portion of the line to swing back, so as to face the enemy, now on this flank. Pending the execution of this movement, the enemy advanced in such force as to compel me to fall back and take a new position a short distance in the rear.

In the meantime I had lost in killed and wounded several of my best officers and many of my men. . . .

The second line was promptly formed, and we made a desperate resistance, but the enemy accumulating in our front, and our losses being very great, we were forced to fall back and take up a third position beyond a slight ravine. . . .

By this time the ranks were so diminished that scarcely a fourth of the forces taken into action could be rallied. Corpl. Andrew Wagner, Company F, one of the color guard, took the colors, and was ordered by me to plant them in a position to which I designed to rally the men. He was wounded in the breast and left on the field. I now took the flag from the ground, where it had fallen, and was rallying the remnant of my regiment, when Private William Kelly, of Company E, took the colors from my hands, remarking, as he did so, "The colonel of the Twenty-fourth shall never carry the flag while I am alive." He was killed instantly. Private Lilburn A. Spaulding, of Company K, seized the colors and bore them for a time. Subsequently I took them from him to rally the men, and kept them until I was wounded.

We had inflicted severe loss on the enemy, but their numbers were so overpowering and our own losses had been so great that we were unable to maintain our position, and were forced back, step by step, contesting every foot of ground, to the barricade. I was wounded just before reaching the barricade, west of the seminary building, and left the field. Previous to abandoning our last position, orders were received to fall back, given, I believe, by Major-General [Abner] Doubleday.

The command of the regiment now devolved upon Captain Albert M. Edwards, who collected the remnant of it, and fell back with the brigade to Culp's Hill, which it held for the two succeeding days.

Shortly after I was wounded, Captain Edwards found the colors in the hands of a wounded soldier, who had fallen on the east side of the barricade. He was reclining on his right side, and was holding the colors in his left hand. I have not been able to ascertain the name of this brave soldier in whose paralyzed hands Captain Edwards found the flag. Captain Edwards describes him as being severely wounded, and he is, therefore, probably among our dead. His name may forever be unknown, but his bravery will never die.

Captain Edwards behaved very gallantly at this time in rallying the men under a murderous fire.

The field over which we fought, from our first line of battle in McPherson's woods to the barricade near the seminary, was strewn with the killed and wounded. Our losses were very large, exceeding, perhaps, the losses sustained by any one regiment of equal size in a single engagement of this or any other war. . . .

Nearly all our wounded, myself among them, fell into the hands of the enemy when he took possession of the town of Gettysburg. When the enemy evacuated the place, on the night of the 3d instant most of the wounded were left behind.

The War of the Rebellion: A Compilation of the Official Records of the Union and Confederate Armies, ser. 1, vol. 27, part 1 (Washington, DC: Government Printing Office, 1889), 267–73.

UNDER CONFEDERATE AND UNION FIRE

Writing from Georgia shortly after the battles of Resaca and Cassville, Henry G. Noble of the 19th Michigan Infantry describes the ordeals of combat and points to battlefield confusion that sometimes resulted in soldiers' being shot by their comrades—described by a later generation as "friendly fire."

Camp Near Cassville, Georgia
May the 21st, 1864

Dear Ruth. . . .

Since I wrote to you our regt. has seen some pretty hard times. . . . For more than two weeks we have been either hearing of the booming of cannons and the rattle of musketry and not one day in that time has passed without our hearing the dreaded cannon as it belched forth its content so destructive to human life. Although our regt and Brigade was so near the enemy we did not get into any action until sunday the 15th of May and I have reason to believe that there are many of our Division that will remember that day to the latest period of their lives.

We had been lying back in sight of where our troops skirmishing with the enemy for about ten days and had not seen the rebels in any force. But Sunday morning our Corps commanded by Gen Hooker was ordered forward. We marched some five miles around on one of the enemies [*sic*] flanks and joined Gen Howard['s] Corps which had been desperately fighting the day before. He found the enemy pretty strongly fortified and in a strong position. Of course we privates knew nothing of the strength of their numbers and position at that time but we had a chance to test both ere night set in[.] I cannot describe to you how I felt when I saw the battle flag and knew that we were about to go into battle but at any rate it was no very pleasant sensation that I experienced at that time, there were several lines of battle in front of our regt or Brigade when we got into position but when ordered to advance the front lines with the exception of the one in advance did not move. We were under the fire from the rebel batter[i]es at that time and the Grape & Canister were flying around us at a rate in no wise pleasant or agreeable, and we were all lying flat on the ground [a]s the front lines did not stir. [O]ur Brigade was ordered to charge past them and forward we went walking right over them and just as we passed the one next [to] the front those in the rear came up behind us and without seeing a rebel commenced firing right through our lines[.]

[W]e were on the side of a hill and they were a little above us this is all that saved us from being shot down by our own men[.] As it was there was more men in our Corp[s] killed & wounded by this piece of carelessness than by any firing that that [*sic*] the rebels done[.] It was a trying time, the smoke from the guns was almost blinding and the bullets whistled past our ears so close in some instances that they could be felt. Dexter Baird [i.e., George L. Baird] was shot through both arms one ball taking effect in his wrist and the other above the elbow, this was done by our own men. . . . We drove the rebels from a fort and captured four pieces of artillery and then our regt having become considerably scattered by other regts charging in among us we fell back to get organized again, the fighting continued all day and in the night the rebels skedaddled leaving us in full possession of the field[.]

Henry Noble to Ruth, May 21, 1864, Noble Papers, Bentley Historical Library, University of Michigan.

CUSTER AND THE MICHIGAN CAVALRY BRIGADE AT YELLOW TAVERN

Most remember George Armstrong Custer as a brutal Indian fighter who died while leading the 7th US Cavalry to its decimation by a combined force of Sioux, Cheyenne, and Arapaho at the Battle of the Little Big Horn in June 1876. His reckless demise obscures Custer's brilliant career as a Civil War cavalry general. Custer, a sometime resident of Monroe, Michigan, graduated last in his class at West Point in 1861 and became the US Army's youngest general officer two years later. As general, Custer took command of the Michigan Cavalry Brigade, consisting of the 1st, 5th, 6th, and 7th Michigan Cavalry Regiments. In this report, Custer describes his brigade's participation at the Battle of Yellow Tavern, in which US cavalry killed Confederate general J. E. B. Stuart and routed his cavalry.

July 4, 1864. . . .

On [May 11, 1864] the enemy's cavalry, under Maj. Gen. J. E. B. Stuart, was met at Yellow Tavern. . . . The enemy was strongly posted on a bluff in rear of a thin skirt of woods, his battery being concealed from our view by the woods, while they had obtained perfect range of position. The edge of the woods nearest to my front was held by the enemy's dismounted men, who poured a heavy fire into my lines until the Fifth and Sixth Michigan were ordered to dismount and drive the enemy from his position, which they did in the most gallant manner, led by Colonel [Russell A.] Alger, of the Fifth, and Major [James H.] Kidd, of the Sixth. Upon reaching the woods I directed Colonel Alger to establish the Fifth and Sixth upon a line near the skirts of the wood and hold his position until further orders. From a personal examination of the ground, I discovered that a successful charge might be made upon the battery of the enemy by keeping well to the right. With this intention I formed the First Michigan Cavalry in column of squadrons under cover of the wood. At the same time I directed Colonel Alger and Major Kidd to move the Fifth and Sixth Michigan Cavalry forward and occupy the attention of the enemy on the left, Heaton's battery to engage them in front, while the First charged the battery on the flank. The bugle sounded the advance and the three regiments moved forward. As soon as the First Michigan moved from the cover of the woods the enemy divined our intention and opened a brisk fire from his artillery with shell and canister. Before the battery of the enemy could be reached there were five fences to be opened and a bridge to cross, over which it was impossible to pass more than 3 at one time, the intervening ground being within close range of the enemy's battery. Yet, notwithstanding these obstacles, the First Michigan, Lieutenant-Colonel [Peter] Stagg commanding, advanced boldly to the charge, and when within 200 yards of the battery, charged it with a yell which spread terror before them. Two pieces of cannon, two limbers, filled with ammunition, and a large number of prisoners were among the results of this charge. . . .

[I]t is impossible to mention the names of all the officers of the First Michigan Cavalry who distinguished themselves by their gallantry in this charge. . . . The united efforts of the First, Fifth, Sixth, and Seventh Michigan, assisted by [Lieutenant Edward] Heaton's battery [2nd United States Artillery], and the First Vermont, under the gallant Colonel [Addison Webster] Preston, proved sufficient, after a close contest, to rout the enemy and drive him from his position. His defeat was complete. He fled, leaving a large number of dead and wounded in our hands. Among the dead was found the body of the notorious Col. Henry Clay Pate.[19] From facts obtained on the battle-field and from information derived since, I have every reason to believe that the rebel General J. E. B. Stuart received his death wound from the hands of Private John A. Huff,[20] Company E, Fifth Michigan Cavalry, who has since died from a wound received at [the Battle of] Haw's Shop [May 28, 1864].

The War of the Rebellion: A Compilation of the Official Records of the Union and Confederate Armies, ser. 1, vol. 36, part 1 (Washington, DC: Government Printing Office, 1891), 815–20.

ENVIRONMENTAL DEVASTATION ON THE VIRGINIA FRONT

This unnamed correspondent of the Lansing State Republican *went to the front in Stevensburg, Virginia, for the dedication of a building at General Hugh Judson Kilpatrick's headquarters—an event that both Michigan senators and four-fifths of the Michigan US House delegation also attended. After the dedication ceremony the correspondent ventured outside the camp to witness the specter of environmental desolation—a landscape savaged by almost three years of war. Venturing there in the winter, he also witnessed opposing soldiers at close range. Everyone realized, though, that with the onset of spring this militarized border would be the site of intense fighting.*

Washington, Feb. 27th, 1864. . . .

And alas, the wild work which war has made with the whole region, from Fairfax to the Rapidan! For a distance of fifty miles, along the railroad route, you see scarcely a dwelling. Barns, out houses of every kind, fences, bridges, door-yards, gates, fruit trees, shade trees, shrubbery, implements of husbandry, horses, cattle, sheep, hay, cornstalks, are all gone. The fruit trees of any value have been cut down and burned for fuel or used as encampments, and the life of others been destroyed by cavalry horses, picketed to them, gnawing off the fresh bark and leaving the tree to dry. The whole route, as you go on, echoes on your ear but one word—desolation! desolation!—and until your own eyes shall see the sad spectacle, you cannot properly estimate the folly, the wickedness of this causeless and wanton rebellion. . . . The very fields, as they undulate across valley and hill, seem to reproach the criminality of the authors of the strife; [the landscape], trodden and poached up by the tread of the cavalry, cut with deep ruts by the artillery wheels and the tires of the heavy army wagons, whose trains sometimes stretch along for many miles, seem to throw a ghastly grin—a grin of despair and death, at the unspeakable crime. . . .

A portion of our party, among whom was Senator [Jacob] Howard, then proceeded under the escort of Lieutenant Colonel [Ebenezer] Gould, of the 5th Michigan cavalry, to the Rapidan, near to what is known as Morton's Ford, and took a view of the rebel pickets on the other side of the river. The stream is perhaps half the size of Grand River at Lansing and flows sluggishly through bottoms of considerable width. We saw some scores of grey backs on the other bank, leisurely walking to and fro and seeming to understand that the visit of our party was one of mere amusement and no menace. There was no firing from the one side to the other, as, by general consent, the barbarous practice of picket shooting had been dropped. Col. Gould, however, did not fail, very courteously to admonish certain enthusiastic ones of our party against approaching so near to the grey backs as to enable them to draw a bead on the intruder and thus attract him *across the river.*

Lansing State Republican, March 9, 1864.

THE 2ND INFANTRY'S ADDRESS TO THE PEOPLE OF MICHIGAN

Political partisans often used soldiers to advance their agenda. Consequently soldiers in the field sometimes published their own newspapers to present their perspective to the public. The only known issue of the Union Vidette, *published by the 2nd Michigan Infantry in Lebanon, Kentucky, demonstrates soldiers' fierce patriotism, their determination to fight the war to the end, and their displeasure with some civilians—the implication being Copperhead Democrats—for their less-than-complete support for the war. At least two civilian newspapers republished this manifesto from the* Vidette, *one that the author privately revealed "took all my spare time for three days" to write.*[21]

At a meeting of the Line Officers of the Second Michigan Volunteers, held at Newport News, Virginia, March 17th, 1863, the following address to the people of Michigan was adopted:

Believing that the most perfect understanding should at this time exist between the people and the army, we take this means of communicating with our friends at home. We believe and desire that the war should be prosecuted till our victory shall be final and complete, and till the enemy shall be reduced to unconditional submission. We will give our cordial and united support to any and all measures adopted by the Government . . . for the rigorous prosecution of the war. We have been, and still are, cheered and encouraged by the loyalty and patriotism of the body of the people. Our labors are lightened by your sympathy, and our hearts moved by your unceasing efforts in behalf of the sick and wounded.

There is, however, a class among you, whose conduct is alike a disgrace to themselves, and the communities where they are allowed to exist. While partaking of all the blessings which the kindest Government can bestow, they strive, with the vicious activity of cowardice and treason, to ruin it by depreciating its currency; harboring deserters; preventing enlistments; by circulating false reports of the demoralization of its army, and by urging a peace more ruinous than defeat itself. In our estimation, such men deserve the bayonet, the halter, and the universal contempt of mankind.

We are now about entering on our third year of service. Our torn flag, and thinned ranks, testify that we have experienced the realities of war. When we say "Prosecute the war," we well know what those words mean, and who will be the first to fall. Nevertheless, give us your support, and we will, with ten-fold ardor and enthusiasm, again . . . "bear our colors proudly and defiantly against the enemy."

Our success has not always been equal to your expectations. We know of no remedy except to try again. Conscious of our own defeats, we are doing our utmost to correct the errors of inexperience, and to perfect organization and discipline. Animated by the same feelings as when we left the State, we are ready to give all we have for the cause. Let the North but give twentieth part as much, even, and ere another year the Star Spangled Banner will float victorious from the lakes to the gulf. Refuse, and we shall soon have to look back to the day when it was honorable to be called an American.

Brand the coward; drive the traitor and deserter with the bayonet, if need be, from your midst; put your hands to the work you promised to do when we left the State, and as for a time you did; let our former companions, if there be any pride or patriotism in them, show it by coming forth at once, without the delay and expense of the draft. The enemy dictated the war—let us dictate the peace and its terms will probably be satisfactory.

Union Vidette, undated [April 1863].

HOW THE SOLDIERS FEEL ABOUT THE WAR

Many soldiers' frustrations—low pay received irregularly, hardships their families suffered, a sense that the war's duration defied common sense—found a welcome audience in Democratic newspapers, whose editors were always on the watch for political advantage. While this pseudonymous letter may have confirmed Democrats' belief regarding the war's inefficient conduct—or futility—it candidly reveals sentiments held by many soldiers.

   Camp 3d Michigan Cavalry, near Jackson, Tenn., Jan. 19th, 1863. . . .
Our boys are healthy, cheerful, and becoming more disciplined in the science
of the soldier. . . . [W]e have strong hopes that this hard work will not be required
of us a great while longer, for we look forward to a speedy termination of this
unnatural war. But we must admit the prospects seem dark. How our fathers,
and brothers at home, look upon it, we don't know, but we hope to them the
future looks brighter than it does to us. I have heard more troops were called for
in the North. Can it be that *more* brave men must enroll themselves as soldiers
for the Union, and fail, and [become] sacrifices to [the] inefficiency, and selfish
men in leaders we have? True, the only honorable, and creditable way of ending
this war, is by putting down the rebellion by force of arms; but there must be a
change in our system of management. We are loyal—the last drop of blood which
courses through the veins of him who is fighting for the preservation of this once
unbroken Union, is free as the waters of the brooklet . . . but it is discouraging,
disheartening to us, to learn of such military reverses as we have had recently.
A terrible carnage at Fredericksburg; at Vicksburg a disgraceful repulse; at
Murfreesboro, the victory amounts to nothing more than a terrible slaughter of
precious human lives! Why these reverses, when the Government has even *now*
twice the number of troops that the South has? Is there any reason for it? We, as
soldiers, loyal to the good old Union, would like to know.
   We have received no pay since the 30th of June, 1862. Letters are received
daily in the regiments, from wives of soldiers asking for money with which to
purchase the simple necessities of life, for which they are actually suffering! Still,
the prospects of any pay for the present, are very dubious, indeed. Seven long
months, nearly, and no pay. 'Tis thus with most of the army of the Southwest.
As a poor Infantry private remarked to me a few days ago[,] "One of three things
must happen—either the Government must pay me for my services, my wife and
children must *starve*, or I must *desert!*" Would a man be justified in *deserting* the
service, to keep his wife and babes from starving? Yet, such is the feeling among a
great many. Now, will some one suggest to the poor private soldier, who serves for
the small pittance of $13 per month, a plan of operation, in case of getting no pay

for his services? Another thing—when is our State going to do anything for her sick and wounded soldiers? These are significant questions, and should be answered.

Adrian Daily Watchtower, January 27, 1863.

TENSIONS IN THE RANKS

Because Civil War soldiers within a regiment often came from the same community, officers and enlisted men frequently knew one another from their prewar civilian lives. The expected return of soldiers to those communities after the war's conclusion initially moderated the traditional hostility between a regiment's enlisted men and its officers. The strains of war, however, often led some soldiers, like Daniel G. Crotty of the 3rd Michigan, to despise officers who exercised their prerogatives.[22]

About the first of August [1862] we commence our backward march on the Peninsula. The marching is very disagreeable on account of the severely warm weather and dusty roads. Water is very scarce along the route, and there is much suffering from the want of it. When we camp nights, if there are any nice springs around, there is soon a guard put over them, and, of course, it is reserved for the officers. Like a certain tree at the battle of Fair Oaks [May 31-June 1, 1862]. In the heat of battle a certain officer, well known to us all, took a position behind a huge pine. A couple of soldiers thought they would like to take shelter there too. But the gallant Captain drew his sword and told them to be gone, for this tree is reserved for the officers, and none others. Of course, the poor soldiers give way, for they dare not disobey the order of an officer, even if he was a coward, for he would be courtmartialed, his pay stopped, be made to march in camp with a stick on his shoulder, or be bucked and gagged and forty pails of water thrown on his head, or, if he did not like all this, by way of a change, be tied up by the thumbs to the limb of a tree. Oh, yes, all the good things are reserved for the officers, and the poor soldier has to roam over the fields and hunt some cow track for some water to cook his coffee. But we have one consolation. The soldier is here to save this country, and suffer for it, while such cowardly officers as the one at Fair Oaks are here for pay. I will say here, that I thank God that such officers are scarce in our army, and we have some as humane and as good men as live—but the bad ones have influence, and the good ones cannot do much against them.

Daniel G. Crotty, *Four Years Campaigning in the Army of the Potomac* (Grand Rapids: Dygert Bros. & Co., 1874), 58–59.

A WOMAN AND A SOLDIER

Women's activities in support of the war included the exploits of a few who disguised themselves as men and enlisted. The best-known Michigan woman to embrace this role was Sarah Emma Edmonds, whose semifictional memoir, Nurse and Spy in the Union Army *(1865), became a postwar best-seller. Edmonds, who enlisted as Franklin Thompson in the 2nd Michigan, later received a federal pension after the members of her regiment attested to her valuable service. Another woman served under the name of Frank Martin in the 8th Michigan. Less well known is Annie Lillybridge, who gave this account of herself to a reporter in the spring of 1863.*[23]

She gave her name as Annie Lillybridge, of Detroit, and stated that her parents reside in Hamilton, Canada West. Last Spring (1862) she was employed in a dry goods store in Detroit, where she became acquainted with a Lieutenant W., of one of the Michigan regiments, and an intimacy immediately sprang up between them.[24] They corresponded for some time, and became warmly attached. During the ensuing Summer, Lieutenant W. was appointed to a position in the Twenty-first Michigan Infantry, then rendezvousing in [Ionia] county.

The thought of parting from her lover nearly maddened the girl, and she resolved to share his dangers and be near him. No sooner had she determined on this course than she proceeded to act, and, purchasing male attire, she visited [Ionia], and enlisted in Captain Kavanagh's company of the Twenty-first Regiment. While in camp she managed to keep her secret from all; not even the object of her attachment, who met her every day, being aware of her presence.

Annie left with her regiment for Kentucky, passed through all the dangers and trials of camp life, endured long marches, and slept on the ground without a murmur. At last, before the battle of Pea Ridge, in which her regiment took part, her sex was discovered by a member of her company, upon whom she enjoined secrecy after relating her previous history.

On the following day she was under fire, and from a letter in her possession it appears she behaved with marked gallantry, and shot with her own hand a rebel captain who was in the act of firing upon her friend, Lieutenant W. But the fear of being discovered continually haunted her.

After the battle she was sent, among others, to bury the dead, and among the first corpses found by her was that of the soldier who had discovered her sex. Days and weeks passed by, and she became a universal favorite with the regiment; so much so, that her Colonel (Stephens) frequently detailed her as regimental clerk—a position that brought her in close contact with her lover, who at this time was major or adjutant of the regiment.

A few weeks subsequently, when out on picket duty, she received a shot in the arm that disabled her, and, notwithstanding the efforts of the surgeon, her wound continually grew worse. She was sent to the hospital at Louisville, where she remained several months, when she was discharged by the post-surgeon, as her arm was stiffened, and rendered useless.

She implored to be permitted to return to her regiment, but the surgeon was unyielding, and discharged her. Annie immediately hurried homeward. At Cincinnati she told her secret to a benevolent lady, and was supplied with female attire.

She declares she will enlist in her old regiment again, if there is a recruiting officer for the Twenty-first in Michigan. She still clings to the lieutenant, and says she must be near him if he falls, or is sick, and that where he goes she will go.

Chicago Post (May 1863), as reprinted in *United States Service Magazine* 3 (March 1865): 273.

MICHIGAN ANNIE: A REGIMENTAL DAUGHTER

While Civil War armies usually had significant female support staff employed as nurses, launderers, and cooks, a distinguished few became "daughters" of their regiments. Anna Etheridge—"Michigan Annie"—became the most renowned of these regimental daughters; as one historian concluded, "In her own time and after, Annie Etheridge was undoubtedly the most famous Civil War army woman."[25] Etheridge initially accompanied her husband, James, following his enlistment in the 2nd Michigan in 1861. Remaining with the army following her husband's discharge for disability in 1862, Etheridge later served with the 3rd Michigan and the 5th Michigan. While not a combatant, Etheridge generally carried a pair of pistols and was one of two women to receive the Kearny Cross, a military decoration awarded for bravery. In addition to the battles listed below, Etheridge also served at Antietam, Chancellorsville, Gettysburg, and Spotsylvania. She was never compensated for her labors during the war, but in 1887 the United States Congress authorized the federal government to pay Etheridge a twenty-five-dollar monthly pension.[26]

[Mrs. Anna Etheridge] was born in this city, and is now twenty-three years of age. . . . On the breaking out of the rebellion, she was visiting her friends in this city. Colonel [Israel] Richardson was then engaged in raising the Second Michigan volunteers, and she and nineteen other females volunteered to accompany the regiment as nurses. Every other has returned home or been discharged, but she has accompanied the regiment through all its fortunes, and declares her determination to remain with it during its entire term of service. She has for her use a horse, furnished with a side-saddle, saddle-bags, &c. At the commencement of a battle she fills her saddle-bags with lint and bandages, mounts her horse, and gallops to the front, passes under fire, and, regardless of shot and shell, engages in the work of staunching and binding up the wounds of our soldiers. In this manner she has passed through every battle in which the regiment has been engaged, commencing with the battle of Blackburn's Ford, preceding the first battle of Bull Run, including the battles of the Peninsula, and terminating with the battle of Fredericksburg.

General [Hiram G.] Berry, the present commander of the brigade to which her regiment is attached, and who highly distinguished himself for bravery and gallantry in all these fights, declares that she has been under as hot a fire of the enemy as himself. On one occasion a soldier was torn in pieces by a shell while she was in the act of binding up his wounds previously received, and on many occasions her dress has been pierced by bullets and fragments of shell, yet she has never flinched and never been wounded. Her regiment belongs to the brigade commanded by the lamented Gen. [Philip] Kearney till his death, and in consideration of her dauntless courage and invaluable services in saving the lives of his men, Gen. Kearney commissioned her as a regimental sergeant. When not actively engaged on the battlefield or in the hospital, she superintends the cooking at the headquarters of the brigade. When the brigade moves, she mounts her horse and marches with the ambulances and surgeons, administering to the wants of the sick and wounded, and at the bivouac she wraps herself in her blanket, and sleeps upon the ground with all the hardihood of a true soldier.

Anna is . . . about five feet three inches in height, fair complexion (now somewhat browned by exposure), brown hair, vigorous constitution, and decidedly good looking. Her dress on entering into battle, is a riding garment, so arranged as to be looped up when she dismounts. Her demeanor is perfectly modest, quiet and retiring, and her habits and conduct are correct and exemplary; yet on the battlefield she seems to be as one possessed and animated with a desire to be effective in saving the lives of the wounded soldiers. No vulgar word was ever known to be uttered by her, and she is held in the highest veneration and esteem by the soldiers, as an angel of mercy. She is indeed the idol of the brigade, every man of which would submit to almost any sacrifice in her behalf. She takes the deepest interest in the result of this contest, eagerly reading all the papers to which she can obtain access, and keeping thoroughly posted as to the progress of the war. She says she feels as if she stood alone in the world, as it were, and desires to do good. She knows that she is the instrument of saving many lives and alleviating much suffering in her present position, and feels it her duty to continue in so doing.

These facts can be substantiated by testimony of the highest character, and they deserve to go forth to the world to show that if England can boast of the achievements of a Florence Nightingale, we of America can present a still higher example of female heroism and exalted acts of humanity in the person of Anna Etheridge.

Bangor Whig (Maine), as published in Detroit Advertiser and Tribune, February 17, 1863.

THE MICHIGAN COLORED REGIMENT

In 1861 federal policy prohibited African Americans from serving in the United States military. A year later the war's unexpected length, the increasing need for

soldiers and sailors, declining enlistments, and white Unionists' growing support of
emancipation opened the door to blacks' serving in the military. Congress passed the
Militia Act in July 1862 authorizing African American enlistments; Abraham Lin-
coln's final Emancipation Proclamation on January 1, 1863, announced that blacks
would "be received" into the United States military.[27] *Active recruitment of blacks*
followed the War Department's creation of the Bureau of Colored Troops in May
1863. By the war's end, almost 200,000 African Americans answered this call. The
federal government initially paid all black soldiers only ten dollars per month—less
than white soldiers, who received thirteen dollars per month with a clothing allow-
ance of $3.50. Congress later corrected this injustice in June 1864 and also provided
retroactive pay.[28]

In July 1863, Secretary of War Edwin Stanton authorized Governor Austin Blair
"to raise one regiment of infantry to be composed of colored men,"[29] *the recruitment*
of which began on August 12, 1863. By the end of the war, as many as 1,673 men served
in this regiment, with at least 1,300 enlisting in Michigan (some of whom came from
other states, and Canada, to enlist).[30] *Members of the 1st Michigan Colored Infantry*
were mustered into federal service on February 17, 1864, and left Detroit almost six
weeks later, eventually arriving in Hilton Head, South Carolina, on April 19. The
following month the regiment was redesignated as the 102nd US Colored Troops.
Aside from a four-week stint in Florida in August 1864, the regiment remained in
South Carolina for the remainder of the war, where it constructed fortifications, per-
formed picket duty, and countered Confederate forces in several skirmishes.[31] *In this*
document, an unnamed white officer of the regiment recounts its most significant
engagement—at Honey Hill, South Carolina, on November 30, 1864. As with almost
all black regiments in the Union Army, the unit's officers were entirely white.

[At] the time of the organization of the 102d . . . it was almost a by-word, and
those connected with it subjects of derision. But now its praises are on every one's
lips, and here, at least, it is an honor to belong to what was once known as the 1st
Michigan Colored Regiment.

You have already heard, no doubt, that another expedition has been set on foot
in this department, the object of which is to interrupt the Savannah and Charleston railroad, and, if possible, destroy it altogether. The expedition numbered, all
told, about 6,000 men, mostly colored troops. It landed at first on what is called
Boyd's Bluff. . . . Our forces advanced along this neck of land for several miles
in the direction of Gorhamsville. . . . There had been skirmishing for most of
the way, but here they met the enemy in force and here a sanguinary battle was
fought, which was the first real fight in which our regiment was ever engaged. On
one side of our little detail of 300 men the 54th Massachusetts (colored) was drawn
up, on the other a white regiment, the 127th New York. Here our forces sustained

a charge from the enemy, and charged in turn. In this affair the 102d covered themselves with glory. It is acknowledged without stint on all hands that our regiment maintained the steadiest line of battle and fought with the greatest determination of any troops on the ground. Many who were wounded quite severely refused to go to the rear, but kept on fighting, while the blood was flowing from their wounds. But the enemy's position was found too strong to be taken, and our forces were withdrawn. The enemy's fire having been very severe upon our artillery, and so many horses having been killed, they were obliged to abandon two pieces of artillery on the field, and while all were falling back, and after the retreat had been sounded, two companies of the 102d hauled off the two pieces of artillery by hand. For several days fighting and skirmishing were kept up quite briskly near the same place, during which time the 102d not only maintained their credit, but were constantly gathering new laurels. The white regiment which fought next to ours held our men in the highest estimation, and expressed their preference to fight beside our regiment rather than any other regiment in the department.

The attempt to reach the railroad by this route was finally abandoned, and the troops were taken to a point near Pocatallago Bridge, and landed on a strip of land called Bull's Neck. Here again they had several skirmishes and one severe fight, where the 102d fought as well as any troops ever fought, no other Michigan regiment excepted. There were men in my company who were shot through and through the fleshy part of the arm who have not gone to the hospital, but after having their wounds dressed have come to their company quarters, remained there, and seemed scarcely to notice their wounds. If such a thing had occurred in the regiment I formerly belonged to, such a wound would have been good for a three-months' stay in some hospital at Philadelphia or Baltimore. There are others who are wounded in the neck and side, but still have the full use of their limbs, who would go back to the field at once if they were permitted to do so. The same is true of men of every company of the regiment. Now such bravery I never saw before. I have known men to fight as well and bravely as men ever fought, but never before have I known men to fight on after being severely wounded, and anxious to return to the field as soon as their wounds were dressed. After having been three and a half years in the field and participated in sixteen different engagements, I never before saw men exhibit such unyielding bravery in battle.

John Robertson, *Michigan in the War*, rev. ed. (Lansing: W. S. George & Company, State Printers, 1882), 490–91.

INDIGENOUS PEOPLE FROM NORTHERN MICHIGAN
FORM A COMPANY OF SHARPSHOOTERS

The Odawa and Ojibwe peoples of northern Michigan fared better than most Native Americans, as they remained on their ancestral land rather than being forcibly removed westward. Despite northern Michigan's near-frontier conditions, by the 1850s white immigration caused the region's native peoples to worry that they, too, might soon be required to leave.

Since Michigan generally did not recognize Native Americans' right to vote or to hold office, it also excluded them from serving in its regiments. By 1863, though, the state's demand for soldiers diminished this resistance, giving the Odawa and Ojibwe an opportunity to gain leverage in their efforts to remain on their ancestral lands. Company K of the Michigan Sharpshooters became the unit that Michigan Indians joined; eventually it became "the most famous Indian unit in the Union army fighting Confederate forces east of the Mississippi."[32] Odawa comprised the majority of the company, but it also included Ojibwe, Delaware, Huron, Oneida, and Potawatomi. Key to the recruitment of this company was Garrett A. Gravaraet, from Little Traverse Bay. Fluent in four languages, Gravaraet personally recruited over one-fourth of the company's original members and eventually became the company's second lieutenant, despite his lack of previous military experience. Amos Farling, serving in one of the regiment's other companies, describes the battlefield death of Gravaraet's father, Henry G. Gravaraet, on May 12, 1864, at Spotsylvania, Virginia, and Garrett's mortal wounding on June 17, 1864, that led to his death three weeks later.[33]

An incident in front of Fort Hell, Petersburg:—Lieutenant Graversat and father, of Co. K, First Regiment Michigan Sharpshooters, both Indians. By the request of the members of Co. K the young man was promoted Lieutenant. In all the battles in which the Regiment participated this young hero bore himself conspicuously, winning the admiration of the commanding officers and making a record which the noblest and most distinguished soldier in the army might emulate, if he did not envy it. [I]n the fight in front of Fort Hell this Lieutenant was in the trenches with his father , and had the misfortune to see his father shot dead by his side. He bore the body of his parent to a safe spot, where, weeping bitterly, he dug a grave in the sand with an old tin pan and buried him. This done he returned to the battle. Many a rebel was laid low by his unerring aim, but at last he fell himself, wounded badly in the arm. He was brought to Washington City, where his arm was amputated at the shoulder, which resulted in his death. If the Indian is so willing to shed his blood in defense of the country which he can scarcely call his own, how much more readily should we take up arms and go forth to do service in a cause so near and dear to us—a cause in which our Nation's interests and the interests of every man, woman and child in the loyal States are at stake.

Amos Farling, *Life in the Army: Containing Historical and Biographical Sketches, Incidents, Adventures and Narratives of the Late War* (Buchanan, MI: Published by the Author, 1874; reprinted by Berrien County Historical Association, Berrien Springs, MI, 2005), 15.

~

FIVE

Conscription, Commutation, and Dissent

$\mathcal{M}$ OST UNION SOLDIERS served in regiments organized by political leaders in the soldiers' home state. The federal government determined the number of soldiers it needed and left to the states the responsibility for meeting the federally determined requisition. At first, meeting those quotas proved easy; in the spring and summer of 1861 the United States military could not accommodate every Unionist who wanted to serve. As enlistments across the North declined sharply in mid-1862, the importance of cash bounties grew. The federal government began offering $100 cash bounties to enlisted soldiers in the summer of 1861 and in 1863 increased the amount to $300 for new recruits and $400 for reenlisting veterans.[1] Meanwhile, local and state governments offered additional cash incentives to encourage recruitment. Addressing the Michigan legislature in January 1863, Governor Austin Blair explained that the various amounts paid in different locales had created a "vicious" system that had "been the cause of endless trouble." He continued:

> [T]hose seeking to enlist have been induced to offer themselves wherever the highest bounty was offered. The result has been a very injurious bidding between different places, and very much higher bounties have been paid than reason would dictate. Appeals have been constantly made to the cupidity instead of patriotism of the citizen to enlist, to that extent degrading the service. In consequence some have enlisted merely to obtain the bounties, and have then deserted disgracefully.[2]

Michigan's bounty laws, and the amounts volunteers received, underwent revision throughout the war as draft calls and federal bounties increased.[3] Because appeals to patriotism and cash bounties could not supply the needed troops, the state and federal government turned to conscription—a step the Confederacy previously had taken when it enacted its first conscription law in April 1862.

Michigan conducted its first conscription in February 1863 when the state met an unfulfilled federal call for troops, made the preceding August, by drafting 1,278 men to a nine-month term of service.[4] All drafts made in Michigan thereafter occurred under the provisions of the Enrollment Act, passed by Congress in March 1863, which established the conscription system that lasted for the remainder of the war. Under the Enrollment Act, the federal government assessed the number of men required of each congressional district.[5] If enlistments matched the assessment, then the draft would not apply to that district. Hoping to avoid having the draft affect their constituents, local officials stimulated recruitment by offering larger cash bounties, often raising the bounty money by assessing higher local taxes. Separate drafts held in July 1863 and in March, July, and December 1864 resulted in conscription of an additional 1,809 Michiganians.[6] Although conscripts made up only 3.4 percent of Michigan's 90,000 Civil War soldiers, they constituted 7.1 percent of those who served after January 1, 1863. The small percentage of draftees belies the importance of conscription, as the threat of being drafted spurred many to enlist.

Those drafted into the military could fulfill their obligations by finding a substitute or by paying a $300 commutation fee. These commutation fees became a source of federal revenue, but many soldiers complained that moneyed men simply paid the commutation fee and avoided military service. Widespread protest against this $300 exemption led to its repeal in July 1864. Subsequently the cost of finding a substitute soared. Many men subject to the draft formed local associations that pooled individuals' contributions toward paying a substitute for those drafted. By mid-1864 the growing federal demand for soldiers made finding substitutes increasingly difficult, regardless of the amount an individual could pay. As one historian concluded, as "bounties went progressively upward . . . the quality of the men obtained went progressively downward."[7] Communities across the North sent representatives elsewhere in search of substitutes, a practice that often set communities against one another. Draftee-hired substitutes constituted 4.1 percent of Michigan soldiers who served during the last two years of the Civil War.

Although the provisions of the draft were never popular, most eligible Michigan men complied by enrolling with the local provost marshal, an office created by the 1863 Enrollment Act. If drafted, they paid the commutation fees, found a substitute, or entered the army as a conscript. Worried about the prospect of being drafted, many more Michigan men simply set the terms of their service, and selected their regiment, by volunteering and collecting all the bounties for which they qualified, whereas conscripts received only the federal bounty but not the more lucrative state and local ones.[8]

Others, though, took explicit steps to resist or to avoid the draft. Frustrated by the war's length and by the prospect of conscription, Detroit whites rioted in March 1863 and attacked their city's African Americans. Some left the state for Canada and waited for the war to conclude before returning to the United States.[9] Those living in remote corners of the state believed they could easily hide from provost marshals—who were also responsible for apprehending draft resisters, deserters, and spies—and never bothered to report for duty. As the officials responsible for enforcement of the draft laws, provost marshals often arrested and imprisoned, without trial, citizens who evaded the draft.

Besides draft evaders, others faced imprisonment without trial. The United States Constitution authorizes the federal government to suspend habeas corpus "when in Cases of Rebellion or Invasion the public Safety may require it." In September 1862 and again in September 1863, Abraham Lincoln suspended habeas corpus throughout the United States—acts that permitted federal officials to arrest individuals and to hold them without charging them or presenting evidence to a court. While the government arrested some for enemy collaboration, many others were "citizens of the Confederacy, blockade runners, foreign nationals, returning Southern sea captains," or "carriers of contraband goods."[10] Nonetheless, some prisoners languished without being informed of the charges against them—and many Democrats frequently declared these individuals to be political prisoners.

HOPING TO ESCAPE THE DRAFT

Charles Cleveland, an Adrian merchant, was twenty-five when the Civil War began. Although he voted for Stephen A. Douglas in 1860, Cleveland counted himself as a firm supporter of the war. Cleveland embraced Lincoln's leadership of the war, supported the president's reelection in 1864, and met with severe disapproval from his Democratic friends for taking these positions. Cleveland, though, had no interest in going to war himself. On June 13, 1861, Cleveland wrote in his diary: "Were I young, unmarried—not having a wife and a boy absolutely dependent on my labor for their support—my love of excitement and adventure, & my desire to serve my country in the time of her affliction, would certainly lead me to the battlefield." Over a year later, as prospects for a quick and painless war diminished, Cleveland spoke less confidently of his abilities as a prospective soldier. Cleveland worried incessantly about being drafted in 1864 and 1865, but he successfully avoided Civil War service.

For fear of an immediate draft, hundreds are now rushing to the recruiting offices. . . . One company in this city—J.D. Hinkley's—is about full. . . . It is said that there have been 65 new enlistments in this city since this morning. No difficulty will now be had in filling up companies. For myself, I shall stand [the] draft, and if compelled to go, shall endeavor to go in the Telegraph Corps. I know I should be of little service if were compelled to shoulder a musket. I would be in hospital quarters in less than ten days. If could leave my family well provided for, would not hesitate a minute in going—Now anxiously await the draft, relying on my good luck to escape it.

Charles Cleveland Diary, August 6, 1862, Cleveland Family Papers, Bentley Historical Library, University of Michigan.

DETROIT'S ANTIBLACK RIOT, 1863

The Civil War brought economic challenges to Detroiters, whose wages failed to keep up with wartime inflation. Among many Detroiters who objected to the increased demand for federal troops, large numbers disrupted a military rally in July 1862. The following year, war weariness and vehement opposition to a federal draft contributed to Detroit's first race riot in March 1863.

Rape charges against William Faulkner, a mixed-race tavern keeper, precipitated Detroit's riot. Faulkner's trial began on March 5, 1863, the same day Detroit received the first news of a recently passed federal conscription law. Faulkner's conviction the following day enraged Detroit whites who believed blacks to be the chief cause of the Civil War. Some of these whites formed a mob that attacked Detroit's African Americans and their property. The state's militia eventually dispersed the mob, which contemporaries estimated at between fifty and one hundred people. Fires set by the mob destroyed thirty buildings. Only six rioters received convictions. Six years after his conviction, Faulkner received a pardon when his accusers recanted their testimony.[11]

STATEMENT OF THOMAS HOLTON—. . . . We were aroused by the yells of the mob, and, on going to the street, heard windows smashing and hammering against doors, with dreadful curses of "Kill the Nigger."

A crowd rushed up to my residence, and commenced their work of destruction in every possible way, with bricks, stones and other destructive missiles, and the torch was soon set to our house. Myself and wife, with one child, now had to make the best of our efforts to escape with our lives.

They rushed after us with demoniac rage, and their curses and yells were terrifying. We would, most certainly, have fallen a prey to them, had not the hands in the Morocco Factory, just in the rear of our lot, called to us to run through there. We took it as a great favor, for no one could tell in what direction to go—all the streets seemed to be filled with the mob.

Without a moment's time, to even put on cloak, bonnet, or shawl, we started and wandered out to find a friend's house in the suburbs of the city, but losing our way, we found, on inquiry, way in the night, that we had been three miles and a half from the city. Being now at Cork Town, I feared to let them know who we were, for they might be a part of the number who had driven us from our homes.

We wandered all that night in the woods, with nothing to eat, nor covering from the cold, till morning light. With frosted feet and all our property destroyed, did the morning sun rise upon us, as destitute as when we came into the world, with the exception of what we had on, and without a friend to offer us protection, so far as we could learn. Oh, Detroit! Detroit, how hast thou fallen! No power in noonday to defend the helpless women and children from outlaws, till they have fully glutted their hellish appetites on the weak and defenseless. Humanity, where is thy blush!

STATEMENT OF BENJAMIN SINGLETON—I lived at the corner of Fort and Beaubien streets, and have been sick for the last two years. I am so afflicted with blind[n]ess, that while I stand right up to you I can't discern the eyes in your head. All I could hear or understand were the yells and curses of, "Kill the Niggers," &c. A shower of stones, &c. made me understand that I was not to escape. They set fire to my house, and I was not able to get out; but some white ladies came to my relief. They broke a board off my fence, and came through the back way and dragged me out, or I should have been burned up with my house and all that I had.

I had a horse hitched at my door, and some of the mob came to cut his throat, because he belonged to a "nigger." And it was only by a white man coming up and declaring the horse was his, that they were deterred from their brutal act.

Here I was, blind, sick and helpless in the midst, as I had always supposed, of a civilized, yea, christianized people; and to find my property destroyed in broad day light seemed almost impossible. But it was a dread reality.

A Thrilling Narrative from the Lips of the Sufferers of the Late Detroit Riot, March 6, 1863, With the Hair Breadth Escapes of Men, Women and Children, and Destruction of Colored Men's Property, Not Less Than $15,000 (Detroit, 1863), 10–11.

PREVENT CONSCRIPTION BY INCREASING BOUNTIES

By late 1863, supporters of the war recognized that appeals to patriotism could no longer muster the troops necessary to suppress the Confederacy. Many of these supporters, though, loathed conscription, and viewed cash bounties—even if those bounties increased local taxes—as preferable to the draft.

According to the last call of the president for three hundred thousand men, a draft will be made on the fifth day of January next, provided the requisite number are not raised by volunteering before that time.[12] In view of this, we would suggest the propriety of calling a session of the Board of Supervisors, for the purpose of taking the necessary steps towards the payment of a bounty to volunteers, in addition to that offered by the Government. The bounty now paid is three hundred and two dollars to enlisted men who have never been in the service, and an additional hundred to those who have served nine months or more; and if a county bounty of one hundred dollars should be offered in addition, the necessary men to fill the quota for our county could doubtless be raised. In addition to this, each township could offer still further inducements in the shape of a bounty, if thought best, as a town by raising the requisite number of men, and having them properly credited, can escape the draft. Our county . . . would require the raising of twenty-two volunteers, if we would avoid another draft.

It is now supposed that the next draft will be made from the second class, or from both the first and second; therefore, those who felt perfectly secure, and in some cases wholly indifferent as to the result of the last draft, will stand an equal chance of being called into the field in January next, with their younger neighbors, if both classes are included, and if the second class are only called upon, it behooves the middle-aged citizens of the county to bestir themselves in the matter of raising volunteers. . . .

[A] draft is universally repugnant to the feelings of the American people, and they would rather pay any amount of taxes to support the Government, than to have their personal liberty interfered with. We have too long enjoyed perfect freedom of speech and of the person, to go or stay at will, to obey with a smiling face the peremptory call of the Government to shoulder gun and knapsack, and start for the camp or battle field; and nothing is more natural for a Yankee to do, than to resist any attempt at interference with his personal liberty by his neighbor or his Government. We do not say this to induce any citizen of our country to resist its laws, as no loyal man will openly refuse to obey the call of his country in her hour of need; but nothing can entirely eradicate the feeling of opposition which will inevitably arise in the mind of every American citizen, at any attempt to force upon him the performance of military duty. Taking this into consideration, the most popular course for the Government to pursue would doubtless be to offer sufficient pecuniary inducements to volunteers, to fill all calls for troops, thereby rendering another draft unnecessary.

Mecosta County Pioneer, November 26, 1863.

A SOLDIER'S REACTION TO COMMUTATION FEES

Few things underlined the divide between soldiers in the field and civilians more than the way conscripted men could buy their way out of military service though commutation—the payment of $300. Many soldiers, such as Samuel H. Keasy of the 19th Michigan, a sergeant from Constantine, loathed commutation. Six months after he sent this letter to his hometown paper, Congress repealed the law that permitted this practice.

McMinnville, Tenn., December 29, 1863. . . .

The aggregate present in the field of the Company is seventy enlisted men. All are in good spirits, and apparently satisfied with the results of late army movements, but all appear equally at a loss to understand the motives by which our friends at home are prompted to action. Before we enlisted, all united in proclaiming the magnitude and justness of the cause, and the necessity for prosecuting the war with vigor and determination; and, so far as mere verbal assertions are of any value, the same fact still exists. They boast of the prowess of Union soldiers: speak hopefully of the future; of the limited resources of the rebellion and its consequent doom; but let a draft be made, and the commutation fixed at $300, and every man will do his utmost, even to accepting a contribution, in order to avoid carrying a musket in defence of the Government that protects him. And to render escape certain, leading men advocate the raising of money enough to exempt their townships from military duty altogether.

And then, talk patriotism! Yes, patriotic, indeed! Each one has paid $300, or perhaps, joined a club and paid $25 to have some one do his fighting who has been less fortunate in obtaining wealth. But does he think the pittance given is equivalent to the life that must be hazarded on the battle field instead of his own? Is not every life lost on the bloody fields of Gettysburg, Antietam, Shiloh, Stone[s] River, and scores of others, worth more than all the money raised by commutation for the draft of October? The reply may be, that our late successes have rendered more troops unnecessary. But if we would have speedy peace, let us prepare for vigorous war, and thus profit by the advantage we have gained. Those who are already in the field pretty generally detest the $300 clause of the conscription act entirely, believing it to be the duty of every drafted man either to go or furnish an acceptable substitute.

Constantine Mercury and Advertiser, January 14, 1864.

AVOIDING THE DRAFT BY POOLING RESOURCES

The first document provides the minutes of an August 1864 war meeting in Saginaw that assessed twenty dollars upon the town's enrolled men who hoped to escape the draft, with the second, from Saginaw's Republican newspaper editor, urging those enrolled men to pay their voluntary assessment.

War Meeting

In pursuance of a previous call, a meeting of our citizens was held at Buena Vista Hall on Tuesday evening [August 2, 1864], to devise ways and means for raising our quota of men, and avoiding the draft under the present call.—The meeting was well attended, and something of the spirit and enthusiasm that animated the people when the war first broke out, evidently prevailed. There was no sign of desponding or of flinching from the necessary demands upon us; no talk of resisting the draft; but, on the contrary, a spirit of determination to raise our quota and freely comply with the call of the government for more men. . . . After some discussion . . . as to the best means of providing bounties and raising recruits, the following resolutions were adopted:

Resolved, That an assessment upon the enrolled men of the city liable to draft of $20 each be made, and the amount so raised to be paid as additional bounties to volunteers credited to this city, and that the amount be collected by committees in the different wards—Supervisor and Aldermen to constitute such committee, with power to add. Also that the committee call upon all men not liable to draft and solicit subscriptions for any amount, from five to one thousand dollars or more.

Resolved, That all men that have come to thi[s] city for the purpose of getting recruits to be accredited to any other place, be immediately requested to leave, or take such measures to compel them to leave, as they, in self-protection, may see proper to take, with full power to call upon any and all the citizens of this city for the assistance necessary to compel them to leave. . . .

After a few brief remarks by Mr. Driggs, giving a hopeful and cheering review of the progress of military affairs, as they appeared to him after viewing the scene of army operations under Gen. Grant, and giving it as his opinion that six months would close up the war, the meeting adjourned.

~

Don't Hang Back.!

If *every* enrolled man liable to the draft would promptly come forward and pay his $20, the committee would have the means of paying the extra bounty offered, with a fair prospect of filling our quotas and avoiding the draft. But without the money the committee can do nothing. Recruits cannot now be obtained for anything less than $500, total bounties; and the $100 to be raised by assessment of $20 each on enrolled men, is a necessary part of it. We are sorry to learn that some individuals refuse or neglect to pay their assessments. This should not be so. No one should hang back, expecting that the money and efforts of others will clear him. Such a course is not right or honorable, and no man that *is* a man will do it. With the present high wages of laboring men and mechanics of all kinds, there are scarcely any that can plead *inability*.—And unless this fund is raised, we may be sure there will be a draft for a portion of the quotas; and in case any of these men who have refused to pay should be drafted, they can expect no favor or assistance. Those who do pay, will get, in case they should be drafted, the $100 bounty in place of the $20 paid in.

Saginaw Enterprise, August 4, August 18, 1864.

THE CHALLENGES OF HIRING SUBSTITUTES

John H. Richardson of Tuscola served as a major in the 7th Michigan and a lieutenant colonel of the 27th Michigan Infantry before being honorably discharged for disability in December 1863. His correspondent, William Spalding of Sault Ste.

Marie, served with Richardson in the 27th as a first lieutenant and quartermaster, but resigned his commission and received an honorable discharge in April 1864. Deeply affected by their experiences in the war, and loathing their colonel, Dorus M. Fox (whom Richardson described as "one of the damnedst [sic] scoundrels at our head that God ever suffered to go unpunished"), neither of these officers wanted to return to their regiment, then at Petersburg, Virginia. Despite his previous service, Spalding was conscripted back into the army in the summer of 1864, by which time Congress had repealed the draft's commutation exemption. Spalding subsequently wrote to Richardson for assistance in obtaining a substitute. Richardson, in turn, offered a few suggestions on how this veteran officer could remain out of the army. In September 1864, Spalding hired a substitute for $600; six months later, the price for a substitute had risen to over $800.[13]

I got a letter from bob [Ridley] a few days since beging me to get him out of the Regiment, he sais there is but a few of our old comrads left. Poor fel[l]ows gon[e] many of them through mismanagement, I am glad that you have been rescued from the jaws of Death in that Treacharous country, and on the road to affluence and welth. I wish I were with you, you said in your letter that you had almost concluded to come here and see me. I wish I might have the oportunity of seeing you here and taking you by the hand, and having a good old time.

[I]n regard to the substitute I started at once to [S]aginaw to find one and other places. I found they were paying all prices as high as 950, dollars. I went over to see Col [Thomas S.] [S]prague. [H]e sais he with others had sent south[,] recruiting colard men to fill quotas, and that they has 3 Moor than over Taken up—and I might have one of them for you. [B]ut he would cost you 600, hundred dollars. I told him to save one at any rate[,] and I would write you at once[.] [I]f you want him send me your check and I will see that your name is stricken from the rools by a substatute.

But I have the impression that if you had come down, we might posibly get you clear on a count of Disabilety[.] I am well aquanted with the surgeon of this district. I got two men clear a few days since from disibility[.] I had known them for years, it seems to me you might com down and spend two or three weeks with us, I want to have a long talk with you. I have a thousand things to say that I can't write.

John H. Richardson to William Spalding, August 19, 1864, Spalding Family Papers, Bentley Historical Library, University of Michigan.

DRAFT RESISTANCE IN HURON COUNTY

Michiganians who opposed the Civil War sometimes encouraged men to avoid the draft. In early 1865, Huron County draft resisters responded violently to the local provost marshal and sheriff, who escaped only after surrendering their prisoners.

C.B. Cotterell, Esq., special Provost Marshal of Huron [C]ounty . . . states that on Monday evening, in company with Joseph W. Mankin, Sheriff of the county, he started from Sand Beach to Paris, to arrest several drafted men who had failed to report. When about 11 miles out they stopped at a country tavern in Sanilac County, intending to take an early start in the morning, capturing their prisoners by surprise. At this place the officers were recognized, and the friends of the drafted men were all informed during the night of the intended visit.

The Sheriff and Marshal proceeded on their journey early in the morning, but found the whole country aroused. They succeeded, however, in arresting two drafted men, one a German and the other a Polander, who lived alone in the woods. The men gave themselves up willingly, bade farewell to their friends, were placed in the sleigh and started for the lake shore. After proceeding about four miles on the country road two Polanders were met with shot guns. As they passed the latter fired signal shots, and a short distance beyond, 25 men, armed with rifles and double barreled shot guns, were found drawn up in line of battle by the road-side. A parley ensued. The belligerents demanded the release of the prisoners, at the same time bringing their fire arms to a "ready." The situation was decidedly unpleasant for the officers. The latter to reason the case; but the reason and argument were useless. The Sheriff then started his horses and tried to drive on.

In a moment a dozen rifles were leveled at his team and he was told that if another movement was made his horses would be shot in their tracks. The officers held a brief consultation, and finally thought "discretion the better part of valor," so, making a virtue of necessity, they yielded up the prisoners. Their troubles did not end here. After surrendering the prisoners they had proceeded but a few rods when they were fired upon. One bullet whistled by the head, grazing the hair of the Provost Marshal. Another ball passed through the overcoat of the Sheriff, in unpleasant proximity to his shoulder. Another volley passed over their heads. Three volleys were fired in all. The escape of the officers from instant death is truly wonderful. Mr. Cotterell arrested a drafted man in this section a few weeks since and was chased 13 miles but finally escaped with his prisoner.

Mr. Cotterell states that these men are led on in this course of resistance to the laws by several traders in the interior, one of whom is a German Justice of the Peace named Stitcher, who keeps a low groggery. A company of soldiers will probably soon be sent to this rebellious district where the supremacy of the laws will not fail to be vindicated.

Detroit Advertiser and Tribune, January 9, 1865.

A POLITICAL PRANK SUCCEEDS BEYOND ITS CREATORS' WILDEST DREAMS

Angered by Republican newspapers that continually accused Democrats of conspiring to overthrow the government and resentful of Radical Republicans who sought to make abolition a war objective, Guy S. Hopkins of Lapeer County created a forgery that linked former president Franklin Pierce and Michigan Democrats to the Knights of the Golden Circle, a pro-Confederate secret society with a vastly smaller reach than many Republicans imagined it to have. The prank backfired, as government officials traced the letter back to Hopkins, arrested him and two of his friends, and imprisoned them at Fort Lafayette, New York. Eventually Secretary of State William Seward wrote to Pierce and asked for an explanation. Pierce replied indignantly and demanded a public apology from Seward. Meanwhile, Hopkins eventually won his release from Fort Lafayette after being incarcerated for three months.[14]

FORT LAFAYETTE, *November 29, 1861.*

HON. WILLIAM H. SEWARD, *Secretary of State.*

Sir: On the 20th instant in the city of Detroit, Mich., I was suddenly arrested without being informed of the charge against me further than the general one of disloyalty. . . .

My only guilt, sir, lies in attempting to play off a practical joke upon the Detroit press. . . . Although the Democratic press and people acquiesce with more or less cordiality in the policy of the Administration still beneath it all there is an undercurrent on minor subjects of political rancor which still maintains old party lines. Actuated by such feelings the Democrats charge the Republicans with abolition, while the Abolitionists without any show of reason charge all Democrats with either disaffection to the Government or outright treason. In Lapeer County, Mich., in particular, remote from the wild whirl of political and warlike events, these feelings exist in all their strength—so much so indeed that there is scarcely any communication between members of the two parties.

Some time in September, I think, my enemies having reported me a secessionist, my office was attacked in the night and ransacked and other acts of violence committed, of course by Abolitionists. About the same time I noticed frequent paragraphs in the Detroit papers charging the Democrats with treason, with oft-repeated reference to a secret league favorable to the Confederate States. These events, the accusation of men whom I admired as statesmen and loyal Americans, [and] the disgrace heaped upon me . . . it suddenly entered my mind to sell the Detroit press by writing a letter full of dark innuendoes and hints, but which in reality would mean nothing. The idea was hardly conceived before it was executed. . . .

My furthest expectation was that it would be sent to one of the treason-shrieking presses, and when exploded would produce lots of fun. I fancied such a sell would be apt to quiet their howls. My only belief was that it would be either immediately seen through or if the fish took the bait it would be sent to the [Detroit] Tribune, drawing from that admirable journal and yell of intense satisfaction. . . .

Weeks passing away and nothing being heard from this fanciful practical joke, it passed from my mind until my place of residence was visited by one Jenkins alias Whiting. The name used, his visits to the post-office, &c., caused me to suspect something wrong and to fear more serious results from my joke than I ever anticipated. I was on my way to Ypsilanti to look after some property fallen to my family at the time of my arrest. I was not surprised, but after thinking over all I could remember of that doubly-accursed letter I felt very much distressed. I then for the first time realized what I had done. For myself I did not so much care. I felt I deserved all I suffered. I feared, and greatly feared, that I had been instrumental in casting suspicion on good and loyal men; that they might at that very moment be under arrest with no other evidence against them than such as my folly had furnished. Influenced by such fears I begged they would give me an immediate examination, but either from want of inclination or want of power it was refused. . . .

Very respectfully, yours,

GUY S. HOPKINS.

The War of the Rebellion: A Compilation of the Official Records of the Union and Confederate Armies, ser. 2, vol. 2 (Washington, DC: Government Printing Office, 1897), 1250–51.

A POLITICAL PRISONER WRITES TO ABRAHAM LINCOLN

Phineas Wright began criticizing Lincoln after the president issued the preliminary Emancipation Proclamation. Wright then organized the Order of American Knights as a way of countering what he deemed to be the federal government's growing heavy-handedness. Unsuccessful in generating a following in Missouri, Illinois, or Indiana, and generally scorned by Democratic Party officials, Wright eventually caught the attention of Union military authorities who believed that the Order of American Knights sought to separate states from the Union to create a Northwest Confederacy. Arrested while on a speaking trip in Michigan, Wright spent over fifteen months incarcerated without being charged or receiving a reply to the letter he wrote below. Federal authorities finally released Wright in August 1865.

FORT LAFAYETTE [New York], August 30, 1864.

To Hon. ABRAHAM LINCOLN, President of the United States:

Sir: I have been a prisoner in this fortress four months this day. I was arrested at Grand Rapids, Michigan, on the 27th day of April last, "by order of the President, through General [Samuel Peter] Heintzelman," and by Colonel J.

R[andolph]. Smith, commanding Department of Michigan. Until this hour I am
unadvised of any charge or charges against me, or of any special cause why I was
arrested. My position is most painful and mortifying. In regard to my political
sentiments generally, or my opinions touching the momentous questions of
the day, I am prepared, as I ever have been, to make a frank avowal of them. In
regard to my actions touching the questions at issue, or the parties to that issue,
since the commencement of the war, I have nothing which I desire to conceal.
I am a citizen of the State of Missouri, resident in the city of St. Louis, by
profession a lawyer. The story of my private life, or of my relations, of blood, or
social, cannot interest you just now.

From you, as Chief Magistrate and Executive of my Government, I have the
right, respectfully, to demand *justice*. As a citizen, I would fain appeal to your
humane and Christian sympathies. I am incapable of crime, or of premeditated
wrong. I dislike notoriety of any kind, and now respectfully request that I may
be permitted to communicate personally with some one in whom you may
confide, who shall be empowered to set me at liberty, in the event that he shall
be satisfied that there is no just cause for my further detention. I trust that my
motives in this communication will not be misapprehended.

The welfare of my country, and her restoration to unity, peace, and prosperity,
have been the burden of my highest aspirations. I am not a *criminal*, begging for
mercy, but a *free citizen* demanding *justice*, to know whereof I am accused, and who
is my accuser, to be confronted with the witnesses against me, tried by the law, and
by it be convicted or acquitted.

General [John A.] Dix, as my counsel advises me, and Colonel [Martin] Burke,
have both promised that any communication which I might desire to send to you
shall be promptly forwarded to you, if proper.

I have the honor to subscribe myself with due respect,

P. C. WRIGHT.

American Bastile[sic]: *A History of the Illegal Arrests and Imprisonment of American Citizens During the Late Civil War*,
7th ed. (Philadelphia: Evans, Stoddart & Company, 1871), 227–28.

SIX

~

Civilians Confront the War

$\mathcal{A}$LTHOUGH CUSTOM COMMONLY divides those affected by war into combatants and noncombatants, the worlds of Michigan's soldiers and civilians were closely intertwined during the Civil War. With the war front merely days away from southern Lower Michigan, news, whether by telegraph or by personal correspondence, quickly reached the state, where civilians often discussed the war's developments. And with a long unguarded border with Canada—then a British colony whose neutrality afforded sanctuary to Confederate agents—the prospect of conflict close to home remained a constant in many Michiganians' minds. In 1864, two Confederate attacks from Canada—one in Vermont, the other involving Detroit—heightened these fears.

Michigan's civilian contributions to the Civil War mattered in many ways. Conscious of the unprecedented sums that state governments and the federal government spent on the war, civilians became vigilant regarding abuses by government contractors. While some contractors used the war to enrich themselves, soldiers often lacked crucial supplies that would keep them comfortable and healthy. From the war's beginning, the US Army relied on the United States Sanitary Commission, a civilian organization launched by the federal government to meet soldiers' material needs for items often unavailable on the war front, including blankets, coats, towels, handkerchiefs, socks, mittens, bandages, preserved food, crutches, books, and paper. Mostly operating as a charitable enterprise, the Sanitary Commission oversaw the work conducted by state organizations. Citizens on the home front, women in particular, collected such necessities or the money to buy them. Women also took the lead in distributing these goods among soldiers, often traveling outside the state to do so. Four Michigan organizations worked with the Sanitary Commission, the largest being the Michigan Soldiers' Aid Society. Originally known as the Detroit Soldiers' Aid Society, the Michigan Soldiers' Aid Society eventually had 358 subsidiaries in 45 Michigan counties.[1] Some women also left the state to serve as nurses in hospitals near the front.

Historians have long debated whether the Civil War aided or hindered the North's economic growth. On the Michigan home front, the Civil War brought prosperity to some, but not to everyone. Incomes rose during the war, but most people saw prices increase faster than their wages. The departure of 90,000 men from the state brought hardship to the families that relied on fathers and sons to sustain their households' economies. Recognizing that a soldier's monthly salary could not sustain a soldier and his family, the Michigan legislature unanimously passed legislation in May 1861 that empowered counties to levy taxes or issue bonds to support soldiers' families. These supplemental payments could not exceed fifteen dollars per month—a sum that failed to meet recipients' needs.[2]

The tens of thousands of men who left their farms for the war brought immediate shifts in agriculture, Michigan's economic mainstay. Replacing them in the fields were women, children, the elderly, and immigrants. The continued expansion of farm machinery, the value of which grew by 136 percent between 1860 and 1870 (and surpassed the previous decade's growth of 101 percent), partially offset farm-labor shortages. Some Michigan farmers enjoyed exceptional prosperity during the Civil War years and found ready markets for their output with the army and the North's growing population.

The Civil War also witnessed changes in Michigan's copper and iron production in the Upper Peninsula. Although Michigan's iron mines—located on the Marquette Iron Range in Marquette County—had abundant high-quality ore, these mines were unprofitable before the war owing to their distance from smelters and their inaccessibility during the winter. The war's early months brought about a decline in iron production, but by 1862 iron demand began an upswing that continued until 1865. The war years escalated Michigan's portion of national iron ore production from 3 percent to 12 percent, and Michigan's iron ore tonnage grew thirteenfold between 1858 and 1866 despite a more modest growth in the number of miners from 170 in 1860 to 562 in 1864. The war years also brought blast furnaces to the Upper Peninsula. Transportation projects launched during the war—including a railroad from Escanaba to Negaunee—made Michigan iron easier to access thereafter. By 1880, Michigan led the Union in iron ore production, a position it held for about two decades.[3]

Michigan copper mines produced 73 percent of the nation's copper during the Civil War and defined economic life in the sparsely settled Upper Peninsula counties of Ontonagon, Houghton, and Keewenaw. Copper prices surged during the Civil War (from 19.1 cents per pound in 1861 to 46.3 cents per pound in 1864), as did the number of people employed in copper mines, which rose from 3,631 in 1860 to 5,447 in 1864.[4] Yet inflation made workers' lives more difficult, notwithstanding their higher wages. Nor could miners' wages compete with the bounties soldiers received for enlisting. Both copper and iron mine owners frequently complained of the scarcity of laborers during the Civil War and jointly created the Mining Emigrant Aid Association of Lake Superior to foster immigration from Canada and Scandinavia. While the association claimed to have brought 500 prospective miners to the Upper Peninsula, some of those immigrants left the mines for fear of being drafted into the US Army. Others took advantage of increasing bounties and enlisted. Transient labor, labor unrest, including strikes, and the Upper Peninsula's long winters often brought Michigan's wartime mining to a halt.[5]

Despite Michigan's dominant role in iron and copper production, these metals, so critical for the twentieth century's industrial wars, lacked strategic significance during the Civil War. For example, the iron used to manufacture small arms and artillery amounted to far less than the iron that would have been used to build railroads, the construction of which slowed during the conflict.[6] These economic roads not taken serve as another reminder of the numerous costs imposed by the Civil War.

REFLECTIONS ON DEFEAT FOLLOWING THE FIRST BATTLE OF BULL RUN

Aside from some skirmishes, the first major battle following the Confederate attack on Fort Sumter in April 1861 occurred July 21 near Manassas, Virginia, less than thirty miles southwest of Washington, DC. In what was termed the First Battle of Bull Run by Unionists and the First Battle of Manassas by Confederates ("First" as a way of distinguishing it from an even larger battle that took place on the same site thirteen months later), 35,000 Unionists met 33,000 Confederates. With civilians on both sides expecting a quick victory, Confederates surprised the Unionists by routing their raw adversaries. Confederate inexperience, though, prevented them from capitalizing on their triumph. Many across the North now feared that defeating the Confederacy would take longer than they had initially anticipated. The Detroit Tribune *shared this view, but still erroneously attributed defeat to the Confederates' supposed numerical advantage.*

THE LESSON OF THE REVERSE.

"Sweet are the uses of adversity." We are not sure but the recent reverse the Union troops have suffered at Manassas is one of the best things that could have happened to us. Hitherto, we have not taken defeat into account. We have underestimated the enemy in his numbers and his strength, and as a natural result have not made adequate preparation to meet him. It is within the experience of almost every State, every western State at least, that it has been necessary to urge, and in some instances almost beseech the government to accept regiments. Michigan for instance was called upon for one Regiment, but has furnished four, and would have gladly sent three more which were refused. So it has been with other States, and yet our Army went to Manassas, numbering but 50,000 to oppose a force of 90,000. Certainly after this experience, the reserves who are vegetating in State Camps, and holding watch and ward at unimportant points will be called to Washington, and we hope furthermore that our new levies will be called, and that when we move in future it will be with such bodies of men as could almost command victory by their mere presence. . . .

Finally, we have been carried away with the idea of a short and easy war. "Onward to Richmond" has been the cry, as though it was the easiest thing possible to do. We have as a people scarcely appreciated the magnitude and resources of the rebellion. We must now settle down into a better understanding. Reverses are one change of the battle, and we must expect some of them. It is clear that we need not expect to meet the enemy on the field and crush him by a decisive battle. He will not of his own accord fight us in that way, and we probably cannot force him to do so.—This will make the contest slower, longer and more expensive to us, but we must accept the fact as it is, and prepare to meet it in the best manner for dealing with such a campaign.

Detroit Tribune, as printed in *Allegan Journal*, July 29, 1861.

A MINING ENGINEER RESPONDS TO THE FEDERAL DEFEAT AT BULL RUN

Writing from Houghton County in the Upper Peninsula, John Harris Forster, a mining engineer and superintendent at the Pewabic copper mine, reports the news regarding Bull Run, the reaction in Detroit, and comments on the copper market's prospects.

Pewabic Sunday, 28th July 1861. . . .

The reverses sustained by our brave army last sunday are terrible to contemplate, sickening and depressing in the Extreme. But you know that from the first I have always predicted disaster for our troops in the first great Engagements. [T]his sort of discipline seemed to me to be necessary and inevitable before our people could become good soldiers, then these meddling politicians from whom come all our wars, had to be wiped out and I pray God, that now they have with their insane cry "Onward to Richmond" succeeded in killing off so many brave men and nearly ruined our cause, they will retire into merited obscurity and let the President and Gen Scott alone.

The news of the results of the battle caused great consternation and mourning in Detroit. . . . Was it not a terrible fight? God help this nation! He can rule all for good. . . .

Our mines are doing finely and this month we shall make a handsome profit notwithstanding the low price of copper—In these uncertain times it [is] impossible to say how long we shall hold out—The probabilities are that even should we have to stop mining next fall the companies would want me to remain to look after the property. They have much at stake here—and the work will go on as long as possible, for it would involve great loss if not ultimate ruin to stop work Entirely[.]

John Harris to Martha Mullett Forster Harris, July 28, 1861, Mullett Family Papers, Bentley Historical Library, University of Michigan.

THE CIVIL WAR COMES TO COPPER COUNTRY

Michigan's Upper Peninsula claimed only 21,414 residents in 1860, less than 3 percent of the state's population. Its mines, though, produced the almost three-fourths of the country's copper, which could only be shipped when Lake Superior remained ice-free. Lacking telegraph access to the outside world before 1866, information generally arrived in the copper mining districts only by dog sled during the winter months.[7]

Alfred Swineford, a Marquette journalist, politician, and future Alaska governor, offers a contemporary account of the Civil War years in Copper Country from the perspective of "the copper mining interests"—and one hostile to the miners.

One of the darkest hours we remember for the copper mining interests, was the first year of the war on the Union. Every one supposed that the end had come—that the mines must close down—that nothing was left to do but shoulder the musket and march to the South. Copper stocks fell to a zero point; nobody would want our copper, and it must, perforce, lie in the ground. The price of ingot copper fell to 17 cents. . . . [But] as soon as the government found that it had work to do, a large army and navy to arm and equip, they turned to our own copper fields with eager demand for a supply of copper, which could not be safely procured from . . . foreign lands. This demand greatly stimulated mining, and created active business in all kindred departments. It was not long before the price of copper attained a highly remunerative point, and before the war closed it reached the unprecedented figure of 50 cents per pound. . . .

But there were drawbacks to this prosperity. The demands for the army, the demands for miners and all other kinds of labor, owing to the vigorous working of the old mines and the springing up of new ones in every direction, explorations and speculative movements rendered labor scarce, independent, costly and refractory. Everything cost enormously; everybody was making money, but all wanted more. There was a great blossoming of new men—superintendents and captains of mines, promoted instanter from the ranks. It was a troublous time. . . . Strikes among workmen, upon a large, combined scale, were common during the winter months, and mine officers were much exercised in their endeavors to control and regulate the unreasoning, turbulent masses. . . .

At one time an appeal was made to the Governor for arms, and fifty stand of muskets were sent forward. Mine officers were drilled in the manual, ostensibly for the purpose of fitting themselves for service in the army, but really to be prepared to resist internal commotions. Miners and laborers were composed of several nationalities, but chiefly of Cornish, Irish and Germans. The first two classes were bitterly hostile, and often assumed a belligerent attitude in force, or would indulge in secret personal attacks, which often terminated in murder. . . .

About the second year of the war, laborers became so scarce that the mining corporations determined to send an agent to Europe to induce immigration. An agent actually went to Sweden and contracted with a large number of men who finally made their appearance at Portage Lake. They were billeted off to the several companies, but nine out of ten refused to go to work or to abide by their solemn contracts made in their own country. They had reached this free and independent land without cost to themselves, and they proposed to act a freeman's part and do just as they pleased. The fact that the mining companies had expended $90,000 in their transportation, and that they were required to work at good wages, only a sufficient length of time to reimburse those who had assisted them to reach this country, was of no importance—not worthy of a moment's consideration. But one good came out of this venture at the time. Some forty of the men volunteered to fill the draft quota and were marched off to the wars, where some ill-natured ones charitably hoped they might become food for confederate gunpowder. . . .

But, with the war ended, a more orderly and peaceable era succeeded. Dull times followed, the price of copper fell; many mines suspended operations, and labor was at a discount. Hence, wise men became prudent and circumspect in conduct—they were obliged to or starve. For the last decade there has been no general strikes in the copper mines, even in prosperous times.

Alfred P. Swineford, *History and Review of the Copper, Iron, Silver, Slate and Other Material Interests of the South Shore of Lake Superior* (Marquette: The Mining Journal, 1876), 69–72.

"LET US HAVE NO MORE ROBBERY AT THE EXPENSE
OF OUR VOLUNTEERS AND TAXPAYERS"

With the beginning of the Civil War, private firms rushed to fill government contracts, from which they stood to profit. Some firms received contracts through favoritism or corruption and delivered substandard products to state and federal governments. Duncan Stewart, a director of Detroit's Second National Bank and the author of this document, recognized this corruption early in the conflict. Michigan's quartermaster general Jabez H. Fountain, accused by Stewart of corruption but never legally charged with wrongdoing, retained his post until March 1863. Countering Stewart's charges, John Robertson, Michigan's adjutant general, later described Fountain as a "faithful and energetic officer."[8]

LET US HAVE NO MORE ROBBERY AT THE EXPENSE
OF OUR VOLUNTEERS AND TAX-PAYERS.

DETROIT, Oct. 11, 1861.

I beg to call public attention to the fact that railroad men are here with the view of buying up parties that have the control of government property to be transported from this point. Let public scorn wither the villains and drive them out of the city and State. This trying to steal from the government is hellish, and must be stopped. When the regiment that left here lately were about to move, strong pressure was brought to bear in order to send the troops by rail and swindle the government as it was swindled when moving the 4th Mich. Regiment to Washington, and in bringing back the First from that point, and in paying nearly double to move the Wisconsin regiments that was needed to be paid. This must be stopped. The government moves soldiers in cattle cars, and pays about first class fare. If a volunteer is to be treated like a beast, let him be carried at the price animals are carried for. I protest against the brutal usage of our brave, true-hearted volunteers, and I protest against the two cents per mile charged for carrying troops. It is an outrageous charge for the kind of accommodations our gallant soldiers receive.—In moving regiments in cattle cars, one-half cent per mile is better business than any railroad on this continent can get to do. Should any railroad man deny this, I am ready to prove it.

Had Governor Blair paid no attention to railroad managers, we would not have had the dishonest transactions connected with the moving of the Fourth. Had Governor Blair turned Quartermaster [Jabez H.] Fountain out of office when he first let contracts, and then advertised for bids, we would not have thieves and robbers prowling around the government offices. *A man that plunders the people at this time is a Judas Iscariot. His gains are the price of blood.*

Detroit Tribune, as printed in *Adrian Daily Watchtower,* October 16, 1861.

A DEMOCRAT QUESTIONS WAR CONTRACTS

Northern Democrats called attention to how some individuals used the Civil War to enrich themselves at the public expense. This thinking had deep roots in the party, as many Democrats had long railed against moneyed interests and many continued to align with the party on that basis. President Andrew Jackson well captured this position in his veto message regarding the recharter of the Second Bank of the United States: when the "rich and powerful . . . bend the acts of government to their selfish purposes," the "humble members of society . . . who have neither the time nor the means of securing like favors to themselves, have a right to complain of the injustice of their Government."[9] Thomas F. Bouton, editor at the Jackson Patriot, *became one of Michigan's leading critics of war contractors from this perspective.*

In many cases the war has let loose a perfect golden shower upon some of the Eastern railroad companies, and they have realized larger profits and declared

larger dividends on the business than ever before. But you may as well undertake
to dam the gulf stream, or to satisfy the craving maw of an army contractor, as to
quiet the greed of some of these soulless corporations. Patriotism don't belong
to them. It is the people *individually* who are to be patriotic, and who are called
upon to sacrifice their all, even their lives, to save the country, while corporate monopolies and the rich who have friends in the "government" are rolling up heaps
of wealth and "faring sumptuously["] every day. The people, like poor Lazarus,
may call upon the dogs to lick the sores of the body politic, and beg for the crumbs
that drop from the banquet set before them. The "money changers," monopolies
and army contractors, are hovering around the government like vultures around a
carcass, and scent money in the least puff of official favor. When in our history has
there been so many "investigating committees" sitting with closed doors for the
purposes of examining all kinds of official corruption[?] Both Houses of Congress
have their "investigating committees" each State Legislature has its "investigating
committee," and in each of these committees are raised to investigate pecuniary
transactions growing out of the war.

Somebody must be sick, or it would not be necessary to employ so many
physicians.

Jackson Patriot, February 5, 1862.

AN AFRICAN AMERICAN GIVES UP ON THE UNITED STATES

*After the Civil War began, not all African Americans viewed the national govern-
ment's fight against a slaveholders' regime through the lens of optimism. Less than
nine months before Lincoln issued the preliminary Proclamation, John Jackson, an
African American resident of Monroe, issued the following announcement. Jackson joined some 16,000 African Americans—mostly former slaves whose masters
required expatriation as a condition of their emancipation—who left the United
States in the nineteenth century for a new start in Haiti or Liberia.*

To leave the land of one's birth for a strange land is at all times trying, necessarily sundering many ties, and is well calculated to impress the mind with feelings of
sadness. But after mature reflection I have come to the conclusion to move with
my family to Hayti, believing that there, or in the Republic of Liberia, I may find
all the civil and social rights and privileges of citizenship which I cannot hope to
obtain in this country. I believe in the colonization scheme, and I have no doubt,
from the information in my possession, that thousands in the United States will
have before them and their posterity a far brighter future by emigrating to those
distant lands.

Monroe Commercial, January 9, 1862.

BLACK DETROITERS DENOUNCE WHITE RACISM

Henry Barns, editor of the Detroit Advertiser and Tribune, *directed the recruitment of the 1st Michigan Colored Infantry and became the regiment's first colonel. Barns's longtime rivalry with the* Detroit Free Press *boiled over when the* Free Press *charged Barns with profiting from the bounties that Wayne County paid to the recruits in his forming regiment. A meeting of black Detroiters issued this response to the* Free Press.

At a large and enthusiastic meeting of the colored citizens of Detroit and vicinity, and a portion of the Colored Regiment, the following resolutions were adopted, as expressing the feelings of the meeting. . . .

Resolved, That we recognize the Detroit *Free Press* as the ancient and persistent enemy of the colored man—seeking by every means in its power to rivet upon him for all time the galling chains of slavery, and consign him, if possible, to a [lower] level of degradation than he has heretofore occupied. We know its editors to be the haters and revilers of our race, through many years, always willing to ridicule us, or lie about us or to us that they might make us appear to the worst advantage, and thereby accomplish their hellish purpose of keeping us degraded.

Resolved, That in days past the *Free Press* has abused us as being a pest in this community, a nuisance to be gotten rid of . . . but now, when a bleeding country needs the muscle of every man that can fight, the *Free Press* has fallen so in love with the negro, that it has become his special advocate and defender,—filling many columns in his defence, and doing more by its treasonable course to keep men from our regiment, than any other instrumentalities at work. . . .

Resolved, That we recognize in Col. Barns an old and tried friend—one whose paper for years has been the channel through which we have been safe to make known our wants and wishes to the public, and one who has given us a renewed evidence of his friendship by obtaining for us in Michigan the privilege of becoming American soldiers. He has treated us with marked kindness in camp, advancing money from his own purse to meet the necessities of the men before the [bounty] bonds were ready or could be negotiated. . . .

Resolved, That in the struggle now going on in this country between Freedom on one hand and Slavery on the other, every pulsation of our hearts, every sympathy of our beings, every aspiration of our souls, prompts us to be willing and ready to strike a blow for our own elevation, and, like the Pole or the Hungarian or Greek, to sacrifice home and life, if need be, in defence of liberty; and showing to the world our undying love of Freedom, let us here before God declare that no influence shall alienate love of our country, or the determination to fight till all are free.

Detroit Advertiser and Tribune, November 26, 1863.

A WOMAN'S ANXIETY AND LONELINESS

Few Michigan women saw a live Civil War battlefield. Yet the war was never far from their minds, as half of the state's adult men donned a uniform. In facing loneliness and anxiety arising from her husband's service in Nashville, Tennessee, as a captain with the 1)st Michigan Engineers and Mechanics, Ida Fox's experience paralleled the lot of many other Michigan women who sent their men off to war. And her fear of purportedly aggressive Native Americans, even in Michigan's second largest "city" (with an 1860 population of merely 8,085), underscores another source of anxiety for many of the state's white residents.

Grand Rapids Sept 7th 62

My Dear Husband:

No letter from you since I last wrote you. I feel very anxious about you for we hear [General Don Carlos] Buell is in great danger. For three or four weeks we have [had] very little news from the west in the papers. No doubt owing to the mails being interrupted by the rebels. Many persons here are afraid that the indians in Mich[igan] will make trouble[.] 'Tis said they are already collecting and arming themselves. They have felt bitter against Grand Rapids ever since their burying ground was disturbed by the grading on the west side. It seems to me that troubles thicken, and the end seems farther off, than it did in the beginning. . . .

We had peaches and cream for tea. Many of them are rotting on the tree before they are ripe. I shall commence to can them this week. I dread it for it is such hard work. I wish you could be here to help eat them. . . .

Every thing here is going on after the old way. War. War is the only theme. Arthur Currier starts tomorrow for your reg[iment]. You will of course see him and he can tell you many things of this place, and the people, that I can not write.

I have taken two girls into the house to go to school. They board themselves and I did not like to stay alone nights while one is away, so I have company, and they try to make as little trouble as possible. They have the north east chamber, and of course go up and down stairs, and through my rooms, but tis better so than to stay alone nights as I have since Bill has been sick. . . .

Eddie talks a great deal about you and calls himself Capt. Fox, and I am sure you would laugh to see him strut round and call me L[ieutenan]t. He says he must have pants with two pockets in them, for soldiers don't wear dresses. When are you coming home? It seems to me I can not wait, much longer before you come and I feel the loving clasp of your strong arms, and rest my head on your faithful breast, and listen to loving words from your own dear lips. Come and make the heart of your wife glad.

Good by Darling,

Ida

Perrin Fox Papers, United States Army Military History Institute, Carlisle, Pennsylvania.

THE MICHIGAN SOLDIERS' AID SOCIETY ISSUES AN APPEAL

An auxiliary of the United States Sanitary Commission, the Michigan Soldiers' Aid Society collected and distributed comforts and necessities for Michigan soldiers on the war front and in hospitals. As corresponding secretary, Valeria Campbell effectively served as the society's executive director and coordinated the work of local women-run auxiliaries with the US Sanitary Commission. An official in the US Sanitary Commission recalled that Campbell deserved "special mention for her unwearied efforts on behalf of the sick soldier" and that she stood as "an element of identity and vitality" by being "the most responsible" figure of the statewide organization.[10] Politically well connected, Campbell leaned on state and federal officials for financial assistance for the Detroit Soldiers' Home, another project of the Soldiers' Aid Society.[11]

An Appeal for Our Soldiers.

UNITED STATES SANITARY COMMISSION,

DETROIT, September 8, 186[4]

EDITORS ENTERPRISE:—May I beg the use of your columns for an appeal in behalf of our soldiers, now calling to us from many quarters for the supplies of vegetable food necessary not only to their comfort, but to health and life itself.

We appeal to the ladies and the children especially, to dry, or otherwise prepare all the fruit they can in any way procure, and to put up cucumbers, beans, and other pickles in as large quantities as possible. . . . If any are unable to do much, let them do all they can. One has only to look at the fruit packed in our sanitary store rooms to see how the packages often of a pound or two, or less, fill barrel after barrel, and box after box, till the weight is counted by tons; all of it the work of the little home circle, or, perhaps, of the paring-bee, or the berry excursion. . . . Who would not willingly deny himself to give a soldier from a Richmond prison, or in the hard-worked advance of our armies, as many potatoes, for once, as he can eat, or the pale and haggard hospital patient, the dish of blackberries which would bring back color to his cheek, and strength to his limbs? Any one who has seen the satisfaction with which the soldiers receive these luxuries, or who has read the expressions of pleasure and gratitude in their letters, will need no urging from us.

There is a special need for exertion now. While so many objects fill men's minds, there is danger that the time for sanitary work will pass by unimproved, unless we make earnest and vigorous efforts. Both humanity and patriotism call upon us. Whether we think of our friends sickening in hospitals, or of our armies, manfully fighting for our national existence, we must feel that it is our duty to provide abundantly these health-giving stores, graduating our contributions by the need of our vast armies, not by the costliness of the articles required.

It is hardly necessary to say that money will not be refused. There need be no fear of sending too much of either. . . .

VALERIA CAMPBELL,
Cor. Secretary Mich. Soldiers Aid Society.

Saginaw Enterprise, September 22, 1864.

A MICHIGAN JOURNALIST DESCRIBES A CIVIL WAR HOSPITAL

A prolific writer, Lois Bryan Adams began writing for the Michigan Farmer *in 1853 and eventually coedited and co-owned the paper. After selling the paper in 1863, Adams secured a clerkship in the US Department of Agriculture, moved to Washington, DC, and thus became one of the earliest women to work for the federal government. Adams thereafter served as a correspondent for the* Detroit Advertiser *and* Tribune *and for the remainder of the Civil War kept Michigan readers informed about life in the capital, national political figures, and the wounded soldiers she visited—in this instance, some of the first wounded soldiers from Ulysses S. Grant's 1864 Overland Campaign.*[12]

I have been among our wounded soldiers today. It would be a great comfort to the wives, mothers, and sisters of these brave fellows to know how well they are cared for here. The worst of their experience after being wounded is during the long weary wagon rides over rough roads before they get here. Only the comparatively slightly wounded have as yet been brought this side of Alexandria; most of them are still at Fredericksburg, where nurses and all things necessary for their comfort are forwarded as fast as possible. Those brought here are met at the landing by crowds of good Samaritans who distribute among them coffee, lemonade and food of all kinds; then they are taken by ambulances to the different hospitals, where clean beds, clean clothes and kind attendants await them; their wounds are washed and dressed, they undergo a general cleaning process, and are put into clean new shirts and drawers, and lie down to rest, some of them for the first time in days and weeks. . . .

In Campbell Hospital, the one I visited today, the wounds are comparatively slight; few, if any being of a dangerous nature; but even the slightest are ugly enough. Most of the shots are through the hand, arm or leg; some through the cheek, neck, shoulder or thigh. I was looking for our Michigan soldiers, but found few as yet brought to this hospital. . . .

Among the hundreds of these scarred and battered veterans I talked with, I heard but one murmur or complaint, and that was from the lips of [a] sturdy fellow from St. Johns . . . who said he "didn't think it was half fair to be popped over in the way he was without having a chance to shoot once! He was just getting into position when that ugly bit of lead came along, and spoilt his face, and his chance of returning the compliment." All the others could boast of how many hours or days they had been in action, how many rounds they had fired, and with what effect. They talk with flashing eyes and with eager motions of their wounded hands, as if they would fain be in the battling ranks again. Their enthusiasm for Gen. Grant is unbounded, and their confidence in his success entire. . . .

Our boys now in hospital said they fought in the midst of thick woods and brush, and in many instances had to fire lying flat upon the ground, which was the reason of so many catching bullets in their hands and arms. They all have thrilling stories and adventures to relate, and are in such hearty good spirits that while listening to them it is not easy to realize that one is in a hospital with wounded mangled human beings on every side. Jokes and laughter are not unfrequent [*sic*] among them at their own and each other's expense.

Detroit Advertiser and Tribune, May 17, 1864.

A NURSE'S WORK AT A CONVALESCENT HOSPITAL

On September 10, 1862, Julia S. Wheelock of Ionia learned that her brother, Orville, had received serious wounds at the Battle of Chantilly, had a leg amputated, and then had been transferred to a hospital in Alexandria, Virginia. The following day Julia and Orville's wife departed for Alexandria to aid Orville. After learning that Orville died shortly before their arrival, Julia resolved to remain and "do for others as I fain would have done for my dear brother." The Michigan Relief Association employed her as a nurse for the duration of the war.

This was my initiation month [October 1862]. I spent my time in preparing and distributing supplies to the hospitals in the city [Washington, DC]—of which there were fourteen, including some twenty different buildings—and the surrounding camps. . . .

Our Michigan soldiers were scattered through all these hospitals, and to find out and visit every one was no small task, it being almost a day's work to go through one of the largest. . . .

In my visits to these hospitals I seldom went empty-handed; sometimes taking cooked tomatoes or stewed fruit, at others, chicken broth, pickles, butter, cheese, jelly, tea hot from the stove, and, in addition to these, I would frequently buy oranges, lemons, and fresh fruit, according as the appetite seemed to crave. Besides, I gave out clothing to those most in need—such as shirts, drawers, socks, slippers, dressing-gowns, towels and handkerchiefs, also stationery and reading-matter. During this month I received a nice box of goods from Ionia. Could the donors have known how much good that one box did, they would have felt amply repaid for all they ever did for the soldiers, and encouraged to renewed efforts in the good work.

I made several visits to old "Camp Convalescent"—very properly called "Camp Misery"—which was about a mile and a half from the city. Pen would fail to describe one-half its wretchedness. Here were from ten to fifteen thousand soldiers—not simply the convalescent, but the sick and dying—many of them destitute, with not even a blanket or an overcoat, having little or no wood, their rations consisting of salt pork and "hard tack," whatever else might have been issued[.] [T]hey had no fire with which to do the cooking, consequently much of the time they were obliged to eat their pork raw. . . .

While our hearts were justly filled with indignation toward the rebel government for its inhuman treatment of their prisoners, should they not also have been toward our own, for thus shamefully neglecting those within its reach? I do not pretend to say that this camp equalled Southern prison-pens in degradation and wretchedness; but *they* were beyond our control, while over *this* floated the flag of our country. Think of men sick with fever, pneumonia, or chronic diarrhoea, eating raw pork and lying upon the cold, damp ground, with only one blanket, and, it may be, none, and the wonder will be, not that they died, but that any recovered. . . .

There were, at this time, some two hundred Michigan men in this camp. Their tents were pitched on a side-hill, so that, when it rained, the water would run through them like a river, in spite of the little trench surrounding each one. I was frequently told that when there was a drenching rain they were obliged to stand up all night to keep their clothing from being completely saturated, and, wrapping their blankets around them, they like true soldiers submitted to their fate. . . .

In going to "Camp Misery" I always filled my ambulance—when I had one—with quilts, underclothing, towels, handkerchiefs, pies, stewed fruits, and whatever else I happened to have on hand. . . . This was always a pleasant task; pleasant, because some hearts were made happier, and a few shivering forms more comfortable. And yet there was sadness mingled with all the pleasure experienced in this blessed work. To have so many cups presented as the last spoonful of sauce was dished out, and after the supply of clothing had been exhausted, to hear the appeals—"Say, got any more socks there?" "Drawers all gone?" "Can't you let me have a flannel shirt?" "I've the rheumatis awful." "Haven't another of those quilts, have you?" "Pretty cold nights,"—and not satisfied until they had taken a peep into the ambulance to be sure there was not something held in reserve for some one more highly favored than themselves, would produce a sadness of heart which could be relieved only by a continued distribution of the articles needed. . . .

There was so much needed and so many to be supplied, that the little I could do with the limited means at my disposal seemed like a drop of the ocean. . . .

I devoted my time evenings to cooking and preparing things for distribution at the hospitals next day. The 24th [October 1862] I went to Camp Convalescent with forty-two pies and several gallons of sauce. The boys seemed to think a piece of dried-apple-pie, however plain, one of the greatest luxuries they ever enjoyed. The moment it was known there were pies in camp our ambulance would be surrounded, and we, the occupants, literally taken prisoners; some begging for themselves, others for a sick comrade who was unable to leave the quarters.

Julia S. Wheelock, *The Boys in White; The Experience of a Hospital Agent in and around Washington* (New York: Lange & Hillman, 1870), vi, 37–45.

A CIVIL WAR NURSE WRITES TO HER HUSBAND IN MICHIGAN

Hannah Carlisle of Buchanan, in Berrien County, occasionally accompanied by her young daughter, Bell, served with the 2nd Michigan Cavalry and spent four years nursing wounded soldiers in Kentucky. Meanwhile, Hannah's husband, Daniel, remained in Buchanan, Michigan, running the family farm and tending to the older children. Hannah's letter reveals a woman holding strong political views while keenly preoccupied with domestic concerns more than four hundred miles to the north in Michigan. After the war, Carlisle remained in Kentucky for a year teaching for the Freedman's Bureau. Shortly after the US Congress passed the Army Nurses Pension Act of 1892, the federal government awarded Carlisle a twelve-dollar-a-month pension for her work as a Civil War nurse.[13]

I shall have to write on the hop[.] I have been trying to write ever[y]. . .morning & this is the first leisure moment[.] I think often if you at home had to write under the same circumstances letters would be few & far between. . . .

Miss Johnson, Matron of [the] Soldiers Home, called & asked me to go into the country two & a half miles[.] I accepted the invitation. We visited it is said the only true union man in Kentucky[.] The rebels have done everything but kill him[.] At the last raid they took the last horse from him. Mr. Barton is from Rochester[.] His wife is southern born all her friends are rebels but one Sister. . . .

We visited another place just below one of the rankest sessesh in all rebeldom[.] The first summer of the war he built a brick house[,] it cost thirty thousand

dollars & the furnishing twenty thousand[.] Soon after Our troops occupied Columbus some of them were out to his house. He talked verry mean to them before
morning his house & all it contained was in union [control.] This man[']s farm is
the only one that I have seen in this country that looked like Northern culture but
it [is] a waste now[.] His wife is so bitter[.] Her face was crimson with rage all the
time[,] But [she] dare[d] not express herself[.] She remarked that since the trouble
she had no servants all of them had run off she & her husband had to do their own
labour[.] I thought all right long may it continue[.] She would have been insolent
to the Yankees if she had not been in the presence of the <u>Blue Coats</u>.

Bell enjoyed the ride & visit very much[.] She had the mumps on the left side
of her face last week. . . . She has gone through the ordeal of all baby diseases &
one over (the smallpox)[.] If the Parents of Soldiers could see how foolish [it is]
to keep them from youth diseases & what soldiers suffer[,] theire [consciences]
would be ill at ease for many a one has paid the forfeit of his life in consequence
of the neglect. . . .

O what a sad thought that a country that could be an Eden should be laid
waist by the traitor[']s hand[.] How cheering the news from Virginia[.] My heart
seemed to leap for joy yet when the thought comes[,] What a sacrifice of life & the
desolate home that made one rejoice & weeps at the same time[.] But thanks be to
the giver of all good the day begins to dawn when the dear Old flag shall wave in
triumph over all the land & that land shall go free[.] When this war is over I would
not like to stand in Copperhead shoes. For there is a determination on the part of
every true soldier to avenge themself & rid the country of all such nuisances[.] For
my part I would say Amen & Amen. All Copperheads should be put where David
put Uriah in the fore front of the battle. . . .

Have you the silver or not at home[?] I want it used with care[.] I worked hard
to get it & want to take the good of it[.] Tell Fannie I always answer her letters
immediately[.] I have been wondering why she did not write[.] [S]he must not wait
for me yet I am always prompt[.] How does your socks fit[?] Give Ashley couple
pair if you choos[e] she needs them[.] Do you plant the lots this spring[?] I wish I
could send some tomato plants[,] we have such nice ones. We are makeing [some]
gardens. Mary in her letter did not say any thing about Jamerson[.] Was she at
home or has she gone[?] How does Honey's folks get along[?]

Hannah Carlisle (Columbus, Kentucky) to Dear ones at home, May 18, 1863, Carlisle Family Papers, Bentley
Historical Library, University of Michigan.

A PROSPECTIVE ARMY NURSE INQUIRES ABOUT SERVING

*Women in Southwestern Michigan turned to Hannah Carlisle, renowned in the
region for her work as an army nurse, to learn how they might likewise contribute.*

Carlisle's response to Mary Jordan is probably not extant, but she presumably told Jordan that army nurses received twelve dollars per month. Jordan's concerns about compensation posed no obstacle to Carlisle's taking an immediate liking to Jordan, as Carlisle wrote to her husband on June 7, 1863: "When I reached here I found a letter from Miss Jordon of Dowagiac asking a position as a nurse[.] I think the Dr will write to her in the morning[.] She is a teacher in the school there[.] I like the stile [sic] of her letter[.]" Obviously, both Carlisle and Jordan believed that even self-sacrificing women deserved modest compensation.

Mrs. Hannah Carlisle,

You will be somewhat surprised at receiving a letter from an entire stranger, but the earnestness of my motives and, the sacredness of this cause must be my excuse for the liberty. . . .

I have most anxiously looking for some opportunity to be of material service to our loved land, but for two years, circumstances have not favored me, but now the way seems opening more clearly. I made some effort for a situation in a hospital in Paducah [Kentucky] early in the winter, in Apr[il] a dispatch came for me but it found me where I had not been before for years, on a sick bed, and an associate teacher went in my stead. Since then I have been rapidly improving & now can endure about equal to most women, and when my heart is interested in the work I can surprise myself.

I wish to make inquiries of you on what terms you are engaged or if it is entirely free services you give. Had my widowed mother not been in part dependant upon me, I should never ask the question of money in the work, strength & life ever would be given freely, as it is my duty to her seems to demand that I try to make some provision. Please inform me in regard to that matter and also if it be true whose mon[e]y tell me that a woman in [sic] more in the way than she can profit them in a hospital. Some would be I can plainly see, but is there not a profitable field of labor open to those who only ask to be allowed the privilege of doing something for our country & her brave defenders?

Pardon my trespassing upon your time and patience, as I before said my earnestness is my excuse.

Please let me hear from you soon as may be convenient and command my services in any way that will be a benefit or comfort to a soldier, in doing so you will greatly oblige

Your[s] with respect
Mary J. Jordan

Mary J. Jordan (Dowagiac, Michigan) to Hannah Carlisle, May 27, 1863, Carlisle Family Papers, Bentley Historical Library, University of Michigan.

WAR ACCELERATES THE PUSH TOWARD LABOR-SAVING MACHINERY

Historians have long debated the Civil War's effect on Northern industrialization. Many historians hold that directing the economy toward war hindered many industrial sectors and provided few workers for manufacturing. In agriculture, though, historians generally concede that the absence of male labor pushed women and youths into the fields and encouraged a larger number of Northern farmers to buy horse-drawn machinery that they had previously deemed unnecessary.[14] *Although Charles B. Howell of Ann Arbor may have overstated the trends he described, by 1870 the federal census reported Michigan farmers had more than doubled their investment in farm machinery over the previous decade.*

That "this is a world of compensations" . . . has never been proven more to a demonstration, than since the beginning of the traitors' war on the Union, in so vast amount as there has of labor-saving machinery taking the place of the myriads of laboring men upon the farm who have with patriotic sacrifice, left their plows in the furrow, their scythes in the meadow, and grasping the gun and sword, gone forth with their brethren throughout the North to redeem the land from treason, and purge it of traitors.

Looking at the large manufacture and sale of labor-saving agricultural implements since the War, it would almost seem that the inventors in the last quarter of a century were working their brains for the benefit of their beloved country in its approaching hour of trial, or as if they looked at the future with the ken of a prophet. The ingenuity of a few men has been the means of giving to the country in its time of need, thousands upon thousands of those who otherwise would have been absolutely required to remain at home and till the soil.

I have not the statistics at hand to prove my assertion, but I am prepared to say that the employment of labor-saving agricultural machinery has been for the last three years, four-fold what it was in the three years preceding the commencement of the war.

In the city of Pontiac, during the spring and summer of 1863, there were sold between two and three hundred mowers and reapers. This is item is but a fair specimen of what would make up the statistics, if it were undertaken to show the large sales of agricultural implements since the war began all over the country.

These facts prove that men can seldom see the effects of their acts in all their extent.

Michigan Farmer (New Series) 2 (January 1864): 320–21.

A SOLDIER COMPLAINS ABOUT
INADEQUATE SUPPORT FOR MILITARY FAMILIES

Not long after the war began, the Michigan legislature required counties to "make adequate provisions for all requisite relief and support" of soldiers' families, "not exceeding . . . fifteen dollars per month."[15] *This anonymous letter to Elihu B. Pond, editor and publisher of the* Michigan Argus *of Ann Arbor, points to the economic anxiety that soldiers' families faced in 1864 as prices increased and assistance declined.*

MR. POND:—Will you allow me to make your paper the medium of complaint as to the manner that soldiers' families are treated, while they—the husbands and fathers—are away periling their lives for those who quietly sit at home brooding over the prospects of the war, and their chances of making "something handsome" in some speculation or other. From my wife I learn at different times, of the rise in prices, until I find they have become enormous, and it is a wonder to me how the poor women and children can subsist. We soldiers were told on enlisting, that our fam[i]lies would be provided for. How have these promises been kept[?] I have a wife and four small children. I receive from "Uncle Sam" twenty dollars per month, and by the time paymaster comes around, the sutler or purveyor owns a large share of it; for I must buy and use many little things to come up to the requirements of a Sergeant. Then, there are little luxuries the sutlers bring into the field, which makes the mouth of the soldier, who has so long been fed on nothing but pork and hard tack, fairly water. Then can you blame the poor fellows for purchasing, even at sutler's prices[?]

A private only gets sixteen dollars a month. Now, sir, what can it be expected a man can send home out of his pay? In the cavalry, a man's allowance for clothes is not sufficient to keep him respectable, therefore a part of his earnings is used up in extra clothing. For the past year, and the year before, my wife received from the supervisor a certain sum monthly, varying according to the action of the board. I learn that the allowance has been cut down this present month. I ask, sir, is this just, is this right? when every thing a family consumes is daily rising, and fuel and clothing are more needed than in summer, to deduct from the small pittance I feel that any one that will give the subject a thought, will wonder that any soldier's wife and family can go decently clad, appear, and be respected. I know that women are looked upon very lightly, and treated with contempt by those who should befriend them, when their only crime is being a soldier's wife; or if the poor fellow is killed, she is sneered at as a "soldier's widow." Now, sir, I do not write this on my own account, for I am certain that the Supervisor gives my family all he is allowed to; but there are a number around me, even in less humble position and means than I, who wished me to write their grievance. Those in the townships fare worse than in the city.

Hoping that those who have the power, will do what they can to assist the families of the poor fellows striving to sustain the honor of their country's flag, I have the honor to remain,

Yours, respectfully,
CAVALRYMAN

Michigan Argus (Ann Arbor), December 9, 1864.

LABOR DISPUTES IN THE UPPER PENINSULA'S IRON MINES

The Upper Peninsula's remoteness had long complicated efforts to attract labor to Marquette's iron mines. Troop demands during the Civil War made securing labor for the dangerous mines even more difficult. Knowing of the large dividends that mining companies paid, and recognizing that those companies wanted to maximize iron production—and profits—before the war's end, miners struck in May 1864 with an eye toward securing better pay and reducing their hours from sixty-six to fifty-eight per week. Politicians and the press sided with Cleveland Iron Mining Company, whose officials asked Governor Austin Blair to subdue the strike with force. Blair turned to federal assistance. Secretary of War Edwin Stanton directed fifty-six federal troops, accompanied by a federal gunboat, the USS Michigan, *to end the Marquette strike. Despite arresting labor leaders and otherwise acceding to the strikers' demands, labor shortages in the Marquette Iron Range continued.*[16]

For some time past the iron miners in the Marquette district have been dissatisfied with the pay they have been receiving, and fears were entertained that a strike would be the result of this dissatisfaction. The affair reached a culminating point on Saturday, the 14th inst., when a body of 300 men came over from the mines to Marquette, and refused to work any longer at present prices. A conference was held with their employers, and after considerable discussion, a partial arrangement was effected, and the miners went back to their work, and it was hoped that no further demonstration would occur. We understand that later intelligence from that district brings the news that the troubles have broken out afresh, and have resulted in some violence. The dockmen or stevedores seeing the action the miners took, also made a strike, which assumed large proportions. About 250 of them effected a combination, refusing to work themselves, or allow others to do so. The men whose business is of a fluctuating character, are mainly engaged in loading vessels with iron or ore, and are as a class in character below the miners. The have carried their acts to the criminal length of preventing the willing, peaceable and industrious portion of those laborers from pursuing their avocation. On

Saturday last they marched in a body to the various vessels loading in the harbor, and by violence compelled the men to stop work.

Of course, no such forcible interference with the rights of labor could be tolerated in a civilized community. This riotous proceeding necessitated that prompt measures should be taken to ensure obedince [*sic*] to law, and protection to labor. The *North Star*, of Cleveland, was lying in the harbor at the time, about to leave for that city. The representatives of the Cleveland [Iron Mining] [C]ompany . . . left for Jackson, to see Governor Blair to induce the sending of a large force to the Upper Peninsula to preserve order, and protect not only the interests of the Mining Companies, but the interests of those who feel disposed to work at liberal wages. The dock men have hitherto been paid at the rate of 37–1/2 cents per hour for their work, which is considered by those acquainted with this kind of business, liberal compensation for their services. They now demand the increased price of 50 cents per hour or $5.50 per day of 11 hours. While labor should receive its adequate reward, and bring in the market all that a healthy competition will allow, yet no set or class of men have a right to organize and prevent other men from working at whatever price they see fit. The law of demand and supply should regulate the price of labor as it does every other article of commerce. . . .

We have but little doubt that this state of affairs will be of short duration, and that 100 or 200 soldiers will restore order, and that business will soon be resumed.

Detroit Advertiser, May 27, 1864, as reproduced in the *Chicago Tribune*, May 29, 1864.

THE FAILED ATTEMPT TO RESCUE CONFEDERATE PRISONERS

Michigan's international border with Canada proved to be a continued source of anxiety in the state, largely because of the fraught relations between the United States and Great Britain, which still controlled Canada's foreign affairs and Canada's relationship with the United States. By declaring itself a neutral in the conflict, by recognizing the Confederacy as a belligerent if not a nation, and by permitting the construction of Confederate raiding ships in its ports, British policy only escalated the long-standing antagonism of the Northern US public toward Britain.[17] *And as those relations deteriorated, Canada's long border with the United States brought that growing antagonism close to home. Following the* Trent *affair, Governor Austin Blair called for a preemptive invasion of Canada in his 1862 annual message, declaring that the "British government has concealed designs, and only seeks a pretext for a rupture." With slightly milder tones, the Democratic* Detroit Free Press *reported later that year, "An uneasy feeling has prevailed in this city for some time; an undefined apprehension that Britain is on the eve of the contest with the United States, in which, of course, Canada would be involved."*[18]

Notwithstanding the thousands of Canadians who served in the Union army,[19] Canada became the home to Confederate agents and Confederate soldiers who escaped from Northern prisons, with many openly residing in Windsor, Canada West (now Ontario), less than a mile from Michigan's largest city and separated only by the Detroit River.[20] Hoping, in late 1864, to turn the tide in a war that was looking desperate for their side, Confederates plotted to take control of a commercial ship, the Philo Parsons, *which sailed from Detroit on September 19, 1864, with one Confederate agent aboard. After additional Confederate agents and veterans boarded at Sandwich (now a neighborhood of Windsor) and Amherstburg, Canada West, the Confederates seized control of the* Philo Parsons *and eventually made their way toward Sandusky, Ohio, with their eyes on the USS* Michigan, *the only US armed vessel on the Great Lakes. These Confederates hoped to take control of the* Michigan, *liberate three thousand Confederate prisoners on nearby Johnson's Island, and then use the fifteen-gun* Michigan *to terrorize Lake Erie's cities. Confederates on the* Parsons *discerned that the* Michigan *crew had learned of their plot, however, and returned to Canada after abandoning their plan.[21]*

ACTG. ASST. PROVOST-MARSHAL-GENERAL'S OFFICE,
Detroit, Mich., September 21, 1864.

Maj. C. H. POTTER . . .
SIR: I have the honor to inform you that on Saturday night last, the 17th instant, [Godfrey J. Hyams] called upon me at my hotel and introduced himself to me as having been for some years a rebel soldier, and recently a refugee in Canada. He informed me that some of the officers and men of the U. S. Steamer *Michigan* had been tampered with, and that it was the intention of the rebel agent in Windsor, Jacob Thompson, late Secretary of the Interior under President Buchanan's administration, to send a party from Windsor, who, with the assistance of the officers and men, would endeavor to get possession of the steamer. He said he had been approached [by] one of the party, and had consented to do so; and that he would receive more particular information on the next morning, when the party would leave for Malden [Amherstburg]. He said that with the possession of the steamer *Michigan* they would have control of the lakes for a couple of months, and would levy contributions on all the lake cities; and had offered very large inducements to the officers and men of that steamer. . . . The statement of the man and his earnestness made some impression on me, and I telegraphed to Capt. J[ack]. C. Carter, the commanding officer of the steamer *Michigan*, that night. . . .

[A]fter mature consideration, I came to the conclusion that it would be better to let the steamer [the *Philo Parsons*] go [from Detroit], and place Captain Carter on his guard in a way that it would make an impression on him, so that the whole party could be taken. . . . These plots are being constantly made here. We had the information about this one, and the question was whether it would not be better to let it proceed, and make an example in this case, if the information really amounted to anything. . . .

It seems that after taking possession of [the *Philo Parsons*] the piratical party seized and sunk a small steamer named the *Island Queen*, both occurrences taking place in the waters of the State of Ohio. They then proceeded to within four miles of Sandusky, and not, probably, seeing signals that had been agreed upon, or receiving any assistance that was probably expected from Sandusky, returned to Detroit River and proceeded to Sandwich, Canada West, where they plundered the steamer and cut her pipes to sink her, and abandoned her. The steamer was, however, recovered by her owners in a damaged condition, half full of water, and brought to this side of the river.

It seems that my telegram to Captain Carter led to the arrest of [Charles H.] Cole, who made some disclosures which caused the arrest of other parties in Sandusky, the particulars of which will be doubtless communicated by the commanding officer there. It was unfortunate that Captain Carter did not proceed to meet the *Philo Parsons*, as the whole party could have been captured; but there have been so many rumors and reports here of rebel plots that it is hard to discriminate between those having some reality and those purely fabrications. In this case had I placed soldiers on board, whom I could not spare at this time, or deferred in any way the departure of the steamer, suspicions of the conspirators would have been aroused, and the matter deferred to a time when we would have had no intimation of it.

As the case now stands . . . the persons employed in these acts [are] now residing in Canada, under the protection of the British Government.

The U. S. attorney has addressed a communication to our consul in Windsor, to call upon the authorities to arrest the persons committing these outrages, in anticipation of a demand being made for their delivery, and affidavits will be sent by him to the Secretary of State; and I had an interview this morning both with him and Senator [Jacob] Howard, and everything is being adopted to place the matter in proper legal shape before the Government and the British authorities.

Very respectfully, your obedient servant,

B[ennett]. H. HILL,

Lieutenant-Colonel, U. S. Army, Commanding District of Michigan.

The War of the Rebellion: A Compilation of the Official Records of the Union and Confederate Armies, ser. 1, vol. 43, part 2 (Washington, DC: Government Printing Office, 1893), 233–34.

DETROIT RESPONDS TO ANOTHER ATTACK FROM CANADA

A month after the failed hijacking of the Philo Parsons, *mounted Confederates launched, from Canada East (now Quebec), an attack on St. Albans, Vermont. Confederates robbed banks of over $200,000, killed a civilian, wounded two with gunfire, and burned buildings. After their apprehension in Quebec, a local Canadian judge released the St. Albans raiders on December 13, 1864. Canadian-American relations, and British-American relations, thereafter turned worse, as Americans blamed British and Canadian authorities with assisting the Confederacy.*

Days after the Free Press *published this editorial, US Secretary of State William Seward imposed passport controls on the US-Canadian border—controls so rigidly enforced that the* Free Press *changed its mind and joined with the Republican* Advertiser and Tribune *to lobby for repeal of the passport restrictions, declaring that costs to Detroit business were too great and the protections offered by passport control were minimal. Although Seward rescinded this passport order in early March 1865, Detroiters' frightened response to Confederate raids from Canada, and their insistence on ending passport controls, exhibited their complicated relationship with Canadians, who stood as neighbors, economic partners, and potential adversaries. The failed Confederate cross-border attacks also contributed to increased defenses along the Detroit River and to assigning the newly mustered 30th Michigan Infantry there during the last months of the war. It also led to the US decision, on March 17, 1865, to withdraw from the Canadian-American Reciprocity Treaty of 1854 (also known as the Elgin-Marcy Treaty), a withdrawal that took effect a year later.*[22]

WHAT CAN BE DONE TO PROTECT US FROM CANADA?

The duty of the Canadian government to protect us against the incursion of any persons who reside there is too clear for debate. But we are pained to see, by the telegraphic reports, that the judiciary of Canada have determined, so far as in their power, to protect these "raiders," rather than punish them, for making incursions across the borders, and plundering our banks and warehouses, and, when resisted, murdering our citizens.

The Canadian government having failed to perform its duty, what shall we do to protect ourselves? It is very plain that we are now drifting into a war—not with England, unless she elects to take part in it, but with Canada. We cannot remain passive, and see men, no matter where they come from, or to whom they owe allegiance, congregate in the cities and villages of Canada, and there concoct "raids" upon our people, and, when pursued across the border and arrested, discharged from arrest, and again set free, because there is no law in Canada for the punishment of such crimes. It is not for us to say what laws she requires. It is not for us to dictate to her a code, but we have the right, if her citizens, subjects or denizens come across the border and commit crimes against us, to have redress. Our first demand is for the surrender of these criminals, to the end that they may be punished here; our second is, that if, in committing the crime against us, they also violate the Canadian statutes, or international law, that they be punished there. Now, neither of these reasonable requests have been complied with. . . .

What policy shall then be pursued? We answer that the President, if he has the power, should at once declare a complete and absolute non-intercourse with the Canadian Provinces. If he has not the power, he should lay the matter before Congress, and ask for a law which will enable him to do it. There should not only be non-intercourse so far as trade is concerned, but as to individuals. No person should be permitted to come into the States without a passport, showing who and what he is, and in whatever town or city he visits he should be required to lodge his passport, and when ready to return, he should first obtain a permit before he could leave. The most strict and rigid system should be adopted and enforced, and if, after a fair trial . . . this remedy . . . is found to fail, and if the Canadian government are still remiss in their duty, there will be no other course left but for our government to take the law into their own hands, and seize them wherever they can be found.

We have no desire to see an interruption of intercourse between the United States and Canada. It will be a serious inconvenience, if not great damage, to our city and State, but it is far better to submit to this until the Canadian government can enact such laws as will prevent these raids, or enforce the laws they have, than to have our cities along the border plundered and burned, and our citizens murdered. We prefer the uninterrupted intercourse which existed between the people of Canada and the States along the border before they took to their embrace these unquiet spirits; but if we cannot have this, then we prefer to have a wall of non-intercourse so high and so well-guarded that no human being can pass it, to war. We can subsist without Canada. We can live without intercourse with them far better than to be kept in continual turmoil by a set of men they persist in taking into their homes, and protecting by their laws, who are bent upon precipitating the two countries into a war, because they hope such a war will aid them in their traitorous efforts to overthrow their own government. We commend the whole subject to our authorities at Washington. It requires immediate action.

Detroit Free Press, December 15, 1864.

SEVEN

Michigan's Wartime Politics

 $\mathcal{M}$ ICHIGAN POLITICS REMAINED solidly Republican throughout the Civil War, with the state casting its presidential ballots for Abraham Lincoln in 1860 and 1864. Additionally, Michigan Republicans controlled both US Senate seats, the governorship, and all statewide offices throughout the war. The only political success to which Democrats could point was in the election of 1862, when Democrats joined with conservative Republicans to form a fusionist Union Party, which won 51 seats in the 132-seat statehouse. Though still far in the minority, the Democrat-dominated coalition's numbers were a great improvement over the 12 seats that Democrats held during the previous house session.[1] That election also saw A. C. Baldwin narrowly elected to the US House of Representatives, a seat he barely lost in 1864. Otherwise, Republicans controlled Michigan's four seats in the US House of Representatives before 1863, and six seats thereafter.

The Civil War placed Michigan's Democrats—and Northern Democrats generally—in a difficult position that remained unresolved until years after the war's conclusion. After all, Northern Democrats' longtime Southern political allies left the Union on account of the election of a Republican as president. And Republicans were Northern Democrats' intrasectional rival. Although Northern Democrats almost universally held their national loyalties in higher regard than their partisan loyalties, Northern Democrats continued to have misgivings regarding a war directed by their political adversaries against many of their former political allies. The longer the war lasted, the more insistently Republicans made emancipation into a central war objective. And the more emancipation became a war objective, the more Democrats increased their dissent. When it came to dissenting against emancipation, Michigan's Democrats, and Democrats across the North, resorted to their longtime use of racial epithets to frighten their party's base and to attack their Republican opponents.

With Republicans controlling the federal government and many Northern state governments, party unity came relatively easily during the Civil War. Republicans also frequently equated support for the Lincoln administration's war policies with loyalty to the Union. Not infrequently, Republicans falsely accused Democrats of having Confederate sympathies or of being traitors. Within their party, Democrats divided into "War Democrats" and "Copperheads." War Democrats favored a vigorous prosecution of the war but generally questioned the wisdom of emancipation as a war objective. Louder and more critical of Republicans than War Democrats, Copperheads—derisively named after the venomous snake, which epithet many Democrats embraced—adopted the slogan "The Constitution as it is, the Union as it was." Copperheads not only objected to emancipation but also complained about the wartime expansion of federal authority, including the suspension of habeas corpus. Although less numerous than they were in Ohio, Indiana, Illinois, and Pennsylvania, Copperheads nonetheless formed an important element of Michigan's Democratic Party. Many Copperheads opposed coercing the South's return to the Union, and some sympathized with Southern war objectives. A few Copperheads called for an armistice, which would have effectively recognized Confederate independence, and some went further and conspired with Confederate agents. Republicans frequently underlined Copperhead objections to the war, denounced them as traitorous, and conflated all Democrats under the Copperhead designation. Copperheadism peaked during the summer of 1864 when Union military victories seemed elusive. Ultimately wartime prosperity, the Confederate surrender of Atlanta in September 1864, and Lincoln's reelection two months later undermined the Copperhead movement.[2]

During the summer of 1864, many Republicans, including Abraham Lincoln, feared that Democrats would win the fall election. Union victories during the late summer and fall, however, turned the tide in public opinion and resulted in Lincoln's reelection—one in which the president increased his vote in the Northern states from 53.7 percent in 1860 to 55.0 percent in 1864. Lincoln also won Michigan's popular vote, but saw his proportion drop modestly from 57.2 percent in 1860 to 53.6 percent in 1864. Part of this decline resulted from a Michigan Supreme Court decision, on January 28, 1865, that rejected a state law permitting out-of-state soldiers on military duty to cast ballots in state elections.[3] This decision invalidated 12,361 soldiers' votes, 76.2 percent of which went for Lincoln and other Republican candidates. Had these ballots been counted, Lincoln would have still secured only 55.3 percent of the state's votes. And he lost nine Michigan counties—Livingston, Macomb, Monroe, Oakland, Ottawa, Saginaw, St. Clair, Washtenaw, and Wayne— that he and Republicans had won in 1860.[4] Although still a solid Republican state, partisanship and uncertainty regarding the Civil War's outcome kept most Michiganians from placing Abraham Lincoln in the American political pantheon during the president's lifetime.

A DEMOCRAT'S GROWING FEARS REGARDING ABOLITIONISTS

Soon after the Civil War began, Northern Democrats noticed how increasing numbers of Republicans began to favor an attack on slavery—the South's economic foundation—as a means of defeating the Confederacy. Because most Northern Democrats favored a restoration of the Union with slavery intact, they continued their long-standing front against abolitionism. Unlike most Democrats, this anonymous writer argues for abolitionists being a distinctive force within American politics, radicals driven by religious fervor, and separate from even the Republicans that Democrats regularly linked to abolitionists. Less than two months later, the editor of this Democratic newspaper praised Abraham Lincoln as a "patriotic President who is so earnestly struggling to put down the efforts of the wretched traitors north and south."⁵ Soon, Democrats' deepest fears became realized when the Lincoln administration and congressional Republicans increasingly pursued emancipationist policies, with Democrats thereafter arguing that Republicans placed emancipation above the Union and thus unnecessarily prolonged the war.

ABOLITION AND THE REBELLION.

The indications are clearly discernible that the abolitionists of the North, will, ere long, give the government as much trouble as the secessionists of the South. The contest will not be one of arms . . . but it will be a conflict of opinion which may do the cause of the Union vital injury, by dividing a now United North.

No one can for a moment deny that the success thus far in repressing this formidable rebellion, is mainly due to the *united* efforts of Northern men, of both the great political parties, in sustaining the President and Congress in the performance of their important duties. In order to secure a speedy and successful termination of the present unhappy struggle, it is vitally necessary that past political predilections and prejudices should be for a time laid aside, and give to the executive our united voice and strength, in the prosecution of the war. It is therefore an obligation resting upon every lover of his country, to frown down any and every attempt to renew among us past political differences, or sectional prejudices, whether they come from the unpatriotic spirit of partisanship, the sympathizers of rebellion, or the ministerial and lecture-room disciples of abolitionism. Evidences are daily multiplying, that the abolitionists of the North, with an undivided front, will present to the Administration, at the coming session of Congress, the issue of the unconditional abolition of slavery everywhere, by proclamation, or open and direct hostility to its policy.

Abolitionism has no interest in this war, only so far as it can be made to conduce to its cherished idea. It has no sympathy with the Constitution, and its votaries like the unclean spirit of old, enter into it only to throw up the ground and tear it to pieces. The declaration of Garrison, "dissolution or abolition," is repeated from the pulpit and the rostrum, and emblazoned on parchment and tendered to our fellow citizens for their endorsement. . . .

Are we to believe that the only use and purpose of this war, is to free four millions of slaves? Are we not fighting to maintain the Union and the Constitution, in all their integrity? Are we not willing to abide by the doctrines and lessons of our Revolutionary ancestors? Are we to listen to the assertions that the star emblazoned flag, of which every American is proud, and under which our liberties were won, carries the dogma of abolitionism in its folds wherever it floats?

Adrian Watchtower, December 2, 1861.

DEMOCRATS AS UNWITTING TRAITORS

In the normal give-and-take of nineteenth-century American politics, partisans commonly used unsavory and demeaning language to vilify their opponents. During the Civil War, the harsh tone of political speech became more severe as Republicans commonly linked their Democratic rivals with the hated Confederacy. This pamphlet included testimonials from Michigan soldiers that reported the troops' disgust with the Northern Democrats.

Loyal Democrats of Michigan! . . .

Democratic leaders in this State and the North, who have got entire control of the party, and are using it to embarrass the Government, defeat the army and give aid and comfort to armed traitors! If you heed the voice of our gallant soldiers, you must abandon that party or abandon the soldiers and the only hope of the Union! DECIDE AT THE BALLOT BOX WHICH YOU WILL ABANDON!! A most terrible retribution awaits those who are not found with the army, and friends of the Government in this hour of trial. Listen to the warnings, and the PRAYERS of the loyal Democrats in the army. Come to the rescue of the Union by deserting at the ballot-box the Northern allies of Southern traitors. . . .

It is enough to know that the Democrats of the North are regarded by the REBELS as their FRIENDS AND ALLIES-and that every "Democratic victory" only gives them hope and encouragement to hold out longer, and persevere more vigorously in killing our SONS AND BROTHERS! The Richmond Dispatch of the 9th Feb., 1863, announced that "THE NEXT GREAT DEFEAT OF THE REPUBLICAN HORDES WILL CONSOLIDATE THE WHOLE DEMOCRATIC STRENGTH OF THE NORTH IN OPEN AND DETERMINED RESISTANCE TO THE FURTHER PROSECUTION OF THE WAR."

Thus the loyal voters of Michigan are being used by the rebel sympathising leaders, to give aid and comfort and hope to red-handed treason. A vote for the Democratic ticket now, is a vote of ENCOURAGEMENT TO THE SOUTHERN REBELS and against the prayers and supplications of the gallant soldiers. It adds to their sufferings and hardships. It PROLONGS THE WAR. . . . Do not deliberately vote DEATH and DEFEAT to your sons on the battle-field.

A Bugle Blast from the Army. What the Soldiers Think of Northern Traitors. THEY WILL REMEMBER WHEN THEY RETURN. The Voice of Loyal Democrats in the Army to Traitor Democrats at Home. READ AND CIRCULATE THIS DOCUMENT (Detroit? 1863?).

A SOLDIER COMPLAINS OF ABOLITIONISTS' FAILURE
TO SUPPORT MCCLELLAN AND THE TROOPS

In March 1862, General George McClellan loaded 130,000 US troops and supplies on boats and transported them to Virginia's James Peninsula. There he commanded the Peninsula Campaign that aimed to capture Richmond and end the war. Although his army reached the Confederate capital's outskirts, with a two-to-one troop advantage, McClellan, steadfast in the false belief that Confederate forces outnumbered his, called off the offensive and in August returned to the defenses of Washington.

Writing from Harrison's Landing, Virginia, at the end of the campaign, Hiel P. Clark of the 3rd Michigan Infantry blamed McClellan's failures on the general's Republican and abolitionist critics. Nine months later the Ionia County resident died at Chancellorsville.

[W]e had rather a rainy time of it yesterday last night at midnight was awakend by heavy firing and for about an hour they kept it up with the greatest fury I have not heard what it was for nor how they made of it but from the sound I concluded that sesesh got the wurst of it or it would not have stopt so soon. [F]or it was right where they land all our sup[p]lies and if the rebs should get posession of that we would have to cave, or little move would have to make some bigger splurges than he [McClellan] has yet made, although acording to [Senator Zachariah] Chandler, he [McClellan] has done nothing. [B]ut I would like to know what Chandler has done but wast[e] his time and the Countrys monny preaching from his Nigger text like all the rest of the abolitionests, when they had ought to have been in the field fighting or els[e] urging on the peopel at home to reinforce Gen McClellan[.] [I]t is no use talking, siss, we are fighting against just as good men as the north dare have, and men who have got their harts in the work they are doing and we have got to have an equal number of men to cope successfuly with them. You see all the country we get we have to protect that takes a great many from our army. [T]hat is the reason why we have to have such an enorm[o] us force[,] to bring an equal force into the field against them.

Hiel P. Clark to Carrie Clark, August 1, 1862, Clarke Historical Library, Central Michigan University.

"THIS WAR SHOULD NEVER END UNTIL
THE REBELLION IS COMPLETELY CRUSHED"

Dr. George K. Johnson, the former mayor of Grand Rapids, joined the 1st Michigan Cavalry in 1861 as a surgeon. Despite his commitment to restore the Union, Johnson, a Democrat, says nothing about eradicating slavery, notwithstanding the Emancipation Proclamation's issuance the previous month.

Defense of Washington, Feb. 8, 1863.

But on one subject I am clear. This war should never end until the rebellion is completely crushed and the national authority is restored over all the rebellious States. It would be disgraceful, *infamous*, RUINOUS, to submit to any other result. We have got the power, we have got the money and the men to enable us to put down the rebellion, and to restore federal authority over the revolted States, and it is our *duty* to *do* it, even though it may take five, ten, yea, even fifteen years, to do it. It is a duty we owe to God, to the memory of our fathers who gave us these noble institutions, to our posterity, and to ourselves. We cannot escape from this duty, except in shame and disgrace. And, besides, it would ruin us to do so. To consent to the dismemberment of this nation by Rebellion and Treason would sound *the death knell* of our peace, prosperity, and power, FOREVER. I could easily show that such must be the result of the success of this attempt to disrupt the nation; but I have neither the time nor the space to do so. Nor is it necessary, for you and every intelligent man, who will look at the subject, must see that this must be so.

On the subject then of sustaining the Government in its efforts to vindicate its authority, there ought not to be any difference of opinion. On this vital point, every man, woman and child of the loyal States ought to be completely and earnestly united. As for myself, I never will, I never can, consent to a peace based on the disruption and dismemberment of my country.

Grand Rapids Daily Eagle, March 2, 1863.

A DEMOCRAT QUESTIONS EMANCIPATION

Edward G. Morton from Monroe, a long-standing Democratic member of the Michigan House of Representatives and former Speaker pro tempore, supported the war from the start. But like most Democrats across the North, Morton opposed Lincoln's Emancipation Proclamation, which the president signed on January 1, 1863, and which freed all slaves living within the Confederacy. In a speech opposing emancipation, Morton resorted to Northern Democrats' common refrain of emphasizing widely felt racial prejudice among Northern whites while acceding to Northern whites' hostility to slavery.

Had we of this day treated the subject of slavery as did the Fathers of the Republic, this wicked rebellion would not be upon our country; and before it is settled we shall find it necessary to look at facts as they are, rather than continue to be guided by our sectional prejudices. In fact, sir, it is time, if we would have peace, for us in the North to examine ourselves, and see if our garments are free from the stain of blood. It is no virtue in us to assume the position that we are all right, and the South all wrong. . . .

Our fathers had the same difficulties before them in regard to slavery that we have, but they treated the subject in a different manner and spirit. They were successful, for they cherished the sentiments of union and concession. We have failed because we have allowed our local prejudices to obtain ascendency over national sentiments and patriotism; and hence the present day of calamity, which teaches us that a government founded in compromise can live only in compromise, now repudiated by the extremists in both sections of our unfortunate country. It is only a despotism that can live without compromise. . . .

We are told that we have the right of free speech in a free country. Yes, sir, but not the right to abuse this freedom of speech; and we have no more right to allow our fanaticism to lead us to interfere in the affairs of other States, because they differ with us in their institutions, than we have to slander and misrepresent our neighbors who do not live, think and act as we do. It is an abuse of freedom, and caries with it hatred and disunion. . . .

But it is impossible to give freedom to the slaves. . . . Our highest court says it is right to exclude them from the company of gentleman on our steamers. A few years ago, by an overwhelming vote, the people of Michigan decided that they should not vote and become citizens of the State; and then denounced Judge Taney for expressing the opinion that a slave was not a citizen of the United States.[6] Here is both social and political degradation to the black man; and political parties, for the sake of appealing to a morbid sympathy, and theorizing about liberty, for imposition and power, we may well suspect quite as much hypocrisy as philanthropy in that profession.

The North has no right to complain of the condition of the slaves until they are prepared to place them in a better one. How much we have heard about slavery, merely for agitation, without the least regard to the welfare of the slave. Northern laborers have been told that it was degrading to compete with slave labor. . . . They will never live together on terms of equality—If we had large numbers in Michigan, of that unfortunate race, such is the popular prejudice that they would not be employed unless they underbid white labor, and then would come the animosity which would end in the subjugation of the blacks to slavery, where our laws now place them so far as they relate to their position in society. We have denounced the South for doing what we would have done under the same circumstances. It is time we knew ourselves, and what we really desire to do with slavery. All the flattering promises of the agitators have been only delusions.

Adrian Watchtower, February 7, February 9, and February 10, 1863.

A REPUBLICAN RESPONDS TO DEMOCRATS' OPPOSITION TO THE EMANCIPATION PROCLAMATION

In a speech before the Michigan State Republican Convention the month after Lincoln signed the Emancipation Proclamation, Detroit postmaster William A.

Howard, formerly a member of the US House of Representatives and subsequently
governor of Dakota Territory, lampoons the Democrats' idea that the war should
be fought without attacking slavery. In so doing, Howard emphasizes abolishing
slavery as a war measure and less as a moral issue.

The Democrats of New York, Indiana, and Southern Illinois are opposing the
war in a crafty manner. . . . They dare not openly oppose the war, but howl over
certain incidents of it. We say, if a negro gets free in consequence of the war which
the rebels began in order to tighten his chains, God be praised, (applause) and let
the locofocos [Democrats] howl. A war for slavery, o[r] one against it, is certain to
kill the institution. History shows that slavery cannot stand war at all. Mr. Lincoln
never seems to have been in the fog in this matter. He has endeavored to save the
Government, whatever became of slavery. If the war killed slavery, let it die. . . . What
is the difference between destroying corn taken in a wagon train of the rebels, and
releasing negroes who are engaged in raising or harvesting corn which would go
to feed rebels? The principle is precisely the same.

It is the President's duty to deprive the enemy of every means whereby they
peril the lives of loyal soldiers—whether it be a horse, a jackass, an ox, or a negro-
a white man or a black man. It is our duty to take away the slaves which have
worked for the rebels, and enabled almost every white Southerner to be sent to
the field. Away with everything which stands in the way of putting down this
rebellion!. . . .

Whatever sins the "Black Republican" party has committed, it has never furnished an armed rebel for Jeff. Davis! (Applause.) Our opponents [Democrats], in
their perpetual howl about the incidents of war, are actuated either by prejudice
in behalf of their old party friends at the South, or they have very little sense
or very little patriotism. . . . Now they are howling against the Proclamation of
Emancipation. But that is a question of power, and as fast as our armies subdue
rebel territory, the Constitution and laws which they defy, and the proclamation
which our opponents sneer at will be enforced.

Grand Rapids Daily Eagle, 16 February 1863.

A DEMOCRAT EMBRACES EMANCIPATION

During a debate in the Michigan House of Representatives, William T. Howell, a
Republican, produced a letter from Daniel A. Spicer, a constituent from Newaygo,
then serving as surgeon of the 10th Michigan Infantry. Before the Civil War, Spicer
had been, according to the Grand Rapids Daily Eagle, *"a Democrat of the most*
'conservative' stripe." Spicer's letter suggests how the war's persistence forced him
to jettison his prewar political beliefs.

You know that I never was much of an abolitionist when at home, but I confess to being that just now, that is, if sustaining the President's proclamation makes me such. I have seen enough at the South to convince me that slavery is the pillar of the rebellion, and if so it must be necessary to destroy such support, and if necessary, then I say constitutional. For I reason in this way—the Constitution is the foundation of the Government. . . . Then it follows as a natural deduction, that if slavery is the great power in the hands of vile traitors for destroying the Government, it must be removed. . . .

The laborizing [sic] thousands of the South are the only means of producing supplies for the Southern army, as is witnessed in those portions through which our armies have passed. The thousands of acres of rich plantations formerly devoted to the cotton crop, have been tilled only by slave labor, producing millions of bushels of corn, which would have required at least one-third of the whole rebel army to have produced it by free labor. I have seen large plantations under the best of cultivation, and not a free man on the premises—not even an overseer—but men, women and children, all slaves, in the fields under slave superintendence, working to feed the traitor army. Then, I say, remove this support and the rotted superstructure must fall. Now if you can make the people of the North feel on this subject as the great majority of our troops do for the interests of the contemptible slave-whippers of the South we can finish this business in a short time, and again be permitted to return to a land of civilization in peace—the source of discord between the North and South effectually and permanently removed.

D. A. Spicer (Nashville) to William T. Howell, February 1, 1863, as printed in *Grand Rapids Daily Eagle,* February 26, 1863.

A REPUBLICAN EDITOR ASSESSES LINCOLN IN 1863

Although historians and the American public widely recognize Abraham Lincoln as one of the most—if not the most—capable presidents to serve in the office, most of Lincoln's contemporaries failed to recognize the greatness with which subsequent generations have endowed him. Besides being denounced by Confederates and Democrats, many radicals within the Republican Party criticized Lincoln for not moving more swiftly on emancipation and for not acting more vigilantly against treason. Theodore Foster, editor of the Lansing State Republican, *and an antislavery activist since the 1830s (particularly as editor of Ann Arbor's abolitionist newspaper, the* Signal of Liberty, *from 1841 to 1848), generally sided with Republican radicals. While conceding many of the radicals' criticisms of Lincoln, Foster accounts for Lincoln's appeal to Northern voters and counters that difficult circumstances stemming from the Civil War prevented Lincoln from carrying out the radicals' wishes.*

Mr. Lincoln is the only President we have ever had who may be said to be from the working class of people. Some of his predecessors, like Jackson and Fillmore, had limited advantages of education . . . but no other President has ever worked with his hands for a livelihood after arriving at the full maturity of manhood. This familiarity with the pursuits and feeling of the great laboring class of his countrymen, has doubtless given him some advantages in conducting public affairs, over those Presidents who like J. Q. Adams and Jefferson were educated among books, and associated exclusively with those who never worked for their living with their hands.

This peculiarity in the education of Mr. Lincoln has made his style of writing and speaking unlike that of any other President. . . . Mr. Lincoln's style is plain, simple, blunt, forcible, emphatic, direct, easily understood and carries the conviction to the mind of the reader that he means just that thing which he says, and nothing else. Hence the public letters he has written have raised him in general esteem, because the public find therein good sense and earnest patriotism, put into plain words, which cannot be tortured into any doubtful or overt meaning.

This general regard of the people is further strengthened by . . . a freedom from all appearances of aristocracy and haughtiness, and by a readiness, on all occasions, to sympathize with the condition of those who toil for their daily bread. . . .

Whatever deficiencies the President may have in some directions, he seems to have something of that prescience of the future, with which minds of the highest class are often gifted. . . .

The President has shown his firmness in the obstinacy which he resisted at first all proposals for the exchange of prisoners: in the suspension of the Habeas Corpus act twice: in the persistence with which he has held on to Halleck and Seward and Stanton as his advisers: and in the steady perseverance with which he has labored to organize the negro into an efficient aid to the Government. Those who suppose the President is a mere cipher in the Government, of no value in himself, and only useful as placed by the side of some other person, are greatly mistaken.

As a Republican, the President is of the Seward school. About the same time [US Senator William] Seward made his "Irrepressible Conflict" speech in New York, Lincoln, in Illinois, on a public occasion, expressed precisely the same ideas. For this he was attacked by [Stephen A.] Douglas as a Disunionist, and in the celebrated stumping campaign which followed in that State, Lincoln every where insisted that the two systems of free and slave labor could not always co exist, but, in the end, all the States would become free, or all would become slave States. He is also, in feeling, an emancipationist. In one of his public letters, he has said: "Personally, I desire that all men, every where should be free."

There seems to be nothing cruel or revengeful in the disposition of the President; but on the contrary his mildness and clemency, as displayed in the administration of public affairs, has been a matter of deep regret to thousands of his most strenuous supporters. The President is Commander-in-chief of the army and navy: and it is alleged that it is through his weakness that there has been such a vast number of desertions from the armies; that traitors everywhere have been dealt with too tenderly; that great numbers of semi-traitors have been kept in office: and that instances of most flagrant treason, occurring at and near the seat of government, and sometimes perpetrated by persons in its own employ, are passed over as mere peccadillos, thus encouraging traitors, and making the national authority despised. . . . This class of persons insist, that a Government which shows such weakness, cannot be greatly respected either by its friends or enemies: that in cases of flagrant treason . . . the offender should have been executed as soon convicted. . . .

But it is well to hear both sides: and it may be justly said, in behalf of the President, that the country around Washington and Baltimore is, to a great extent, an enemy's country, inhabited by a great number of families, many of them of much wealth and respectability, who have lived there for one or two generations: that they are not open traitors, although strongly southern in their feelings and family connections: that it would be impracticable to remove them south: that they are held, like the people of New Orleans, as inhabitants of a conquered country, on condition of their not committing any hostile acts . . . and under these circumstances it is better to pursue a moderate rather than a severe course, the question for the President to ask himself, being not "How can a hundred traitors best receive their just deserts," but "What course will be best for the whole country in suppressing the rebellion?." . . .

By taking this common sense view of things, the President is succeeding largely in the vast undertaking before him. Having no military knowledge or genius with which to devise a general plan of the war, he gets advice from Scott, and Halleck, and others, who are competent. He gathers and organizes men and materials in numbers and quantities proportioned to the immense demand upon them. Not being able to create generals, he chooses the best he can find, assigns them to specific duties, and when they prove incompetent, changes them for others. Thus the great military and naval machinery is set in motion, to subdue the rebels, according to a regular plan, which is being worked out day by day. In this way, to use his own homely but expressive phrase, the President keeps "PLUGGING AWAY" at the rebellion. . . .

There may be those in the nation who would have conducted us through our national struggle in less time, and with more ability, than Lincoln; but if the experiment were tried, we should probably find, that where there was one man who would do better, there would be at least half a million who would do worse.

Lansing State Republican, October 7, 1863.

MICHIGAN'S LONE DEMOCRATIC REPRESENTATIVE ADDRESSES THE US CONGRESS

Augustus Carpenter Baldwin (1817–1903) served as Michigan's only major Democratic officeholder during the Civil War. Speaker pro tempore in the Michigan House of Representatives in 1846 and a delegate to both Democratic National Conventions in 1860, Baldwin argued strongly for a vigorous prosecution of the war while being harshly critical of Republicans and of the Lincoln administration. Baldwin served but one term in the US House of Representatives before narrowly losing his reelection bid in 1864. After his defeat, and in the closing weeks of his congressional term, Baldwin and fourteen other Democrats voted with the entire Republican caucus to abolish slavery through the Thirteenth Amendment.

It is but a few years since an American citizen could look upon the broad map of his country, and with a laudable pride truthfully exclaim, "It is the only free one upon the globe!." . . . [O]urs was indeed a happy country. . . .

But three years have passed, and our citizens are incarcerated for months in loathsome dungeons, and then discharged, even without their offence or the cause of the arrest having been made known. . . . The writ of *habeas corpus* has been denied, the freedom of speech interfered with, and our rights as freemen imperiled; the whole industrial pursuits of the country diverted, our commerce nearly banished from the ocean, a debt already counted by thousands of millions of dollars incurred. . . . We have also a bloody, intestine war, and a divided country.

The historic annals of no nation present such a rapid change as ours. We have descended from the height of prosperity to the depths of a profound abyss, where we find ourselves without a guide, and no apparent way of escaping. . . .

During this Administration its particular devotees have endeavored to make the terms "Administration" and "Government" synonymous, and to charge the person as either a traitor or a rebel sympathizer who had the temerity to canvass the wisdom of any of the acts adopted by the dominant party, or to doubt their expediency. . . .

The Democracy[7] of this country have no sympathy or favor for the rebellion. In all their acts and speeches they have evinced as sincere devotion to the Union as have the peculiar friends in the majority. They have rightly deprecated the cause that has precipitated the war upon us. . . . We have voted men and money for that purpose;

we have encouraged the enlistment of our friends in the gallant army, and have bid them Godspeed and a glorious success in their efforts to restore the whole Union. . . .

At the commencement of hostilities it was distinctly avowed that the war was not upon the local institutions of any portion of the country, but to retain the unity of the whole, and when that was accomplished strife would cease. . . .

I fearlessly assert that if no change in the programme had been made, the rebellion would ere this have ceased. What these changes have been is too fearfully evident. Fanatical radicalism has gained the ascendancy, and the war for the last eighteen months has been prosecuted, not for the restoration of the Union, but for the destruction of the South; and in the blow aimed at them we believe it is the intention that all the reserved rights of the States of the Union to be obliterated, and a vast centralized Government formed. . . .

I insist, sir, that the Administration has never appreciated the power of the enemy, but has had a too overweening confidence in itself, and that it has adopted ultra paper fulminations when it ought to have relied upon the stern realities of war, with the sword in one hand to subdue the armed forces of the South, and the olive-branch in the other, to welcome any recusant and repentant State that was ready to return to its allegiance and submit to the requirements of the Constitution. . . . Mr. Lincoln and his advisors are responsible for changing the original object of the war, and aiding the rebel leaders in educating a now almost unanimous South.

Congressional Globe, 38th Congress, 1st sess., 1981–83 (April 30, 1864).

A GOOD CAUSE RUINED BY BAD MANAGEMENT

With no Democrats holding statewide office, the Detroit Free Press *served as Michigan's most important Democratic voice. Generally siding with War Democrats, the* Free Press *nonetheless objected to how Lincoln's policies had divided the North and united the South against reunification. Significantly, this editorial protests how Lincoln sought to destroy "the very foundations" of Southern society without specifically mentioning "slavery."*

There is not, on the pages of history, a record of a rebellion so entirely without any just cause, as that which now threatens to destroy and blot from the map of the world the very name of the United States of America. How is it possible that such a rebellion should be successful, is a question which has continually recurred to the mind of almost every man in the community. . . .

We start, then, with the proposition that [at the war's commencement] the sentiment was unanimous in the North in favor of sustaining the Constitution and laws by force, if necessary, and divided in the South in favor of the rebellion. At an early day the North adopted, with entire unanimity, the [proposition] . . . that the paramount object of the war was the maintenance of constitutional and lawful authority, and that when unlawful resistance to such authority should cease, the war should also cease. . . .

But in process of time, the administration of Mr. LINCOLN changed the objects of the war, and in effect declared that it was no longer to be prosecuted for the purpose of restoring the Constitution and lawful authority of the United States. While its whole purpose and objects were confined to the restoration of the Union, there could be little, if any differences of opinion, but when the whole purpose and scope of the war was changed, then dissension arose wherever discussion was permitted. For this change, and all the consequences which have or may flow from it, the administration are responsible.

If the government fails, it will fail because of this change of policy, a change from objects dear to every patriot in the land, to a policy which, in the end, if successful, will be as fatal to the vital principles of the Constitution, as a success of the rebellion. The present policy of the administration avows it to be necessary to uproot and overthrow the very foundations of society as now constituted in the Southern States. It is a radical revolution, and the South, which began this accursed rebellion, without real cause, is now fighting as one man for the maintenance of all that is dear to them in life. This change of policy fully explains why it is that there are no Union men in the South. . . .

Mr. LINCOLN himself is so thoroughly committed to his policy that he cannot change it. . . . If the country is to be saved from utter ruin, there must be a change of policy and a change of rulers; without it success is impossible, and the Union is gone forever.

The [re]election of Mr. LINCOLN under the present circumstances, would be the end not only of all hope for the safety of this Republic, but of republican forms of government; for no one who studies the history of the past can satisfy himself that republican institutions in the North or South can long survive the dissolution of the Union.

Detroit Free Press, July 3, 1864.

DEMOCRATS HAVE BEEN SUPPORTIVE OF THE WAR

In response to Republican charges that Democrats had not been supportive of the war, Democrats countered that their sacrifices on behalf of the government needed no apology and proclaimed Republicans had bungled the war and turned patriotism against the Democrats for political advantage.

It is a favorite charge of our Republican friends that Democratic speakers do not spend all their breath in denouncing JEFF. DAVIS and his rebel colleagues; but that, instead, they bestow their censure upon ABRAHAM LINCOLN and his administration.

This bugbear will frighten no reasonable man. Democrats have had no sympathy with secession, and they have no sympathy with the rebellion. Democrats have sent their sons, and paid freely of their money, to aid the Government in its struggle against the rebels, and having done so it is wholly unnecessary for them to spend their time and strength in protesting their loyalty. Democrats have always acknowledged their fealty to the Constitution, they have never been accustomed to make "mental reservations" when swearing to support it, and it is wholly unnecessary to spend time and strength at this juncture in fulminations against the rebels, fulminations which would be like LINCOLN's own estimate of his proclamation, a "Pope's Bull against the comet."

LINCOLN and his Administration are now on trial before the grand inquest of the country; it is the time set apart by the Constitution for bringing him to account, and the Democracy are now dealing with his policy, his measures, his abuse of power, his usurpations, his violation of the solemn guarantees of the Constitution. When the jury shall have rendered a verdict in favor of the people, and against Mr. LINCOLN, then will the Democracy do what Mr. LINCOLN has not been able to do, *put down the rebellion and restore the Union.* Now, we have not only to obey the laws, but a still higher duty to perform, to change, in a lawful manner, the law makers. That is the work the Democracy has in hand at this time.

Michigan Argus (Ann Arbor), October 21, 1864

A ONE-TIME SUPPORTER OF LINCOLN RENOUNCES THE PRESIDENT

Ezra C. Seaman, editor of the Republican Ann Arbor Journal, *was a conservative in his party. After Lincoln's election in 1860, Seaman declared Lincoln to be "a National Republican of the Henry Clay school, and no abolitionist."[8] During the war, Seaman denounced federal efforts to undermine the Confederacy through attacking slavery. In 1863 he published a book that criticized Lincoln's embrace of emancipation and charged the president with usurping power that Seaman believed rested with Congress and the states.[9] Although Seaman remained a Republican, he became a favorite among Democratic editors across the North who frequently reprinted his writings, including this editorial and another the following month in which Seaman endorsed George McClellan, the Democrats' 1864 presidential nominee.[10]*

[A]s the political campaign for the election of President and Vice-President of the United States is about to commence, and the undersigned differs widely in opinion from the leaders of the [R]epublican party, on some of the leading measures of national policy adopted by Mr. Lincoln, and approved by the late Baltimore convention, he thinks it proper that he should define his position.

Being opposed to slavery as a great moral, social and political evil, as well as unjust to the slave—and . . . believing that the repeal of the Missouri compromise was a political outrage upon the free States, designed to aid in extending slavery into the territories north of the compromise line, and throw the balance of power in our government into the of the politicians of the slave States—on the breaking up of the [W]hig party I became a [R]epublican; but I ever have been a national, not a sectional [R]epublican. . . .

[H]aving confidence in Mr. Lincoln, I supported him for the Presidency in 1860. Believing also in the great importance of the Federal Union, in the necessity of overturning the Confederate government, and suppressing the rebellion by military power, and enforcing submission to the Constitution and laws of the United States in all the States, I earnestly supported Mr. Lincoln's administration, until after he issued his first Emancipation Proclamation, in September, 1862; and have supported all the legitimate war measures of the administration, until the present time, and shall continue to do so.

But believing that to change the main purpose of the war; to convert it into a crusade against slavery—by making the emancipation of slaves and the destruction of the institution of slavery in the Confederate States one of the principal objects, and really the leading o[b]ject of its prosecution, would intensify the feelings and prejudices of the Southern people towards those of the North, and tend to unite them in support of the Confederate government . . . I could not approve the policy which was inaugurated by that proclamation. . . .

The opposition to the inauguration of the abolition policy has induced the adoption of other measures, infringing, and to some extent crushing out the freedom of speech and of the press, endangering the liberties of the people, undermining, partially overthrowing, and threatening to destroy the internal and municipal sovereignty of the States, and to establish a consolidated national despotism. . . . I am in favor of the restoration of the Federal Union as it was, as near as practicable, under the Constitution as it is. . . . I see no ground to hope for peace and the restoration of the Union upon any other basis.

Believing that the war is now prosecuted for an impracticable purpose-that the Union can never be restored and a permanent peace established between the free and the slave States, so long as the emancipation and restoration policies of President Lincoln are participated in[,] I am in favor of a change of policy, and of making an effort to restore the Union on the old basis.

Ann Arbor Journal, as reproduced in the *Detroit Free Press*, August 10, 1864.

A DEMOCRATIC APPEAL FOR THE SOLDIER VOTE

Democrats realized the political information that soldiers received would favor Republicans and expected that most soldiers would vote Republican. Nevertheless, Democrats appealed to the soldier vote by repeating the same political issues that

they raised on the home front. In the end, only the 1st, 15th, and 16th Michigan In-
fantry Regiments saw majorities for McClellan. Three-fourths of Michigan soldiers
supported Lincoln, but all soldiers voting out-of-state saw their ballots invalidated
by the Michigan Supreme Court.[11]

SOLDIER SUFFRAGE.

ADDRESS OF THE DEMOCRATIC STATE COMMITTEE OF
MICHIGAN TO THE SOLDIERS FROM THAT STATE.

To the officers and soldiers of Michigan Regiments now in the field.

By an act of the Legislature you are to vote at the next election (Nov. 8) for Presidential Electors, members of Congress, and the various officers of the State. The
right to vote is valuable only as it is free. It has been claimed by Republicans that
your votes will be a unit for their candidates. This is an insult to intelligent freemen.
Obedience in military matters is indispensable, but a free ballot is your right.

The Commissioners who will go to you will be sent by Republican authority.
Perhaps your sources of knowledge will not be under the same dictation. Seek
light from Democratic sources. Believe not the slanders uttered against Democrats
and the Democratic party. The term "traitor" and other opprobrious epithets do
not belong to them. Call to mind the personal and pecuniary sacrifices of Democrats in raising troops, in furnishing means for the war, in sustaining your families
at home, in sending sanitary supplies to you in the field, and in volunteering to
fill your ranks. They still continue to sustain you and provide for your families at
home. They are with you and for you in every emergency.

You are about to express by the ballot your opinions as to the policy which
should govern in our present national difficulties. You, with the voters at home,
are to decide whether peace and a Union of all the States are preferable to the
policy now announced of unending war for negro equality.

This was not the policy under which the veterans enlisted. No; that policy
was to put down the rebellion and restore the Union under the Constitution. But
the President has changed, Congress has changed, the Republican leaders have
changed. They are now ultra Abolitionists. But many conservative Republicans
will vote with us for a restoration of the old order of things.

If you think they are right, unite with these conservative men and with us for
this object. Let us have a change of Administration. Would you have the war carried on, provided it be necessary, solely for the Union and the restoration of peace,
then vote for a change. The present Administration can only unite the South, divide public sentiment at the North, prolong the war indefinitely, and end finally in
dissolution.

Changed to a Democratic Administration and you may hope to see a restored Union, an early return to peace, and that blessed re-union with friends at home, who are watching your every peril, rejoicing in your every success, and waiting your return from the dangers and sufferings of war.

Seek for correct political information, and follow not blind political guides and speculating shoddyites, who for personal gain would plunge the country into financial ruin, leave your families destitute, and destroy our armies in pursuing their chimerical phantoms—of abolitionism.

Campaign Age (Philadelphia), September 8, 1864.

KALAMAZOO REPUBLICANS' APPEAL ON THE EVE OF THE 1864 ELECTION

Days before the 1864 presidential election, the Kalamazoo County Union Republican Committee issued the following manifesto. Declaring the war nearly won, Kalamazoo Republicans proclaim that the Union cannot be restored without the destruction of slavery, that Confederacy's defeat offers the opportunity to end slavery once and for all, and that reelecting Abraham Lincoln provides the path to achieve both objectives. Exuberant over the expected demise of slavery, Kalamazoo's Republicans say nothing about the changes and challenges that emancipation would bring and little about the candidate who spoke in Kalamazoo eight years previously.

A decisive hour in the history of this nation is at hand. It is an hour that admits of no faltering, no mistakes, no doubts. The existence of the Union, the re-establishment of enduring Peace, the overthrow of Treason, the suppression of Disloyalty, the destruction of Slavery, the future greatness of the United States and the cause of Freedom everywhere are in the issue of the hour. . . .

A gigantic conspiracy against Freedom and Humanity, after long years of silent, yet not un-noted preparation, suddenly broke out into bloody insurrection against the integrity of our country and the authority of its laws. Its pretext was the election as President of ABRAHAM LINCOLN; but that pretext it had awaited, courted, sought. Its real impulse was Slavery's instinctive hatred of Liberty, stimulated by the contrast inevitably presented between a region blest with Free Labor, Free Schools, Free Men, and one wherein the Laboring Class are bought and sold like cattle and it is [a] felony to teach their children to read. Of course, the Free section rapidly outstrips the Slave in Industry, Art, Intelligence, Production, Wealth, and every element of Progress, leaving to the distanced community hearts rankling with all the malice of Cain.—Hence our most sanguinary, devastating Civil War. . . .

But the end of the War visibly approaches. The colossal fabric of Treason, which so lately threatened us with subjugation, now visibly totters to its fall. . . .

We are on the brink of Peace. Shall it be a real, hearty, enduring Peace? Or shall it be a mockery, a sham, a fleeting illusion? The answer is to be given by your votes. If slavery is made to share the doom of the Rebellion it has fomented, then no child who now lives who will ever again see this country distracted and desolated by Civil War. If Slavery shall survive, it must and will renew the struggle to regain the ground it has lost. . . .

If you care nothing for the rights of the Slaves, we entreat you to consider the case of the staunch Unionists whose homes are in the South. . . . To re-establish Slavery is to put these under the feet of their Rebel enemies. It is to expose every open, active Unionist in the South to the deadly hate of the baffled, beaten oligarchy which, though not strong enough to overthrow the Union, will still have power to wreak vengeance on their neighbors who were its steadfast champions.

Let Slavery die the death it has deserved, and all will be changed. Rebellion will have lost its motive power. Hate of the Union will rapidly vanish, never to return. Southern Unionists will rest secure in the homes of their youth. A flood of emigration [sic], bearing on its bosom new arts, new industries, new hopes, will rapidly rebuild and beautify the waste places of the devastated States.—Twenty years of Free Labor will so strengthen and enrich the South that her people will bless the authors of the Rebellion for the unintended good they did in upheaving the foundations of Slavery. . . .

Let us close the contest with Liberty everywhere, and Slavery nowhere throughout this broad land, and their earthquake shout of glad surprise, of joyous exultation, shall tear the cobwebs of Tradition and break the fetters of Caste. American Slavery has too long been the stumbling block of reformers, the reproach of Democracy, throughout Christendom. Let us firmly resolve that it shall serve the ends of despotism no longer.

Electors of Kalamazoo County! By the aid of your vote Abraham Lincoln was made President of the United States. You imposed on him that high trust in defiance of a formidable, skillfully combined and most determined opposition, with full knowledge of his inexperience, but trusting that he would be faithful to the Union, to Justice, and to Freedom.—Has he not justified your confidence? He has doubtless made mistakes; he has seemed to some too fast, to others too slow; but, though most reluctant to draw the sword, he has never since faltered in his determination that the Union should be upheld and the Rebellion put down.

Kalamazoo Telegraph, November 5, 1864.

DETROIT BLACKS APPEAL TO MICHIGAN LEGISLATURE FOR FULL CITIZENSHIP

Michigan law finally recognized African Americans' right to vote after the Fifteenth Amendment's ratification in 1870. Before that time, the state's black population

made numerous appeals to the state's lawmakers to rescind Michigan's discriminatory laws, particularly those that prevented black males from voting. During the
Civil War, Michigan's African Americans recognized that service to a country in
need required that the state and nation recognize their full citizenship rights. As
they worked to achieve that recognition, Michigan's African Americans confronted
numerous obstacles. When John D. Richards, Robert L. Cullen, and James D. Carter
presented this memorial to the Michigan House of Representatives on January 18,
1865, they were initially excluded from "the bar of the House"—that is, from presenting their appeal under the same conditions as white petitioners—a condition
that the House overturned by a vote of 75 to 15.[12]

To the Hon. Senate and House of Representatives of the State of Michigan:

We, "the colored citizens of the city of Detroit," respectfully pray, that your
honorable body will so amend the constitution of this State, as to permit the colored men within its borders to exercise the elective franchise. We ask that the
word "white" be stricken from the constitution, that it may not stand as a bar to
the exercise by us of the privileges of freemen. We ask this as our right, and desire
to show briefly the reasons upon which the claim is based.

We believe that the highest welfare of this great State will be found in erasing
from its statute books all enactments discriminating in favor or against any class of
its people, and by establishing one law for the white and colored people alike. . . .

Formerly our petitions for the elective franchise were met and denied upon the
ground that while colored men were protected in person and property, they were
not required to perform military duty. . . .

But now even this frivolous, though somewhat decent apology, for excluding
us from the ballot-box, is entirely swept away. Two hundred thousand colored
men, according to a recent statement of President Lincoln, are now in the service, upon field and flood, in the army and navy of the United States. Many of
them are from Michigan, and every day adds to their number. . . . Friends and
enemies, rebels and loyal men, each after their kind, have borne conscious and
unconscious testimony to the gallantry and other noble qualities of the colored
troops. . . .

Are we good enough to use bullets, and not good enough to use ballots? May
we defend rights in time of war, and yet be denied the exercise of those rights
in time of peace? Are we citizens when the nation is in peril, and aliens when
the nation is in safety? May we shed our blood, under the star-spangled banner,
on the battle field, and yet be debarred from marching under it to the ballot
box? Will the brave white soldiers, bronzed by the hardships and exposures
of repeated campaigns—men who have fought by the side of black men—be
ashamed to cast their ballots by the side of their companions in arms? May we

give our lives, but not our vote, for the good of the republic? Shall we toil with you to win the prize of free government, while you alone shall monopolize all its valued privileges?. . . .

But, again, why are we so urgent for the possession of this particular right? We are asked, even by some Abolitionist, why we cannot be satisfied, for the present at least, with personal freedom; the right to testify in courts of law; the right to own, buy, and sell real estate; the right to sue and be sued? We answer: because in a republican country, where general suffrage is the rule, personal liberty, the right to testify in courts of law, the right to hold, buy and sell property, and all other rights, become mere privileges held at the option of others, where we are excepted from the general political liberty. . . .

Give the colored men of this State the elective franchise, and you will see no mobs driving them from places where they obtain honest livings, but you will go far towards making them respectable and respected citizens. The possession of that right is the keystone to the arch of human liberty, and, without that, the whole may at any moment fall to the ground, while with it, that liberty may stand forever—a blessing to us and no possible injury to you. If you still ask us why we want to vote, we answer: because we are men, and want to be as free in our native land as any other men.

Journal of the House of Representatives of the State of Michigan at the Biennial Session of 1865 (Lansing: John A Kerr, 1865), 159–65.

~

EIGHT

The Civil War Changes Michiganians' Relationship to Slavery

$\mathcal{M}$OST NORTHERNERS INITIALLY expected the seceded states could be brought back into the Union without affecting slavery. The US House of Representatives overwhelmingly embraced this position when it passed the Crittenden Resolution on July 22, 1861, which affirmed that the federal government only sought to "defend and maintain the supremacy of the Constitution and to preserve the Union" and it was not waging "war . . . in any spirit of oppression, nor for any purpose of conquest or subjugation, nor purpose of overthrowing or interfering with" slavery.[1]

This view, however, had already been challenged two months earlier, when enslaved people sought freedom within Union lines. In May 1861, General Benjamin Butler had refused to return fugitives after a Confederate officer requested their return under the terms of the 1850 Fugitive Slave Law. Because they had been working on Confederate fortifications near Fortress Monroe, Virginia, Butler declared the fugitives "contraband of war" and refused to return them. Soon fugitives streamed toward Butler's lines, where Butler put them to work building Union fortifications. In August 1861, the US Congress codified Butler's policy declaring that any slaveholder who employed his or her slaves in the Confederate war effort would "forfeit . . . claims" to those slaves. Later known as the First Confiscation Act, it was followed in 1862 by a treaty between the United States and Great Britain to suppress the international slave trade, by Congress ending slavery in the District of Columbia and in the federal territories, and by Congress passing the Second Confiscation Act that declared secessionists' slaves "forever free."[2]

When President Abraham Lincoln issued the preliminary Emancipation Proclamation in 1862, then, he was simply continuing a policy direction that he, his administration, and Congress had launched previously. The preliminary Proclamation declared slaves living in areas remaining under Confederate control after January 1, 1863, would be "forever free" once Union authority reasserted itself, with Lincoln's January Proclamation affirming this position. The Proclamation also made clear that the federal government tied its war objective, restoring national authority, to abolishing slavery. As it invaded the Confederacy, the Union army enforced the Emancipation Proclamation, and with the Confederacy's defeat, slavery effectively came to an end. Congress's passage and the states' ratification of the Thirteenth Amendment to the Constitution in 1865 prohibited slavery from ever being reintroduced.

Even in Michigan, where slavery had long been outlawed and never had as much as a meager existence, emancipation proved to be one of the Civil War's most divisive issues. Most Michigan Republicans embraced emancipation as soon as they recognized that the war would not end quickly. Governor Austin Blair expressed this sentiment in his message to the legislature in January 1862:

> The people of Michigan are no idle spectators of this great contest. . . .
> [They have] furnished adequate means, both of men and money, to crush
> the rebellion, have a right to expect those men to be used with the utmost
> vigor to accomplish the object, and that without any mawkish sympathy
> for the interest of traitors in arms. Upon those who caused the war and
> now maintain it, its chief burdens ought to fall. No property of a rebel
> ought to be free from confiscation—not even the sacred slave. The object
> of war is to destroy the power of the enemy. . . . To undertake to put down
> a powerful rebellion and at the same time to save and protect all the chief
> sources of the power of that rebellion, seems, to common minds, but a
> short remove from simple folly. . . . To treat this enemy gently is to excite
> his derision. To protect his slave property, is to help him to butcher our
> people and burn our houses.[3]

The state's Democrats, in contrast, believed that making emancipation a war objective would unnecessarily prolong the war by strengthening Confederates' resolve. Many of Michigan's Civil War soldiers, like their counterparts from other Northern states, initially opposed emancipation, but most changed their minds after viewing slavery themselves, usually for the first time. Believing that slavery was the cause behind a war they were eager to finish, Michigan soldiers often attributed the differences they observed in the South to slavery and became even more convinced regarding the rightness of their cause.

By 1864 Republicans across the North concluded that slavery should be abolished through a constitutional amendment. The US Senate passed a constitutional amendment to end slavery in the United States—the future Thirteenth Amendment—by a vote of 38 to 6 on April 8, 1864. Securing two-thirds of the US House of Representatives proved more challenging, falling 13 votes short on June 15, 1864. Passage finally occurred on January 31, 1865, by a vote of 119 to 56—with merely 2 votes to spare and only after considerable lobbying by the recently reelected Abraham Lincoln and others from his administration. The amendment then went to the states. Michigan ratified the amendment four days later and became the third state to do so. To become operative, three-fourths of the thirty-six states (including those that had been in rebellion) needed to ratify the amendment. Georgia became the twenty-seventh state to ratify the amendment on December 6, 1865, with slavery formally ending in the United States on December 18, 1865, when Secretary of State William Seward issued a proclamation declaring the amendment adopted. By that time, Kentucky and Delaware were the only states where slavery remained legal.[4]

INCREASED HOSTILITY TO SLAVERY YET QUESTIONING EMANCIPATION

After several months of fighting—and recognizing that the war would last longer than most people initially expected—many Northerners grew increasingly impatient with slavery. They recognized that disagreements over slavery had led the nation into civil war and understood that slave labor freed white Southerners to fight. By late 1861, some Northerners argued that emancipation provided the quickest path to victory. Yet as this Republican editorial demonstrates, emancipation's prospects left some in Lincoln's party unsettled.

It is wonderful to look back over the history of the past six or twelve months and note the changes which have taken place in the public mind on the subject of slavery—indeed the changes are almost incomprehensible. If public opinion should in the six months to come, undergo so great a change in the same direction, as it has in the past, where would we then stand? In the early part of this rebellion we repeatedly stated in these columns that while the war to repress the rebellion would not be a war against slavery, it would still inevitably result in a blow to that institution so terrible, so deadly, and so potent, that it would never again lift its hydra head in a war for supremacy, but on the contrary, at the close of this struggle, would be in progress of gradual extinction. . . .

Appearances indicate that the slavery or contraband question is to be the leading question for discussion and agitation in Congress during the present session. . . . There are undoubtedly many in our national councils who will seize upon the present as a favorable time to push their ultra measures of emancipation and reform to the utmost extreme. . . . But the utmost care should be taken by all to whom have been committed the responsibility of aiding in the conduct of the Government, not to go too fast in that direction. The present is a time when deliberate, cool judgment, sound and practical common sense, and honest patriotism, should hold undisputed sway in the national capitol. Slavery is unquestionably a giant evil; and the radicals will let us strike one full blow at the monster, and rid the land forever of the curse. Let us not tamper with a thing which has brought a war costing such immense treasure, such vast and frightful suffering, and so horrid in all its consequences. . . . An evil so huge in its proportions even if Congress have all the necessary power to do with it as it will, must not be dealt with in this summary manner, lest in disposing of one evil another almost equally as great be brought upon us. . . .

The great element of strength of this government is its adherence to the Constitution. . . . And while we are fighting to maintain Constitutional liberty, let us beware how we interfere with the sacred rights of the people as guaranteed them by that instrument. What to do with slaves after they shall have confiscated or emancipated is certainly a grave question, and will increase in magnitude just in proportion as the number of slaves increases who shall so be set at liberty.

But the question of what attitude the Government shall assume towards slavery must be decided. . . . We believe this policy should be to strike no blow at slavery, only as we strike at all property held by rebels. Wherever the armies of the Union penetrate, let slavery stand or fall, as the fortunes of war determine. There is certainly no reason why slavery should be placed above other personal property, and it is also certain that it should have no special exemption from the savages of war. And when slaves of unquestionable Union men shall obtain their liberty through the fortunes of war, they should be paid for out of the public treasury. . . . And the idea of arming the blacks as our armies penetrate the slave states is open to fully as many objections. While there is no sense in leaving the enemy in possession of his slave property—a species of property which aids him more than any other in carrying on and extending this war—we can see no reason why arms should be placed in their hands, to turn upon their masters in brutal retaliation for the wrongs they have suffered. If we have not already men enough in the field to quell this rebellion, then more can be furnished from the free white population of the North. Deprive the rebel armies of their slaves, and set those slaves at work within our lines, on our fortifications, &c., paying them for their labor; or if labor cannot be furnished them, leave them at liberty to go where they will, until means can be provided to colonize them.

Monroe Commercial, December 12, 1861.

DEMOCRATIC REACTION TO "ABOLITION FANATICISM"

While most Republicans were not abolitionists, hostility to slavery permeated the party's ranks. Believing the Northern public's enmity to abolitionists to be stronger than its dislike of slavery, Democrats had conflated abolitionists and Republicans since the latter party's emergence in 1854. From the start of the Civil War, though, many Republicans called for attacking the Confederacy by taking aggressive action against slavery, including emancipation and enlisting blacks as soldiers. By the end of 1861, as Democrats recognized the shifts in public opinion, they pleaded with the public to consider the costs of fighting a war to end slavery.

Abolition fanaticism is making alarming strides, and developing by designs, its long concealed designs to control the policy of the present civil war. . . .

[T]he abolition programme for conducting the war, is to emancipate and arm the slaves. Three or four months ago the slightest hint of such a project, was received by the American people with the most utter disgust, and considered worthy to emanate only from the pandemonium of extreme abolitionism, and if old John Brown had been living, he and Hinton Rowan Helper would have been charged with the sole authorship of such a degrading and atrocious proposition. Yet it is now before us in all its hideous reality, and its proportions enlarged, in that its advocates have increased, and are increasing from day to day, not only in numbers, but in character and political position.

It is becoming a fixed idea in the public mind, that the use of the slave population of the rebel States is essential to the conquest of those States, and even members of Congress have openly declared that without the aid of the negroes, the rebellion cannot be suppressed. The proposition had its origin in the spirit of vengeance against the rebel States, and a mortal hatred of their social institution; but a persistent adherence to it by its fanatical advocats [*sic*], has had the effect desired, to impress upon the minds of others that it is a measure of necessity. . . .

To see the negro slaves of the South armed with a pike and bowie knife, to murder indiscriminately the men, women and children of the South, is the culmination of abolitionism, the haven of its hopes; and when this is once begun, then, and not till then, will its exacting spirit be appeased. We have already had six months of civil war, a war of sections, and a large portion of the Northern people have misconceived its effect upon the slave population of the South. It was considered a reasonable apprehension by many, that on the commencement of hostilities, the negro slaves would become turbulent and insurrectionary, and that in many localities there would be mutinies and insubordinations, followed by outrages against the planters and their families. This was what the abolitionists expected, and wished to see, and for this they invoked the manes [spirit] of John Brown. . . . They have been most egregiously disappointed, and now to palliate their mortifying discomfiture, they call upon Congress and the President to inaugurate a war policy, which of itself is revolting to humanity and civilization, and involves an exercise of power not confided to the General Government by the Constitution. . . . Is it for the *negro*, or the Union *with* the Constitution, that thousands of human lives are to be sacrificed and millions of treasure squandered?

Jackson Patriot, December 18, 1861.

A MICHIGAN SOLDIER OPPOSES PROSPECTIVE EMANCIPATION

Even Republicans who favored having their party take aggressive actions against slavery, including emancipation, worried whether soldiers would sustain such a policy. Such concerns, and sentiments expressed by this unnamed soldier from the 9th Michigan, prompted Lincoln to move slowly on emancipation. By the fall of 1862 most Union troops welcomed the enlistment of additional soldiers, regardless of their race, and few objected to Lincoln's preliminary Emancipation Proclamation that September.

Elizabethtown, Kentucky
January 18, 1862

We read the reports of Congress every morning, and most generally the first thing offered is some proposition to emancipate the slaves, by some abolition fanatic. This is a critical juncture in the affairs of this government. The party in power have, and are still driving into the rebel army, thousands of as true and loyal citizens in Kentucky as ever the sun shone upon. The Union cause in Kentucky has already lost more strength by the agitation of the abolition question in Congress, since it convened, than was lost by our defeat at Bull Run. If these antislavery members possessed good common sense, and were actuated by an honest purpose to restore the Union, they would cease this agitation altogether. It is a fact, that a large portion of the Southern army is composed of men who have been deceived by their leaders: they have been taught that the North and the Northern army are abolition[ists]. The speeches of Northern abolitionists are read in the rebel camps, and there is no way to counteract the evil but for the Northern press to stop publishing such incendiary speeches and documents as we often see. Oh what a fearful responsibility rests upon those men, North and South, who by their sectional and disunion speeches have stirred up this rebellion. They are alike parties of the same crime, and have mutually aided in plunging this once happy country into the horrors of civil war. . . .

Abolitionism in our Congress has a fearful effect on our army, and the fools think they have got us fastened, and that we must fight any way, but when the abolition bill passes, and the army to be considered as fighting for the liberty of the slaves, you will see commissions thrown up by the hundreds, and to place new officers over the privates will make an interesting time. Men will revolt, and attempt at coercion will produce a civil war among ourselves. Our soldiers have sword to fight under and for the constitution, and this vow they will keep. We are held here with nothing to do but guard each other and bury our own dead, while politicians and office seekers, and army contractors are getting rich out of the war, and while too, soldiers are suffering the common wants of army life. There must be a changing soon, or there will be more rebels to the administration in the North, than there are among the secessionists.

Jackson Patriot, February 5, 1862.

HERALDING LINCOLN'S SIGNING OF THE EMANCIPATION PROCLAMATION

Most Republicans supported—or celebrated—the news of Lincoln's signing the final Emancipation Proclamation on January 1, 1863. Some however, questioned the loyalty of those who felt otherwise.

On the first day of January, as announced on the 22d of September last, the President, by virtue of his Constitutional prerogative as Commander-in-Chief of the military and naval forces of the United States of America, ordered and proclaimed the freedom of the slaves in all that portion of the United States then in rebellion against the Government. To a portion of our people, this measure has been of all others most desired. To another portion it comes as the sore extreme of a beleaguered government in putting down a monstrous rebellion. Both classes welcome the proclamation as a most expedient and necessary measure at the present stage of affairs, and both will cordially support the Government in carrying it out.

To the rebels and those who sympathize with them it is very objectionable. They object to it, because *it hurts them*. It hurts no loyal man. Their objections furnish the strongest argument in favor of the proclamation as an appropriate measure.

Constantine Mercury and Advertiser, January 8, 1863.

DEMOCRATIC OBJECTIONS TO THE EMANCIPATION PROCLAMATION

Despite being now celebrated as one of the Civil War's most important developments, Lincoln's Emancipation Proclamation met with hostility not only in the Confederacy, but among many, if not most, Northern Democrats. Here the editor of the Niles Republican, *perhaps Michigan's fiercest Democratic newspaper, states criticisms that many Democrats made regarding the Proclamation.*

The long expected proclamation is before the country, and a more lame and impotent conclusion was never arrived at before. . . . It would be laughable, if the folly of rulers was not always a serious matter. Who it will please is beyond our comprehension. The abolitionists, certainly, will not be grateful for an emancipation policy which excludes . . . all places in which the Federal government can *not enforce it*.[5] The conservative masses of the country, on the other hand, will be pained because the President is so weak as to lean upon so fragile a reed as an implement of war. The spectacle of a ruler addressing a subject caste, far within the limits of the territory of a victorious enemy; preferring freedom to men surrounded by hostile bayonets, which he has in vain essayed to break through; advising them to labor for wages when he knows that such labor is impossible to them; enjoining them to peace, when peace is a perfect nullification of his proclamation. . . .

[W]hat shall be said of the President of the United States, who has lost all the opportunities which united and fervent patriotism has cast upon him, who has fritt[er]ed away the strength of hundred of thousands of soldiers and wasted hundreds of millions of dollars at the dictation of those who desired to wrest this proclamation from him? The struggle of the radicals to obtain emancipation has overwhelmed the struggle of the people to preserve the constitution. . . . Strong in the delusion that freedom to the niggers would be the trump card in his hands, Mr. Lincoln has played the game languidly, throwing away all other cards, to find that his trump, when thrown out, cuts a very sorry figure after the uninterrupted defeats to which his folly has subjected him.

In only one quarter will there be joy over the proclamation. Jeff. Davis will seize it as kindling to fire the Southern heart. Every rebel in arms will grow sturdier in his hate and opposition to a government whose head takes pains to convince him that it is abolitionized, determined to destroy the constitution. In every Southern State the proclamation will be bruited abroad as the conclusive evidence . . . that secession from the rule of the republican party was a just and necessary act of self defense. The delusion created by Jeff. Davis will be kept alive by Abraham Lincoln. . . . The proclamation is in all respects only a continuation of the fatuity which . . . has made the administration of Abraham Lincoln from beginning to end an uninterrupted violation of the constitution.

Niles Republican, January 10, 1863.

A MICHIGAN SOLDIER OPPOSES
THE ENLISTMENT OF AFRICAN AMERICANS

The vicious racism displayed during the 1863 Detroit Riot also found expression, without the overt violence, among many soldiers, particularly those whose politics leaned Democratic. As the enlistment of black troops increased in 1863, some observers predicted that protests from white soldiers objecting to black enlistments would damage the war effort.

Writing within days of the War Department's creation of the Bureau of Colored Troops, an organization that orchestrated the recruitment of black soldiers, this soldier from an unidentified regiment repeated these fears and others commonly

expressed by many nineteenth-century white Americans. Contrary to this soldier's
expectations, the expected protests never occurred. Most Union soldiers—and the
Northern public—quickly recognized that African American soldiers were valuable
recruits who would diminish the need for conscripts and help end the war sooner.

FAIRFAX COURT HOUSE, VA.,
May 30[t]h, 1863

The great question of negro soldiers has at last been settled. The government
has commenced to raise regiments of negroes in the city of Washington. . . .
They will degrade the position of a soldier. This is "putting it on too thick" for
me. I love the old flag, and God knows I would fight for it to the last, but I cannot
suffer the government to place me on the same footing as a negro. I *cannot* and
will not stand it. I love our government—our old government—and would do
nothing to injure it or the administration, but I cannot consent to be the same
to them as a negro. I know that by some my feelings would be thought disloyal,
but, as Heaven is my judge, I do not entertain a single traitorous thought. I
know full well that if my sentiments were known, they would blast my military
prospects, but I cannot help it. . . .

Many of the brave fellows who now wear the cloth of the United States
are gentlemen, and when at home hold good positions in society. They have
given up their homes and comforts and stepped forward in the cause of their
country, and are ready to fight and die for it. Now what has the black given up
that *he* should share the same honors with the volunteer soldier? His position
as a soldier is far better than as a slave. I repeat, that if the government wish
to make the black of use in this war, they can do so, and yet not make him a
soldier. Let the government put the negroes at work on fortifications—and
other military works—in fact, let them do *all* the work of the army, which the
soldiers now do. Such a course would at once send back to their regiments
more than thirty thousand white soldiers, now employed as teamsters and
laborers of all kinds.

The whole thing is, to my mind, an insult to the soldier, and the whole army
(or at least most of it) think the same. . . . But if they make negroes soldiers
and place them on an equality with the white soldier, they *must* give him all the
rights and privileges of a white soldier. Equal political privileges must soon lead
to equal social privileges, and then the intelligent, well educated negro, though
black as night, will come to these people and demands their fair daughters, and
take them too. If the government must and will have negro soldiers, may God
help it and our cause, but I cannot and will not do so in company with negroes.

Detroit Free Press, June 10, 1863.

MICHIGAN WHITES RESPOND TO AFRICAN AMERICAN SOLDIERS

The persistence of Confederate resistance caused many Northern whites to welcome the enlistment of African American soldiers. This document also reveals how racial prejudice made it difficult for whites to view these prospective soldiers as equals while also causing whites to believe that blacks would easily transition from slave to soldier.

The late telegraph reports say that a Union meeting at Helena, Ark., by General Thomas a few days ago, 25,000 colored roldiers [*sic*] were enlisted in the short space of twenty four hours. If this report is true, it is an earnest of the willingness of the blacks of the South to fight for the Union that we did not expect. They have from the beginning of the war shown a zeal and sympathy for the cause of the North, that has been of the greatest service to our armies during the campaign, and now that the President has determined to use them as soldiers, they come forward with an alacrity that is truly surprising.

That they will make good soldiers there is not a doubt. Having been raised in the warm climate of the South, they will not have to go through the process of climatizing, which has taken off so many white soldiers[.] Being accustomed to privations, hardships and toil in every form while slaves, they can endure that fatigueing [*sic*] duties of a soldier much better than our Northern troops, while their knowledge of the enemies [*sic*] country, strength and ways will make them incalculable value during the marches of our armies through the South. Their lifelong position as slaves will make them obedient to the commands of their officers and less clamorous for pay and less persistence [*sic*] in enforcing their own opinions as is the case in most armies of the world.

It is no longer a question as to their bravery. The fact is already established that they are no cowards. They will fight with an energy and determination second only to the brave veterans of the Union army. In the recent battles in Florida where they have been used they fought with that coolness and bravery that is the only convincing proof that powder and death has [*sic*] no terrors for them while fighting for the Government. No panic or fears of a defeat will cause them to break ranks and flee before the enemy. They are blood, bone and brains of the Southern people, and possess all of the elements for making good soldiers that they do, which has only to be developed by military discipline to make an army that can successfully meet all the traitors of the South.

We say then, as a means of saving the country, and the lives of our gallant northern men, arm the negroes and put them in the front ranks. Every one taken from the Southern plantations leaves the rebels with so much less help to produce food for their army. If the rebellion is to be *starved* out we know of no more effectual way than this. Soon the white men of their army will be obliged to leave the rank and go to work in the field and raise bread or starve, and when this point is reached the rebellion is forever ended.

Ingham County News, April 29, 1863.

WAR WILL CONTINUE SO LONG AS SLAVERY EXISTS

In writing to her cousin, David O. Coleman of Oshtemo and the 25th Michigan, Clara Phillips of Kalamazoo displays the intensity of her political views and underscores how Michigan civilians came to link the end of slavery with the Confederacy's defeat. Her letter also reveals how writing to soldiers constituted both a political and a patriotic act.

Kalamazoo June 28, 1863

Dear Cousin[,]

It is a bright and beautifull Mourning in June and as I sit thinking of the dayes that have gone no more to return my thought wanders back to the Seenes of my Childhood when a fond Mother watched over me, but what a Change there has been within the last 6 years. Those we loved best were the first to go: but Gods will be done. David perhaps you have forgoten me, but I have not forgoten. I did not know untill the other day that you enlisted to fight for your country. You are fighting in a good cause and I hope our Heavenly Father will grant you a safe return and I hope we shall not have to wate many Monnths before your friends shall Wellcome you Home. I was reading a piece in the paper the other day about Writing to the Soldiers and haveing just heard that you had joined the army & thought I would address a few lines to you hoping they Will be gladly received. I Wonder When this Rebellion will close & do not think it Will close as long as slavery exist[.] How I wish it was in my power to come south and free all the slaves and kill all the Rebbels and then come back and Shoot all the Copperheads whose hearts are as heard as a Millstone if they [have] any heart at all and then I guess this rebellion Would ceasse. Oh the Horrors how little we at the North know how much the South endure they are true to there principles and I wish the North was half as true & pity the Children at the South and was agoing to say the Women but I do not know as I had better say that[,] for I think they can do as much hurt as the men. David I am true to the Union and I know you are Shoot[ing] all the Saucy Scamps and do not let these eskape.

Clara Phillips, Kalamazoo, to David Coleman, June 28, 1863, Jack B. and Barbara Riegel Collection, Archives and Regional History Collection, Western Michigan University.

THE SOUTH UNDERSTOOD THROUGH THE LENS OF SLAVERY

A Lansing physician before and after the war, Joseph B. Hull became the surgeon for the Ohio Volunteer Sharpshooters. After arriving in Kentucky, Hull, like many other Northerners, interpreted the South's differences as stemming from slavery.

After three days absence from Lansing, I arrived in Louisville, Ky., a place of about 75,000 people. The transition in passing from free to slave territory can be imagined by any one, but can only be appreciated by experience. In freedom everything looks prosperous, lively and life like; in serfdom, everything looks stolid and dismal. Louisville boasts of doing more business than ever before, yet the streets are filthy and ragged, notwithstanding all their advantages in water works which are sufficient to wash every street perfectly clean: but they are too lazy to do it. . . . At heart to day Louisville is rebel, yet there are many good Union men there: raiders and guerillas are tolerated by the *Union inhabitants* to within ten miles of the city, and would come nearer if it was not for U. Sam's army there.

J. B. Hull to J. A. Kerr, August 19, 1864, *Lansing State Republican*, September 7, 1864.

FREEDOM'S UNDERSIDE: A CIVIL WAR REFUGEE CAMP

One of Michigan's earliest abolitionists, Laura Haviland was also active in the Underground Railroad and assisted numerous enslaved fugitives, many of whom settled in Canada. A resident of Raisin Township in Lenawee County, Haviland, with her husband, launched the Raisin Institute, a school that admitted students of both sexes and of all races. Haviland's commitment to racial equality led her to teach school to former slaves in Canada and to venture to the South to assist fugitives from slavery. By 1863 reports of soldiers' languishing in hospitals and the indigent condition of recently emancipated slaves—the "freedmen"—in refugee camps led Haviland to take leave of the Raisin Institute and venture south. There, she confronted the Civil War's greatest biological and public health crisis—one that resulted in at least one-fourth of the South's former slaves becoming seriously ill or dying between 1862 and 1870.[6]

There was also great suffering in the camp of freedmen [in Cairo, Illinois]. The officers wished me to aid them in persuading these people to go down to [Island Number 10, Missouri], as they were afraid of being returned to slavery at the close of the war, and desired to push as far into the free States as possible, and very loath to go back "an inch," as one of the officers expressed it. I took the names of these almost nude people, whom I instructed to come to my tent; as the officers said I should have one for the purpose of giving out clothing to the most needy among them. They assured them that their freedom was a fixed fact; that they would never see the day again when they would be separated by being sold apart. This, I found, was a greater inducement for them to consent to the request of the officers to go to the island than all the clothing I could promise.

But one poor woman came to the captain weeping, saying, "My poor baby is dying' an' I can't leave him. He is my only chile left me." In the great hurry and bustle of business the quick reply was, "Go back and I'll see to it." . . . An hour later and the baby of eight years was in the spirit world.

"Now, missus, I can't go an' leave my dead baby for de wharf-rats to eat, an' de boat goes out at three o'clock."

I reported the death of the child and of the distress of the mother. "Tell her," said the officer, "we will see that her child is buried this afternoon, and I want her to go on this boat." I told the mother of the captain's wish, and that I would see that her child was buried. . . .

The grief of this poor mother was distressing in the extreme. She knew not whether her husband and three older children, sold away two years previously, were still slaves or living, as she had never heard a word from them since they were taken from her. Those sad separations, she said, were much harder to bear than the death of this child. But she consented to go, on my promise to see that her child was buried before night. After she left for the boat I went to the captain to see his promise performed. He seemed very indifferent.

"What is the difference if that child shouldn't be buried this afternoon or whether wharf-rats eat it or not?." . . .

Said the captain, "You won't allow such things as these to break your heart, after being in the army a little while and seeing our soldiers buried in a ditch, with no other coffin or winding sheet than the soldier's dress. For the time being we bury hundreds just in that way; and when from five to fifteen die in one day, as sometimes is the case in these large camps, we can not make coffins for them, but we roll them up in whatever they have. If we can get a piece of board to lay them on when we put them in their graves we do well." "But here you have lumber and plenty of carpenters, and you can have a plain coffin for the dead, and I do hope one will be made for this child. As I told the mother I would see that a coffin was made for her child and have it buried this afternoon, I will do it." He called the sergeant and gave the order for a carpenter among the soldiers to make it, and I saw the pine board coffin go to the burying ground with the child just before sunset.

Laura S. Haviland, *A Woman's Life-Work: Labors and Experiences of Laura S. Haviland* (Cincinnati: Walden and Stowe, 1882), 246–48.

Laura Haviland (1808–1898) holding slave irons. Source: *A Woman's Life-Work: Labors and Experiences of Laura S. Haviland* (Cincinnati: Walden and Stowe, 1882), 292 (facing)

WE ARE NO ADMIRER OF SLAVERY

Less explicitly racist than other Democratic editors, Elihu B. Pond of Ann Arbor's Michigan Argus nonetheless repeated arguments frequently made by other Democrats: that emancipation as a war measure violated the US Constitution and unnecessarily prolonged the war.

We are no admirer of the institution of slavery, no hater of the negro; and have no desire to see the former perpetuated out of ill-will to the latter. But slavery existed at the formation of the government, it was recognized by the Constitution, and without such recognition the Constitution could not have been adopted and the Union created. It is a local institution, and can be regulated and abolished by the States alone, and not by Congress or the President. We shall be glad to see its existence terminated whenever it can be done for the benefit of both master and slave, but we protest against the war being perverted from its legitimate object, the putting down of the rebellion, and indefinitely prolonged for the immediate extinction of slavery. To prosecute it for this object, and to its ultimate accomplishment, in to violate the Constitution,—and that once buried in wreck and ruin, we hold our rights as States and citizens at the mercy of Abraham Lincoln and his swam of military subordinates,—to slaughter millions of white men, to pile up untold debt, of which we can not pay even the interest, and all to confer a doubtful benefit upon the colored race. We say doubtful, for while gradual emancipation might benefit the white race of the South and elevate the black, we fully believe that immediate, unconditional emancipation will sow the seeds of destruction in the black race.

So thinking, and so believing, we shall vote for George B. McClellan on Tuesday next, confident that if he is elected the war will be prosecuted on Constitutional grounds, the rebellion put down, the Union preserved, and an early and honorable peace given to the country.

Michigan Argus (Ann Arbor), November 4, 1864.

MICHIGAN RATIFIES THE THIRTEENTH AMENDMENT ENDING SLAVERY

After passing the House of Representatives on January 31, 1865, the Thirteenth Amendment went to the states for ratification. Telegraphing the news to Governor Henry H. Crapo, Senator Jacob Howard and Representatives John F. Driggs and John W. Longyear hoped that "Michigan may be the first to ratify—don't delay." The amendment passed the state senate quickly by a 21–2 vote. The dissent in the statehouse was more vocal but the amendment still passed on the same day, February 2, 1865, by a vote of 56 to 12. Legislators pleased with the speed of Michigan's early ratification must have been disappointed to learn that Illinois and Rhode Island had already ratified it.

Recognizing the momentousness of this amendment, nineteen House members and one senator who were absent at the time of the vote had their chambers recognize their votes after the fact. Three House members who opposed the amendment also saw to it that the House recorded their vote after the fact. And one of the senators who voted against the amendment, Loren C. Treat of Oakland County, had the senate publish his dissenting remarks.[7]

JOINT RESOLUTION RATIFYING THE PROPOSED AMENDMENT TO THE CONSTITUTION OF THE UNITED STATES.

Whereas, The Congress of the United States, after solemn and mature deliberation therein, has, by a vote of two-thirds of both houses, passed "a joint resolution submitting to the legislatures of the several States, a proposition to amend the constitution of the United States," which resolution is in the following words:

Be it resolved by the Senate and House of Representatives of the United States of America, in Congress assembled, That the following article be proposed to the legislatures of the several States, as an amendment to the constitution of the United States, which, when ratified by three-fourths of said legislatures, shall be valid to all intents and purposes, as a part of the constitution, namely:

ARTICLE XIII.

Section 1. Neither slavery nor involuntary servitude, except as a punishment for crime, whereof the party shall have been duly convicted, shall exist within the United States, or any place subject to their jurisdiction.

Sec. 2. Congress shall have power to enforce this article by appropriate legislation.

And whereas, American slavery, in its wickedness and infatuation, has added to its many other heinous sins, the crime of waging a causeless, cruel and bloody war for the avowed purpose of dividing and destroying the nation, whereby it has forfeited all right to further toleration, and has clearly demonstrated that its continuance is wholly incompatible with the safety and preservation of a free republican government, and that in order to form a more perfect union, establish justice, insure domestic tranquility, provide for the common defense, promote the general welfare, and secure the blessings of liberty to ourselves and our posterity, it has become necessary to utterly destroy this barbarous foe of civilization, humanity and religion; therefore

Resolved by the Senate and House of Representatives of the State of Michigan, That in the name and in behalf of the people of this State, we do hereby ratify, approve and assent to the said amendment.

Resolved, That a copy of this assent and ratification be engrossed on parchment, and transmitted by His Excellency the Governor, to the United States, in Congress assembled.

Approved February 2, 1865.

Acts of the Legislature of the State of Michigan Passed at the Regular Session of 1865 with an Appendix (Lansing: John A. Kerr, 1865), 777–78.

NINE

~

The Civil War's End and Reconstruction

*C*ONFEDERATE MILITARY SETBACKS during the late summer and fall of 1864—the loss of Atlanta, the failed attack on Nashville, weakening defenses around Richmond and Petersburg, the inability to stop William Tecumseh Sherman's march through Georgia, recurrent defeats in Virginia's Shenandoah Valley by Philip Sheridan's cavalry—and the reelection of Abraham Lincoln spelled the Confederacy's doom, even though many refused to recognize the inevitable outcome at the time. A renewed federal assault on Petersburg in March 1865 broke the Confederate line and caused Robert E. Lee's Army of Northern Virginia to flee south in the hopes of joining with Joseph Johnston's diminished Army of Tennessee in North Carolina. With Ulysses S. Grant's Army of the Potomac blocking his retreat, Lee surrendered to Grant at Appomattox Court House, Virginia, on April 9, 1865. In less than two months all major Confederate forces had surrendered and Confederate officials had either been captured or escaped into exile. Soon the Union army discharged most of its regiments, and soldiers quickly became veterans.

The Confederacy's defeat did not settle all the questions the Civil War raised. For years, Republicans and Democrats disputed the terms by which Confederate states would reenter the Union and debated the political standing of the defeated Confederates, the formerly enslaved, and of African Americans generally. Once slavery ended, how would law and custom define freedom for the recently enslaved? Disagreements on Reconstruction, though, began before the war started. No sooner had states seceded than federal officials began to use the word "Reconstruction" to address how those states might reenter the union.[1] While not firmly committed to any single plan of action, President Abraham Lincoln favored Reconstruction being administered by the executive branch. In December 1863 he issued a Proclamation of Amnesty and Reconstruction that provided for a seceded state to begin its Reconstruction once a certain number of its citizens—10 percent of its voters in the 1860 election—both swore loyalty to the United States and accepted emancipation. Lincoln then looked to Louisiana as an experimental ground for launching this policy. The results of this policy in Louisiana fell short of most Republicans' expectations, including Lincoln's.

Most Congressional Republicans insisted that Congress set the terms for Reconstruction, favored a higher bar regarding the readmission of Confederate states, and rejected Lincoln's "Ten-Percent Plan." While Lincoln, in turn, pocket-vetoed the Wade-Davis Bill that Congress passed in 1864, he broadly agreed with congressional priorities and maintained a flexibility regarding Reconstruction policy that would have certainly prevented the conflict spurred by the bullheaded-ness of his successor, Andrew Johnson.

While accepting slavery's demise, particularly after the Thirteenth Amendment's ratification in 1865, Northern Democrats favored quick reunification, just as they had during the Civil War. They sided with President Andrew Johnson, who parted ways with congressional Republicans regarding the conditions for seceded states' readmission to the Union. Johnson's battles with congressional Republicans ultimately led to his taking the unprecedented step of actively cam-paigning against Republicans in the 1866 congressional elections—a failed effort that included a whistle-stop tour through southern Michigan.[2] Following those elections, congressional Republicans enacted the Reconstruction Acts of 1867 after overriding Johnson's presidential veto. This legislation placed Confederate states under military authority. Before these states could reenter the Union and have the military authority lifted they needed to ratify the Fourteenth Amendment and to recognize the voting and citizenship rights of African American adult males. Persistent conflict with Congress ultimately led to Andrew Johnson's impeach-ment by the House of Representatives, and to his near-removal from office by the Senate, in 1868.

Reconstruction demonstrated the lasting poignancy of sectional conflict long after the Civil War's guns went silent. All Republican presidential nominees between 1868 and 1900, save one, served as Union officers during the Civil War. Union veterans became a powerful interest group. In 1890 their organization, the Grand Army of the Republic (GAR), secured pension benefits for all disabled Civil War veterans and in 1904, the US Commissioner of Pensions issued an order that provided pensions to all Union veterans aged sixty-two and older.[3]

The Civil War endured in Michigan, too. As they had during the war, many Republicans still questioned Democrats' loyalty to the Union or reminded voters that Democrats' national allies were former Confederates. Michigan Democrats supported Andrew Johnson's plan to readmit the former Confederate states, and argued that white Southerners had paid the price for their disloyalty and had dis-avowed the Confederacy. To underline their commitment to the federal union, Democrats not only nominated a slate of high-ranking army veterans, as the Re-publicans did, they went further and nominated Major General Alpheus S. Wil-liams for governor (the Republicans renominated the incumbent governor, Henry Crapo).

Michigan voters' attachment to the Republican Party during the Civil War continued in 1866 and for years thereafter, with veterans being more likely to vote Republican than other voters (in the 1864 election, three-fourths of Michigan soldiers voted Republican).[4] These soldiers, their families, and others whose lives had been transformed by the Civil War cared deeply about the politics of Reconstruction. Further, most Michigan Republicans, at least during the 1860s, embraced the party's radical wing, which included an aggressive policy against the Confederacy and opposing easy terms for those states' readmission to the Union, vigorous attacks on slavery, and a commitment to citizenship rights for African Americans. Indeed, Michigan's principal Republican politicians during the Civil War and Reconstruction—governors Austin Blair and Henry Crapo, and senators Kinsley Bingham, Zachariah Chandler, and Jacob Howard—were Radicals. The party's radicalism frequently offended party conservatives, who formed coalitions with Democrats in 1862 and 1866. In the 1872 election, a similar dynamic occurred when Michigan's Democrats, like the national party, aligned with the so-called Liberal Republicans.[5]

Michigan's congressional delegation, overwhelmingly Republican during the eighteen years following the Civil War, took leading roles in advancing Reconstruction, with its senators widely recognized by contemporaries as Radicals within their party. Senator Jacob Howard served as one of the Senate's foremost legal authorities during Reconstruction. He maintained that the defeated Confederate states were "ward-provinces" of the United States and that the power for determining these states' relation to the Union rested with Congress. From 1865 to 1867 Howard shaped Congressional Reconstruction policy by serving on the Joint Committee on Reconstruction. He also authored the Fourteenth Amendment's citizenship clause, introduced the amendment into the Senate, guided its passage through that body, and formulated the rules of procedure during Andrew Johnson's impeachment trial. Senator Zachariah Chandler favored keeping former Confederate states out of the Union as long as possible, advocated black male suffrage at an early date, and embraced the Ku Klux Klan Act of 1871, which aimed to suppress neo-Confederate terrorist groups by making their offenses subject to federal prosecution. All six of the state's members of the House of Representatives voted to impeach Andrew Johnson, and both senators voted to remove Johnson from office.[6]

Reconstruction in Michigan often consisted of local debates regarding national issues and of the roles played by Michiganians in crafting national policy. It also included greater attention to African American rights and suffrage. Having long been denied the right to vote in Michigan, African American males appeared to be on the verge of having their suffrage rights recognized when the proposed 1867 state constitution explicitly recognized black males' right to vote.

The rejection of this 1867 constitution by the electorate on April 6, 1868 (likely for reasons besides its suffrage provision), proved to be a temporary setback, however. The Fifteenth Amendment's ratification in February 1870—which prohibited states from denying voting rights on the basis of "race, color, or previous condition of servitude"—effectively ended voting restrictions against Michigan's African Americans, and Michigan's blacks began voting in the April 1870 elections (by this time African Americans in the former Confederate states had been voting for two and a half years). A referendum in November 1870 repealed the racially exclusive suffrage clause of the Michigan constitution—already rendered obsolete by the Fifteenth Amendment. Nevertheless, it passed with just 51.9 percent of the vote.[7]

During the late nineteenth century Michigan eliminated other racially discriminatory laws from its statutes. In 1867, the Michigan legislature outlawed segregation in public schools and sixteen years later legalized interracial marriage. After the US Supreme Court, in 1883, overturned the federal Civil Rights Act of 1875, the Michigan legislature responded by passing the Michigan Civil Rights Act of 1885, which declared that Michiganians were to enjoy "full and equal accommodations" at "inns, restaurants, eating-houses, barber shops, public conveyances on land and water, theaters, and all other places of public accommodation and amusement." Irregular enforcement of these laws, though, resulted in continued racial discrimination in Michigan.[8]

Although Republicans generally controlled Michigan politics until the 1930s, radicals' control of the party waned during the 1870s, as it did nationally. Jacob Howard lost his bid to return to the US Senate in 1871, as did Zachariah Chandler four years later. Austin Blair lost bids for the US Senate in 1865 and 1869 to fellow radicals Howard and Chandler, and to moderate Republican Thomas W. Ferry in 1871. Blair broke with mainstream Republicans in 1872 to accept the Liberal Republicans' nomination for governor and to join forces with the Democrats—which election he lost.

And while Michiganians contested the Civil War's legacy for another two decades or more, by the 1870s state voters showed renewed interest in matters relating to currency and to economic development. As a way of increasing railroad construction in Michigan, in 1869 the legislature passed a railroad aid bill that permitted localities to offer construction incentives to railroad companies. Even though the Michigan Supreme Court invalidated the law in 1870, railroad construction boomed. Still, such one-sided advantages to corporations at public expense fractured the Republican coalition and diminished the Radicals' influence within the party.

Additionally, Republicans came to be divided into hard money and soft money factions. The former, such as Zachariah Chandler, insisted that hard currency replace the federal currency—"greenbacks"—the federal government issued during the Civil War. Soft money advocates, in contrast, favored keeping these paper notes in circulation. Some Republicans, including Detroit's oldest Republican newspaper, the *Detroit Advertiser and Tribune*, also resented Chandler's powerful political machine, the Detroit Regency, which seemed, at least to outsiders, to be more preoccupied with retaining power than with principles (contemporaries used the term "Stalwarts" to refer to Republicans who cynically reiterated radical talking points while being more committed to the party's success than to social change). And many in the party simply lost interest in reconstructing the South. These circumstances—coupled with anger over corruption in the Ulysses S. Grant administration—contributed to the Liberal Republican movement, which briefly joined with Democrats in 1872. An economic depression that began in 1873 weakened the Republican hold on power across the North and led to loss of their majority in the US House of Representatives in the 1874 elections. Michigan Republicans' diminished majorities in the legislature, and the weaker standing of radicals within the party, caused Zachariah Chandler to lose his US Senate seat in 1875 (before the Seventeenth Amendment's ratification in 1913, state legislatures selected US senators, rather than voters).[9]

Although many Americans continue to think that Reconstruction ended when President Rutherford B. Hayes removed the remaining federal troops from the South in 1877, Reconstruction lacks a clear termination in Michigan and elsewhere. Many Republicans continued to embrace a vision of a strong federal union committed to equal rights even as their main political concerns shifted elsewhere. Michigan's entire congressional delegation voted for the 1875 Civil Rights Act and the state legislature, as noted, affirmed its commitment to the 1875 law's principles a decade later. Zachariah Chandler returned to the US Senate in 1879, where he called for federal voting rights protection and continued referring to former Confederates as traitors until his sudden death later that year.

Meanwhile, most former Confederate states remained Republican strongholds until the mid-1870s, when white racial violence overthrew these state governments. African Americans still voted and held office across the South through the 1890s, albeit in fewer numbers. In 1890 the US House passed legislation that would have authorized the federal government to ensure the exercise of African Americans' voting rights in the South—which legislation the Senate failed to pass. Not long thereafter, though, a US Supreme Court hostile to black rights gave sanction to racial segregation in *Plessy v. Ferguson* (1896) and to voting restrictions in *Williams v. Mississippi* (1898). Another six decades passed before the federal government began to remedy these injustices.

"Capture of Petersburg, Virginia—The Second Michigan Raising the Stars and Stripes Over the Custom-House, April 3, 1865." Source: *Harper's Weekly*, April 22, 1865

THE FEELING IN THE ARMY:
SOLDIERS' REACTIONS TO LINCOLN'S ASSASSINATION

The end of fighting did not quell the anger that many Michiganians felt toward their former foes, whom they held responsible for starting the four-year bloodfest. Writing on April 21, 1865, to his father from City Point, Virginia, George S. Gordon of Grand Ledge, a volunteer in the 8th Michigan Infantry, revealed his continued animosity toward Confederates, expressed outrage over the Confederate treatment of Union prisoners, blamed Confederates for Abraham Lincoln's assassination, and reported that soldiers from both parties saw things as he did.

You know we used to read of the cruelty of rebels to our prisoners, and you know we did not use to believe it could be so. But, as God is my judge, it never was half told.

Oh, it was a heart-rending sight to see the poor fellows we released in Richmond: all rags and filth, and nearly starved to death—nothing but walking skeletons! While the prison yard had hundreds of graves in it, of men who had friends at home as dear to them as I have. And though almost incredible, it is a fact that every 'Yankee son of a bitch' the guards would shoot they got a furlough of twenty days. I know of men shot on the battlefield by wounded rebels while giving the scoundrels water. I have seen this myself, or I could never have believed it.

And to wind up their horrid work, which has placed almost every family in mourning in the land for friends lost, they have killed the President, than whom, I believe, now he has gone, no nobler man lived in the United States. But when the South killed Lincoln, they lost their best friend. He would have pardoned every one of the leaders—even Jeff. Davis. But Johnson, who, you remember, was a slaveholding Democrat all his life, says, "Treason must be punished and not pardoned." I hope he will hang every one of them, so they never can bring war on us again.

I have seen strong Democrats—men that I know voted for McClellan—when the news came that Lincoln was shot, weep like children, and lift their hands to high Heaven and curse the South and all traitors. It was an awful and imposing time. God have mercy on the people, if the army again gets in motion. They will entirely exterminate them; and I believe it is right.

Lansing State Republican, May 17, 1865.

JEFFERSON DAVIS'S CAPTURE

Written for Secretary of War Edwin Stanton fifteen days after Jefferson Davis's capture, Lieutenant Colonel Benjamin D. Pritchard's report explains how he and the 4th Michigan Cavalry captured Confederate president Jefferson Davis on May 10, 1865, near Irwinville, Georgia. They did so just moments before the 1st Wisconsin Cavalry's arrival—but not before the Michigan and Wisconsin forces exchanged gunfire, with each thinking the other to be Davis's Confederate guard. The unintended scuffle killed two and wounded five.

Pritchard, of Allegan County, afterward escorted Davis to Fortress Monroe, Virginia, where Davis remained incarcerated until May 13, 1867, when a court released Davis on bond. The federal government, which originally intended to prosecute Davis under the charge of treason, eventually dropped the case. Pritchard's report—along with other accounts—also became grist for contemporary cartoonists, who depicted the Confederate president trying to escape while disguised as a woman (see illustration, p. 167).

I left Macon, Ga., at 8 p. m. on [May 7, 1865] in command of the Fourth Michigan Cavalry . . . for the purpose of capturing Jefferson Davis and party, who were reported to have left Washington, Ga., on the morning of the 4th instant, traveling southwestward. . . .

[W]e reached [Irwinville] about 1 o'clock on the morning of the 10th instant. Here, passing my command as Confederates, and inquiring for "our train," representing that we were a rear guard left to fight back the Yankees, & c., I learned from the inhabitants that a train and party meeting the description of the one reported to me at Abbeville [Georgia] had encamped at dark the night previous one mile and a half out on the Abbeville road. I at once turned the head of my column in that direction (impressing a negro for a guide). After moving to within half a mile of the camp, I . . . dismounted twenty-five men, and sent them, under

Jefferson Davis's capture. Source: *The Last Ditch of the Chivalry, or a President in Petticoats*, broadside (New York: Currier and Ives, 1865)

command of Lieutenant Purinton, to make the circuit of the camp and gain a position in its rear, and thus cut off all possibility of escape. . . .

After waiting an hour and more, and just as the earliest dawn appeared, I put the column in motion, and we were enabled to approach within four or five rods of the camp undiscovered, when a dash was ordered, and in an instant the whole camp, with its inmates, was ours. A chain of mounted guards was immediately thrown around the camp and dismounted sentries placed at the tents and wagons. The surprise was so complete, and the movement so sudden in its execution, that few of the enemy were enabled to make the slightest defense, or even arouse from their slumbers in time to grasp their weapons, which were lying at their sides, before they were wholly in our power. . . .

As soon as the firing had ceased [with the First Wisconsin Cavalry] I returned to camp and took an inventory of our capture, when I ascertained we had captured Jeff. Davis and family (a wife and four children), John H. Reagan, his Postmaster-General; [Pritchard identifies nineteen military personnel, three women, and "several servants"]. . . . Upon returning to camp I was accosted by Davis from among the prisoners, who asked if I was the officer in command; and upon my answering him that I was, and asking him whom I was to call him, he replied that I might call him what or whom I pleased; when I replied to him that I would call him Davis, and after a moment's hesitation he said that was his name; when he suddenly drew himself up in true royal dignity and exclaimed, "I suppose that you consider it bravery to charge a train of defenseless women and children, but it is theft—it is vandalism!" After allowing the prisoners time to prepare breakfast, I mounted them on their own horses . . . and started on my return. . . .

On the afternoon of [May 22] the prisoners Davis and [former U.S. and Confederate Senator Clement Claiborne] Clay were transferred . . . to the casemates of Fortress Monroe and turned over to Brevet Major-General Miles, the Fourth Michigan Cavalry acting as special escort, after which it was temporarily assigned quarters within the fort. On the afternoon of the 23d I received orders from the War Department, through General Miles, directing me to procure the disguise worn by Davis at the time of his capture, and proceed to Washington and report to the Secretary of War. Accordingly I went over to the steamer Clyde and received from Mrs. Davis a lady's water-proof cloak, or robe, and which Mrs. Davis said was worn by Davis as a disguise at the time of his capture, and which was identified by the men who saw it on him at the time.

On the morning following the balance of the disguise was procured, which consisted of a shawl, which was identified and admitted to be the one by Mrs. Davis. These articles I brought to Washington and turned them over to the Secretary of War; and thus closes my account of the capture and custody, up to the time of his being turned over to the U.S. authorities, of the great conspirator and traitor, Jefferson Davis.

The War of the Rebellion: Official Records of the Union and Confederate Armies, ser. 1, vol. 49, part 1 (Washington, DC: Government Printing Office, 1897), 534–39.

THE WAR IS OVER AND SOLDIERS WANT TO GO HOME

Following the collapse of the Confederacy, much of the army gathered to Washington, DC, for the Grand Review: a two-day parade in late May 1865 that signified for many Americans the war's end. Thereafter the army mustered out numerous regiments and allowed soldiers to return to civilian life.

Some regiments, such as the 1st Michigan Engineers and Mechanics, remained in service for additional months—service that severely tried the soldiers' patience. After writing this letter in Washington, DC, Lambert Luten of Grand Rapids traveled with his regiment to Nashville, Tennessee. There, despite the war's end, they worked on the city's defenses until being mustered out on September 22, 1865.

I will again attempt to pen a few lines for your perusal since I have plenty of time as we have nothing to do and time hangs heavily on our hands. The idea of home is constantly in our minds but as yet we are not on the way. . . .

I don't receive any more mail for some reason or other. I suppose the principal reason is that we are all soon expected home and consequently you have stopped writing. . . .

I am quite tired of the army. The object for which I was enlisted has been accomplished and further army life has no more charms for me. [B]efore enlisting I often heard father rehearse the abuse practiced in the army in Holland, but I had an idea that free Americans could not be made to submit to such abuse, but I find that they can. [I]n one reg[iment] the rank and file are slaves, not so much in the amount of duty to perform, but the division between officers and men. The officers like the Southern slave holders receive all the visitors. They may take a look around the quarters of the slaves amuse themselves a little with some oddities &c.[,] but that is all. Visitors come up from the city and have picnics with the officers. The best we can do is to stand and gase [sic] at them. These are not imaginary visions from a mad[d]ened brain but are facts. In the army a persons [sic] worth is measured by the position he holds. [W]hile many of our officers have not the excellence of character which entitle them and would naturally draw respect. [S]uch being the condition of things in the army I long to sever the ties and once more proclaim myself a free man. I do not suffer in body, but I do in mind. The body is sufficiently provided for at present. . . .

Several of the officers are now trying to make up for their past abuse of the men but I do not think they will succeed much better than copperheads at home. At least they do not deserve to. [E]very dog has his day.

Lambert Luten to Hiram Luten, June 3, 1865, Lambert Luten Papers, Civil War Correspondence, Burton Historical Collections, Detroit Public Library.

JACOB HOWARD ON RECONSTRUCTION

In a US Senate debate regarding Louisiana's provisional government established under the terms of Lincoln's "Ten-Percent Plan," Michigan's Jacob Howard explains in February 1865 why he cannot accept Lincoln's policy.

If I am asked whether I favor the scheme of allowing one tenth or any other minor part of the male citizens of a State to organize a State government and assume to act as a State, I answer no; and for two reasons: first, because as against the will of an actual majority the government of such a minority must necessarily come to a speedy end and thus invite a renewal of the civil war, in that locality at least; and second, because government by a minority is of evil example and inconsistent with the genius of American liberty. Whatever may befall, whatever may be the result of the present great struggle, we cannot, we must not abandon the principle of civil government by a majority. It is the vital principle of republicanism. . . .

But when we speak of government by a majority we speak of a community made up of persons loyal and faithful to it. Traitors and aliens are always excluded from the category. Their hostility or indifference to the Government is universally admitted to be a sufficient cause for their exclusion. But where, as in some of the rebel States, there is an actual majority of the unfriendly or where, as in others, the numbers of the friendly and the unfriendly are so evenly balanced as to leave a contest between them of doubtful result, we are in fact dealing not with a loyal but a hostile community, and the necessity of adhering firmly to the principle becomes still more manifest. In both cases the prevalence of the will of the friendly can be secured only by military force employed to restrain the will of the unfriendly. . . .

Let us adhere with undeviating steadiness to the principle that, the community being loyal, the majority shall govern, which is the pole-star principal of our system—between which and despotism, either single-headed or many-headed—there is but one step, and that a short one.

Congress ought, in my opinion, to take the subject of readmission into their own hands. It is for them and not for the Executive to execute the important guarantee to each State of a republican government, and this duty presses upon us more and more as our victorious arms advance towards the close of hostilities. And in making good this guarantee, the great, the indispensable necessity is loyalty. To establish it, to give it a firm rock on which to rest, the Government must first show to its enemies and to those of hesitating loyalty that its physical power is as irresistible as its motives are benevolent. Its enemies must learn to feel a respect deep and abiding, for the arrows it carries in its quiver as well as for the shelter which its shield affords.

Congressional Globe, 38th Congress, 2nd sess., 1094–95 (1865).

MICHIGAN DEMOCRATS EMBRACE ANDREW JOHNSON

A Tennessee Democrat before the Civil War, Andrew Johnson was the only senator from a seceded state who refused to follow his state into the Confederacy. At their national convention in 1864, Republicans renamed their organization the Union Party, invited War Democrats to join them, and nominated the country's leading War Democrat, Andrew Johnson, as vice president. Upon becoming president following Lincoln's assassination, Johnson clashed vehemently with congressional Republicans, who favored greater rights for emancipated blacks and stricter terms for Confederate readmission than Johnson did.

Recognizing that Johnson shared a common outlook with most Northern Democrats, Edwin H. Lothrop, a former Democratic Speaker of the Michigan House of

Representatives and president of the 1866 Michigan Democratic Convention, urged Democrats at that convention to support a president their party had recently campaigned against.

[W]e behold that for a year and a half the strife of battle has ceased within our land, and that those States which were in rebellion are in a manner restored to their old condition under the Constitution; and yet we find they are not permitted to enter within the halls of our legislature to take part in making the laws of our country. We find that these States have come back asking to be re-admitted as members into the Union, and have, by their acts, declared beyond controversy, that Slavery shall no more exist within our land. They have, through their representative men, acknowledged that they are willing to pay the debt which has been contracted in support of the Union of these States. They have acknowledged that their old doctrine of secession was a heresy. And with all these acknowledgments—and so far as we can judge from appearances, they are sincere—they declare themselves obedient to the Constitution and to the laws of the land. We also find that the President of the United States is doing everything he can to bring about a restoration of the Union, and to give peace to the land. We are here to-day for the purpose of doing our part in devising means by which this end shall be completely accomplished, and I would invoke upon you the spirit of concession, conciliation and patriotism.

Gentlemen, I ask you to extend the right hand of fellowship to ANDREW JOHNSON. Shall we not say to that noble band who have eschewed party—who have given up old associations to rally round Andrew Johnson—shall we not hail them with outstretched hands and say "We are with you?" If we have any old prejudices still lurking in our hearts, it is for us to banish them, and go forth as one man in the accomplishment of the great object of reconstruction. We can contend for many things at a future day which, as party men, we hold essential, but in the meantime it is the part of wise men . . . to unite for that which is of far more vital importance—the full restoration of the Union. . . . Andrew Johnson, who knows more of the character and temper of the Southern people than all of us together, says that they have suffered enough, and that their present conduct is a guarantee that it will be safe to admit them back. And if Andrew Johnson says this, why should we here, who know nothing of it, say anything to the contrary? . . . I hope there is no man in this Convention who will raise his voice and say nay, but that all will reach forth the hand of friendship to our brethren in the South, and say, "We have punished you for your secession, and are, now that you are repentant, ready to take you back and try you once more."

New York Times, September 10, 1866.

"IS THE UNION RESTORED?"

Angered by President Andrew Johnson's Reconstruction policies—policies that permitted former Confederate states to reenter the Union quickly, retained former Confederates in power, severely limited the rights of the freedpeople, and turned a blind eye toward racial violence in the South—Congress passed the Reconstruction Acts of 1867. States could only be readmitted to the Union, and have their state governments restored, after they approved new state constitutions that guaranteed equal suffrage to all adult males regardless of their race or previous enslavement, and approved the Fourteenth Amendment to the US Constitution.[10] Not only did Northern Democrats object to these terms for their once and future political allies, they also argued that the Civil War and Reconstruction changed the conditions of the federal union, for the worse.

Georgia is again, and for the third time, declared to be a member of the Union, and it is now claimed that the work of reconstruction is completed. We do not deny that the Union is reconstructed, but is it the old Union of equal and independent States that was given us by Washington, Madison and Franklin? It is a new Union created upon the ruins of the old one. It is not as much like the old Union formed by our revolutionary fathers as would have been that of the Confederate States, had the rebellion been successful. It is a Union of dependencies, not a Union of equal and sovereign States. The people of the State of Georgia do not enjoy the same privileges of those of the State of Maine, nor do those of Louisiana, the same as those of Massachusetts. It is not a Union of equal States, nor a Union with equal privileges. The citizens of one State are not entitled to all the rights and privileges enjoyed by those of the other States. Those rights and privileges are denied by act of Congress. The Union of 1870 is not the Union of 1860. An attempt was made to destroy the Union of 1860 by force of arms, and failed. That was called treason. The Union of 1860 was destroyed by a Radical Congress—that was called loyalty. What treason failed to do, loyalty has more effectually accomplished. What it was a crime to do by force of arms it has become a virtue to do so by force of Congressional usurpation. Instead of a general government based upon the delegated powers given it by the States, we have States existing only by Congressional sufferance. The whole theory of the government has been changed. The general government is not now the representative of the States, but of their masters in Congress. In short, the Union has been reconstructed; but neither its principles nor its powers have been restored.

A LYNCHING IN MASON, 1866

Not all the country's Reconstruction Era racial violence occurred in the South. Little more than a year after the Civil War's end, residents of Mason lynched an African American youth for allegedly attempting to murder a local white family. Widely condemned at the time and afterward designated, by a contemporary, as "the foulest deed ever perpetrated in Ingham county,"[11] the incident nonetheless reveals the intense racial hatred held by some white Michiganians and suggests the challenges that African Americans in the South would face as they looked for allies in their continued struggle for freedom.

John Taylor, the negro who attempted to murder the Buck family at Delhi, on Friday night, Aug, 23, met a speedy punishment for his diabolical crime at Mason on Monday night. It will be recollected that he attempted to murder the wife, daughter and mother-in-law of Mr. Buck, and then escaped. None of the family have yet died, but it is thought the daughter cannot recover. After his capture he was lodged in the jail at Mason, the shire town of Ingham County. On Monday night, about 9 o'clock, twenty men, armed with rifles, marched into the quiet village of Mason, and proceed to the county jail. They were followed by twenty more armed with revolvers. They were under command of one GEORGE NORTON, of Delhi. They acquainted the Sheriff with their mission, stating they wished to get possession of the negro. The Sheriff and Deputy protested against their action. The crowd then rushed the stairs to the door, and three of them seized the Sheriff and held him. A sledge was then brought and the door of the negro's cell knocked off. He was taken out, when some of the mob proposed to shoot him on the spot, others that he be hung there. Sheriff MOODY came forward and stated that as they had taken the negro from his custody they should not hang him there, and requested them to take him elsewhere. The captain of the gang spoke and said, out of respect to the citizens of Mason and the Sheriff, they would go elsewhere to execute the culprit. They then repaired to a place about half a mile northwest of the village, near the railroad, and halted in front of a thorn apple tree. A fire was kindled, a rope thrown over a limb of the tree, and the noose adjusted around the prisoner's neck. A ring was then formed, and Mr. Buck permitted to question TAYLOR. He confessed the crime with which he was charged, but denied that he had ever killed anyone. The poor wretch trembled in every limb, and so great was his fright that he once fainted. He soon revived, and upon being further questioned stated that he had threatened to kill a man at Pulaski once, but did not carry out his threat. He was then prepared for execution. He asked Buck's forgiveness for what he had done.

Some one here called for a minister to pray for the negro. No one responded. A call was then made for some professing Christian to offer up a prayer. Still no response, when a low, drunken fellow named COOK, from Eaton Rapids, came forward and said he would pray for the d-d nigger. He then began a blasphemous address in the shape of a prayer, concluding by saying he hoped that if the nigger went to Heaven God would put him among the niggers there; but he hoped the negro would go to hell, where all niggers ought to go. When this wretch had finished his blasphemous harangue some one shouted for the captain to give the word, but the captain was not to be found, and the lieutenant was then called upon. He stated he had done all he should, and declined having anything further to do with the matter. COOK then stepped forward and said he would take charge of the affair. He counted one, two, three and gave the word. The rope was quickly pulled, and the body of the would-be murderer was swinging in the air. Not a muscle moved, nor were there any signs of life after he was pulled up. It is thought he died before the word was given, being frightened to death. The body hung for fifteen minutes, when it was cut down. Several wished to shoot at the body while hanging, but were restrained. The lynchers then proceeded to dig a grave at the foot of the tree, in which the proposed to bury the body. The owner of the land came forward and protested against the burial, and the corpse was then thrown into a wagon and carried off. Thus ends the last act of the drama.

The whole affair was characterized by inhumanity and lawlessness, the victim being unmercifully dragged to his death by the cowardly lynchers.

The people of Mason are justly indignant at this lawlessness, and censure the lynchers. The negro was guilty of a heinous crime, but there is a law for the punishment of such offenses, and he would have been punished to the full vigor of the law. We are told that that the mob was composed of men who belong to the lowest order of society, ignorant and depraved, and that the execution was carried on more account of the spirit of caste than revenge. The country has already had enough of mob law, and we hope that the lynchers will be dealth [sic] with as they deserve.

Jackson Citizen, as printed in the *New York Times*, September 3, 1866.

WILLIAM L. STOUGHTON DENOUNCES THE KU KLUX KLAN

During Reconstruction numerous white Southern Democrats joined terrorist organizations, such as the Ku Klux Klan, resorted to violence, and intimidated many Southern Republicans, particularly African Americans, to prevent them from voting. Northern Republicans, such as Representative William L. Stoughton of Michigan, called for increased federal intervention in the South, which Democrats opposed. Stoughton, from Sturgis, and formerly colonel of the 11th Michigan Infantry, delivered this speech in support of the Ku Klux Klan Act of 1871, which Congress later passed and President Ulysses S. Grant signed into law less than four weeks later. While this act temporarily succeeded in using federal power to stem Southern violence, by the late 1870s most Northerners, and many Republicans, became less committed to preserving African Americans' right to vote in the South.

[T]he moderation and forbearance of the American people upon the final subjugation of the rebellion are without a parallel in the history of the world. The lives of the insurgents were spared and their property was restored. . . . It has been the earnest hope of the Republican party and all good men everywhere that the spirit of violence and outrage had passed away in the South and that a better order of things would be established. With this view the State governments have been reorganized and put in operation and all local power freely placed in the hands of the people. The right of suffrage has been generously extended to all classes of men, subject only to the provision that the disloyal white man should never disfranchise the loyal black man. . . . Under these circumstances we have a right to expect and demand at least a quiet submission to just and wholesome laws from our late enemies. Unfortunately, however, our reasonable expectations have not been realized. There exists at this time in the southern States a treasonable conspiracy against the lives, persons, and property of Union citizens. . . .

The evidence taken before the Senate committee in relation to the outrages, lawlessness, and violence in North Carolina establishes the following propositions:

1. That the Ku Klux organization exists throughout the State, has a political purpose, and is composed of the members of the Democratic or Conservative party.

2. That this organization has sought to carry out its purposes by murders, whippings, intimidation, and violence against its opponents.

3. That it not only binds its members to execute decrees of crime, but protects them against conviction and punishment, first by disguises and secrecy, and second, by perjury, if necessary, upon the witness-stand and in the jury-box.

4. That of all the offenders in this order, which has established a reign of terrorism and bloodshed throughout the State not one has yet been convicted. . . .

[T]he Democratic party have from the first denied, and then palliated and excused these outrages. In Tennessee and other southern States the laws which had been passed by Republican Legislatures to suppress and punish the Ku Klux were repealed as soon as the Democratic party came into power. The relation of the Democracy to this order is precisely that of the receiver of stolen property to the thief. The murder of leading Republicans, terrifying the colored population, and putting whole neighborhoods in fear so that the Ku Klux can control an election, is heralded as a Democratic victory. . . .

[I]f this system of violence is to continue in the South the Democratic party will secure the ascendency. If political opponents can be marked for slaughter by secret bands of cowardly assassins who ride forth with impunity to execute the decrees upon the unarmed and defenseless, it will be fatal alike to the Republican party and civil liberty. . . .

The report, Mr. Speaker, to which I have referred shows over one hundred and fifty authenticated cases where persons have either been murdered, brutally beaten, or driven away at the peril of their lives. And the same deplorable state of things exists in South Carolina, Georgia, Mississippi, Louisiana, Kentucky, Tennessee, and Texas. Jails have been broken open, the officers of the law killed while attempting to discharge their sworn duty, and the criminals turned loose upon the community. Revenue officers and mail agents of the United States have in some instances been murdered, and in others driven away from their posts. But a few days ago, over a hundred Alabama Ku Klux made a raid upon Meridian, Mississippi, and carried off their victims for execution. . . .

The whole South, Mr. Speaker, is rapidly drifting into a state of anarchy and bloodshed. . . . There is no security for life, person, or property. The State authorities and local courts are unable or unwilling to check the evil or punish the criminals. . . . [T]he Ku Klux system is ingeniously devised for the express purpose of enabling a few bad men to intimidate the masses of the people, to avoid any conflict with the military power, and to control the State courts and local authorities by perjury and fraud. . . .

It is certain that under . . . the Constitution Congress has power to declare martial law in the insurrectionary districts, to fully investigate these outrages, and to provide for their trial and punishment in the United States courts where perjury in the jury-box and on the witness-stand can be guarded against, and where the military power can be called upon to aid in the enforcement of the laws.

Congressional Globe, 42nd Congress, 1st sess., 319–22 (March 28, 1871).

ZACHARIAH CHANDLER'S LAST SPEECH

Entering the US Senate in 1857 after briefly serving as Detroit's mayor, Zachariah Chandler developed a reputation as one of the most radical members of the Republican Party. He favored a vigorous prosecution of the Civil War and was an early and earnest supporter of emancipation. During Reconstruction, Chandler remained a steadfast supporter of black rights and never hesitated to remind audiences that Southern Democrats had recently fought an armed rebellion against the United States.

After losing his Senate seat in 1875, Chandler served briefly as Ulysses S. Grant's Interior Secretary. When he returned to the Senate in 1879, Chandler found more Democrats in Congress and a Republican president, Rutherford B. Hayes, who seemed to be ignoring white Southerners' violations of black rights. Republicans angry about developments in the South began to herald Chandler as a presidential candidate in the summer of 1879. Chandler denied he was a candidate and announced that he favored a third term for Ulysses S. Grant.

In this speech, given in Chicago on October 31, 1879, Chandler exhibits much of the spirit that made him popular with Republican audiences. When a hotel employee found Chandler in his room the following morning, dead of an apparent heart attack, Radical Republicans—by 1879 a faction in decline—lost their most effective spokesperson.

And the only thing to-day—the Senate and the House both being under the control of those Southern rebels—the only protection, the only barrier between the Treasury of the United States and those rebel claims is a presidential veto [cheers], and thank God for the veto! [Long-continued applause.]. . . .

In the very ordinance of secession which they had signed they had pledged their lives, their fortunes, and their sacred honor to the overthrow of this government, and when they failed to do it, they lost all they had pledged. [Cries of "Good."] They made no claims against the government because they had none. They asked, and asked as a boon from the government of the Unites States, that their miserable lives might be spared to them. [Applause.] We gave them their lives. They had forfeited all their property—we gave it back to them. We found them naked and we clothed them. They were without the rights of citizenship, having forfeited those rights, and we restored them. We took them to our bosoms as brethren, believing that they had repented of their sins. We killed for them the fatted calf, and invited them to the feast, and they gravely informed us that they had always owned that animal, and were not thankful for the invitation. [Great laughter and cheers.] By the laws of war, and by the laws of nations, they were bound to pay every dollar of the expense incurred in putting down that rebellion. . . . [B]ut we forgave them that debt, and, to-day, you are being taxed heavily to pay the interest on the debt that they ought to have paid. [Applause.] Such magnanimity as was exhibited by this nation to these rebels has never been witnessed on earth [applause], and, in my humble judgment, will never be witnessed again. [Cheers.] Mistakes we undoubtedly made, errors we committed . . . but, in my humble judgment, the greatest mistake we made, and the gravest error we committed was in not hanging enough of these rebels to make treason forever odious. [Prolonged cheers.]. . . .

And now, after twenty years—after an absence of four years from the Senate—I go back and take my seat, and what do I find? The self same pretensions are rung in my ears from day to day. I might close my eyes and leave my ears open to the discussions that are going on daily in Congress, and believe that I had taken a Rip Van Winkle sleep of twenty years. [Applause.]. . . .

These rebels—for they are just as rebellious now as they were twenty years ago—there is not a particle of difference—these rebels to-day have thirty-six members on the floor of the House of Representatives, without one single constituent, and in violation of law those thirty-six members represent 4,000,000 people, lately slaves, who are as absolutely disfranchised as if they lived in another sphere, through shot-guns, and whips, and tissue ballots; for the law expressly says, wherever a race or class is disfranchised they shall not be represented upon the floor of the House. [Applause.] And these thirty-six members thus elected constitute three times the whole of their majority upon the floor of the House. Now, my fellow-citizens, this is not only a violation of law, but it is an outrage upon all the loyal men of these United States. . . .

What they want is not free elections, but free frauds at elections. They have got a solid South by fraud and violence. Give them permission to perpetrate the same kind of fraud and violence in New York city and in Cincinnati and those two cities with a solid South will give them the presidency of the United States; and once obtained by fraud and violence, by fraud and violence they would hold it for a generation. To-day eight millions of people in those rebel States as absolutely control all the legislation of this government as they controlled their slaves while slavery was in existence. Through caucus dictation now I find precisely what I found twenty years ago when I first took my seat in Congress. . . . To-day there are thirty-two Southern Democratic senators to twelve Northern, and out of the whole twelve there is not a man who dares protest against anything. [Applause.] I say, that through this caucus dictation these eight millions of Southern rebels as absolutely control the legislation of this nation as they controlled their slaves when slavery existed. . . .

The Republican party was created with one idea, and that was to preserve our vast territories from the blighting curse of slavery. We gave that pledge at our birth, that we would save those territories from the withering grasp of slavery, and we saved them. [Voices, "Yes, we did."] It is our own work. We did it. [Cheers.] But we did more than that; we not only saved your vast territories from the blighting curse of slavery, but we wiped the accursed thing from the continent of North America. [Tremendous cheering.]. . . .

Now, I tell you, Mr. Chairman, the mission of the Republican party is not ended. [Cheers.] I tell you, furthermore, Mr. Chairman, that it has just begun. [Cheers.] I tell you, furthermore, that it will never end until you and I can start from the Canada border, travel to the Gulf of Mexico, make black Republican speeches wherever we please [applause], vote the black Republican ticket wherever we gain a residence [cheers], and do it with exactly the same safety that a rebel can travel throughout the North, stop wherever he has a mind to, and run for judge in any city he chooses.

[{Editorial note by the Post and Tribune Company} This hit at the Democratic candidate for judge of the Cook County Superior Court, who was a rebel soldier during the war, set the audience wild, and they cheered and swung their hats and handkerchiefs frantically.]

Zachariah Chandler: An Outline Sketch of His Life and Public Services (Detroit: The Post and Tribune Company, 1880), appendix, viii–xvi.

THE MICHIGAN CIVIL RIGHTS ACT OF 1885

When the US Congress passed the Civil Rights Act of 1875, it declared governments obligated to "mete out equal and exact justice to all, of whatever nativity, race, color, or persuasion, religious or political." It then legislated that everyone "within the jurisdiction of the United States . . . of every race and color, regardless of any previous condition of servitude" would be entitled to equal access of inns, public transportation, "theaters and other places of public amusement." The US Supreme Court later overturned many provisions of the 1875 act in its 1883 decision Civil Rights Cases, *holding that Congress lacked power to regulate private conduct and that individuals seeking relief from discrimination look to state government.*[12]

C. Fabe Martin, an African American resident of Dowagiac, denounced this "abrogation of the civil rights bill by the supreme court." But taking a cue from the Court's ruling, Martin called upon the legislature "to enact in substance what Congress essayed to do." Martin's representative, Robinson J. Dickson of Cass County, then introduced a civil rights bill in January 1885. Thereafter, citizens from across Michigan called upon the legislature to pass Dickson's civil rights legislation.[13] *In passing this document's resolutions in March 1885, citizens at this Detroit meeting also appointed one committee to "go to Lansing to present the resolutions, and go before the judiciary committee in advocacy of the measure," and designated another committee "to call public meetings for the discussion of matters pertaining to the good and welfare of the colored race." Patterned after the 1875 federal law, the legislation proved far less controversial than state measures recognizing equal voting rights from two decades previous, with the 1885 act passing 56 to 4 in the House and 23 to 0 in the Senate.*[14] *Inconsistent prosecution of the law's violators, however, meant that racial justice in Michigan rarely met the legal ideal.*

A meeting of colored citizens was held last evening at Good Samaritan Hall in Merrill block to consider the Civil Rights bill now before the Legislature. George Soerl called the gathering to order. Walter H. Stowers was selected permanent Chairman with Wm. W. Ferguson as Secretary. The pending bill was read at length and a Committee on Resolutions was appointed as follows: George Soerl, Walter Y. Clark, and Robert Pelham, Jr. . . .

The committee reported the following resolutions:

As this is a free government for and by the people, and firmly believing that the first principles of the same are best served when the rights of the people are most securely guarded: knowing also that there still exists a spirit which may at any time give birth to partisan race feeling and discrimination, because of existing prejudices; be it

Resolved, That for the security and perpetuity of rights to all men under the law, and security from discrimination by places licensed by the law, that we heartily support the civil rights measure as introduced before the State Legislature, and urge upon the members of said body the importance of its becoming a law; be it

Resolved, That we do not ask this as a race or separate people, but as American citizens, entitled to the protection that just laws wisely enacted may provide them; be it further

Resolved, That existing circumstances and cases warrant the asking and the en-acting of such a measure that will protect all citizens alike against discrimination.

Detroit Free Press, March 11, 1885.

WAR LOOKS MUCH DIFFERENT IN RETROSPECT

The 1880s witnessed an outpouring of Civil War reminiscences. Century Magazine *commissioned major political and military figures from the 1860s to tell about the war "from a non-political point of view."*[15] Century *editors hoped that they might foster sectional reconciliation by focusing on military heroics rather than discussing the war's causes and consequences. The success of the* Century *reminiscences revealed a deep interest in the Civil War by people too young to have remembered it, and unleashed a flood of reminiscences, such as this one. Many of these similarly omitted any discussion of slavery and the war's larger issues and remembered the war romantically—or in the case of this anonymous writer, humorously.*

The second day after our arrival at the front [in September 1861] the Fifth Michigan was ordered to relieve the Third Michigan from picket duty. About 9 a.m., amid much handshaking, dubious words of caution and advice from our friends of the Second Michigan, we marched forth to try and keep the Confederates around Munson's Hill busy and impress upon our friends at home the idea that the country was safe. After a two hours' march we reached the picket lines and were assigned a position.

Each post was occupied by a non-commissioned officer and six privates. The squad in which the writer was placed was under command of Sergt. Jim Lane, a good soldier and as full of mischief as a wood-chuck. We occupied a position on the edge of a wood, and about half a mile from Munson's Hill. Between our post and hill was a large meadow, on the opposite side of which the enemy's pickets were stationed. It was our duty to prevent the Confederates nearer approach to the capital. . . .

The Sergeant stationed a sentinel near the edge of the timber. The rest of the squad busied themselves by building a booth out of brush a few yards back in the forest for a shelter during the night for those who were off duty. After completing our arrangements, and not hearing anything from our neighbors in front, Jim sauntered out into the field with a view of becoming better acquainted with the surroundings. All at once zip, zip, came a dozen or more shots, cutting the foliage over our heads, causing our brave commander to drop flat to the ground and wear holes in the knees of his pantaloons crawling back to cover, while the remainder of the squad took refuge behind the largest trees they could find.

As soon as the Sergeant had regained his usual composure he argued that he had been insulted and must have blood in return. Accordingly he ordered his command up to the edge of the wood and directed us to return the volley and "blow the condemned rebellion out of existence." At the word of command we pointed our weapons in the direction of the hill, shut our eyes and pulled trigger. Fiz-z-slosh, ker-thump! and most of us found ourselves on our backs amid the underbrush. Wow-wow! but those old muskets could kick.

After the smoke cleared away and boys had recovered consciousness we looked to see if Munson's Hill had survived the shock, and we soon discovered that the Confederates' nest was intact. Our opinion of the situation was expressed by one of the squad when he said: "By gum! boys, I don't believe we touched a furrow."

Instead of annihilating the enemy we merely excited their ridicule. The distance was too great for oral communication, but the Johnnies were conversant with the "signs of the times," twisted themselves out of shape in pantomining [*sic*] and their views of we'uns. Their gestures were cruelly suggestive, to say the least. They climbed up on their rifle-pits and capered around like goats, interspersing the exercises with signs which none could fail to interpret. We could not help ourselves, for Uncle Sam had placed it out of our power to retaliate by arming us with muskets that were as useful for the work in hand as an ordinary pop-gun.

Detroit Free Press, March 20, 1886.

THE PAINFUL LIVES OF DISABLED VETERANS

Many Civil War soldiers who suffered combat wounds and survived the battle that gave them those wounds recovered and successfully readjusted to life after the war. Numerous veterans, though, carried injuries that left them permanently disabled and incapable of earning a living. While Congress provided disabled Union veterans with pensions—and eventually granted pensions to all Union veterans—some soldiers' disabilities, like those of D. S. Pierce, sometimes became progressively worse and resulted in premature death long after the war's conclusion.

CASE 15. Private D. S. Pierce, Co. B, 1st Michigan, aged 22 years, was wounded at Bull Run, August 30, 1862, and admitted to Ryland Chapel Hospital, Washington, three days afterwards. Surgeon J. A. Lidell, U. S. V., reported: "The patient was admitted to Stanton Hospital from Ryland Chapel, December 5th, with wound in the right leg. The bullet entered the outer part of the front of the middle third of said leg, about midway between the tibia and fibula. The bullet did not go through the limb. It, however, went in so deep that it could not be reached by exploration. The wound has been healed since the middle of October. The missile has gravitated through between the tibia and fibula, and can now be felt deeply seated in the muscles of the calf. It gives him no trouble. The anterior tibial nerve was divided by the bullet, in consequence of which the muscles of the front of the leg are paralyzed. The end of the foot points downward from activity of those on the back of the leg, and the case resembles talipes equinus.[16] The patient walks haltingly, but without a cane, by the aid of a high-heeled shoe. He has suffered but little pain since the wound healed, and considers himself to be slowly improving. He was discharged December 16, 1862."

Examiner D. Hudson, of Lansing, Michigan, reported, May 8, 1863: "Ball passed through both peroneal muscles, dividing the tibial nerve . . . and lodging deep in the soleus muscle. Ankle joint became stiff at an obtuse angle, requiring a heel more than an inch higher on the right shoe than on the left one. Neuralgic pain in foot and ankle daily and hourly."

Drs. J. B. Hull and I. H. Bartholomew, of the Lansing Examining Board, certified, December 7, 1870: "The ball passed down, and now lies under the skin above the inner malleolus. He cannot stand on his leg but a short time, and is getting worse," etc. They also stated that they excised the ball, and reported, September, 1872: "The nerve is diseased, and he suffers great pain through the whole leg; is emaciated and feeble, and growing worse." This pensioner died of "consumption," November 22, 1872, superinduced, in the opinion of the attending physicians, by "the continually depressing effects of the pain and tenderness of his limb."

Joseph K. Barnes, George A. Otis, and D. L. Huntington, eds., *The Medical and Surgical History of the War of the Rebellion*, part 3, vol. 2: *Surgical History*, 2nd issue (Washington, DC: Government Printing Office, 1883), 11.

JANE HINSDALE'S SUCCESSFUL APPLICATION FOR A CIVIL WAR PENSION

After 1890, veterans could obtain a Civil War pension by demonstrating a disability that prevented them from performing manual labor. Before Congress passed the

Army Nurses Pension Act of 1892, though, women could only obtain a pension through a special act of Congress. Jane Hinsdale of Detroit became one of the few to surmount this obstacle when Congress approved her pension in 1891, her illiteracy notwithstanding. After reviewing her pension petition, a House Committee wrote that Hinsdale "served as a nurse for the Union forces in the vicinity of Washington from the beginning to the end of the war. Her services were of a very high order. . . . She suffered great hardships, and is now an old woman in reduced circumstances. Her petition is substantiated by officers and soldiers who received her care." On June 9, 1864, the Detroit Free Press *published an account of Hinsdale's experience at Bull Run on the paper's front page and added that Hinsdale "speaks in glowing terms of her co-laborer, Miss Anna Etheridge."*

In the first part of the war, in the year 1861, my husband, Hiram H. Hinsdale, enlisted in Company D, Second Michigan Infantry. I went with the regiment from Detroit, Mich., to Grovier's Rest, where the regiment encamped. I there acted as matron and laundress for the regiment. The regiment left there for Bull Run. After they had gone I followed alone. I got through the lines by the aid of the Connecticut mail, and got in just as the division was starting for the Blue Ridge. I followed after that division, and during the engagement at the Blue Ridge[17] I was constantly on hand doing what I could for the wounded and dying. I had a small stock of medicine with me, which I used in administering to the wounded and those who had fallen by the roadside from sunstroke. I even carried water in my shoe to them.

I retreated with the regiment to Germantown[18] [Jermantown, Virginia]; after staying there a few hours I started back to the Blue Ridge to try to find my husband, but got lost in the woods, where I remained all night; in the morning I made my way back to Germantown. . . . I staid on the field at Germantown alone . . . until I was taken prisoner by the [Confederate] Black Horse Cavalry. . . . They then consulted together a little apart from me, and finally left two of the Black Horse Cavalry to take me a prisoner to Centreville.

When we got there the South Carolina regiment was drawn up in a line of battle. They kept me there until 5 o'clock in the afternoon, and then took me to Manassas Junction. The rebel countersign was out there; they wanted to put me into the guard house; I told them I never would go there; I would rather be shot on the spot. The head officer then said I was crazy, and for them to put me into a barn, which contained thirty or forty of our Union soldiers. . . . I cared for the wounded in that barn all night; I even tore up the underclothes I had on into bandages and wrapped around their wounds. I called for the Southern corporal in the morning and got a pass from [Confederate] General [P. G. T.] Beauregard to Washington. . . .

Dr. Taylor, of the Sixth New Jersey Regiment, who was a prisoner in the barn, told me I must go to Washington, as I was the only person who had a pass from General Beauregard, and that I could take valuable information to General [Joseph] Mansfield in Washington, regarding the rebel movements at Manassas Junction. Dr. Taylor gave me some papers which I were to take to General Mansfield, and I started for Washington. I walked that day to Centreville, most of the way barefooted, as I had used my stockings for the Union prisoners, and my feet were so sore and swollen that I could not get my shoes on. I had nothing on me but an old blood-stained skirt; no wonder the rebels thought I was crazy.

I slept on the floor in a shanty at Centreville that night, and early next morning started on my way to Washington. I got lost in the woods, and in a ravine were a company of rebel soldiers, who stopped me and demanded who I was. I showed them General Beauregard's pass, and their colonel, Washington, had me put in an ambulance and taken a few miles from them. I was then in a worse way than I was before, but finally succeeded, after great difficulty, in finding my way to Colonel Christian's guards, about 3 miles from Fort Ellsworth. They stopped me and I showed them Beauregard's pass; they said I could not pass on his pass. I then asked them if they were Lincoln's men, and they said they were, and I told them to tell their commander that I was from Manassas Junction, and that I had to get to Washington that night.

They brought their lieutenant, and I took him aside and showed him one of the papers Dr. Taylor had given me for General Mansfield. He said, laughing, you are not so crazy as they would have you to be. . . . I showed the colonel some of the papers I had for General Mansfield. Soon as he read the papers he called the quartermaster of the Twenty-sixth New York and sent him with me to see General Mansfield, and he told the quartermaster not to allow me to speak to any person until I had seen General Mansfield. When we got to Washington we could not find the general, so we went to the hotel to wait for him. . . . We waited up at the hotel until nearly 3 o'clock in the morning before General Mansfield came in. I then delivered the papers to him, and gave him all the information I could as to affairs at Manassas Junction. I told him I wanted to go to my home in Michigan, and he said I could not go, as I was just such a person as they wanted, and that I had done a great deal of good for the Union cause, and that for me to stay and he would see that I was well rewarded. . . .

I continued acting as nurse, and doing all I possibly could do there for the sick and wounded of the different regiments, both in the hospital and in the different camps, until the close of the war.

Jane Hinsdale.
her X mark.

H.R. Doc. No. 3713, 51st Congress, 2nd sess. (1891).

A VETERAN REFLECTS ON THE CIVIL WAR IN 1917

Many Union veterans joined the Grand Army of the Republic (GAR), a fraternal organization dedicated to preserving a Unionist understanding of the Civil War and to promoting veterans' interests, pensions in particular. Nationally, GAR membership peaked at 409,000 in 1890. Over 21,000 GAR members lived in Michigan at this time, and with almost 400 posts in the state, the GAR presence extended into nearly every community.

By 1917, though, Michigan's GAR membership had declined by more than two-thirds. At that year's state convention—its "encampment"—Michigan's GAR Chief Mustering Officer simply reported that "for the past year, I have . . . had absolutely no duties to perform. This is of course owing to the facts that our ranks are necessarily being reduced in numbers and no new Posts are being organized." Another official simply exclaimed, "It will be only a very few years that there will be any Department [of Michigan] Encampment held. We are getting old." Officially, the Michigan GAR continued until 1948, when Orlando LeValley, the state's last surviving recruit, died.[19]

Speaking to Michigan's GAR in 1917, Alison Libby Bryant, a veteran of the 23rd Michigan Infantry, remembered the Civil War while a new generation of soldiers volunteered for the Great War.

Today we step aside and give place to these young men in khaki uniforms. . . . [T]he old boys of the sixties who are left, though marching with bent forms and unsteady step, still hold first place in the hearts of a grateful people who remember. It ought to be a source of pride to each of us that in the discharge of duty so many years ago rendered, we won for ourselves the lasting gratitude of all the loyal people of this great Nation. We are unmistakably the old men in the communities in which we live. . . .

Oh, how the scenes of days long ago crowd into our memories upon occasions like this. How faces once familiar come back to us. Again we stand in line waiting the shock of battle, which comes all too soon. Who that has ever participated can forget the rolling, roaring boom of the cannon. The rattle of the musketry. It seems but yesterday, a comrade went down on either side and with what fidelity you bent down to receive the dying message for the loved ones at home. Who can ever forget the expression on the face of the Comrade, knowing his wound was mortal. And the roll call at the close of the day after the hard fought battle. The dead, wounded and missing must be accounted for.

Sheridan was right, *Yes, Sheridan was right.* How our hearts ought to swell with emotions of gratitude to the fathers of us all for the years vouchsafe[d] to us.

Every old soldier who saw service and is now receiving a pension ought to belong to the Grand Army. I fear too many veterans do not appreciate how much

Civil War veterans (and others) at a gathering of the Grand Army of the Republic, Farmington, Oakland County, 1899. Source: Farmington Community Library Heritage Collection

this organization has done for them in looking after their records, urging pension legislation, and withal cultivating the spirit of comradeship which strengthens as our members lessen. Other than kinship I know no stronger tie than that of comradeship.

Let us hope that the time will never come to this country when treason will cease to be a crime or patriotism a virtue.

May the Nation never forget to remember that the ideas for which the South fought were wrong, wrong then, wrong now, and will be wrong eternally, while the principles for which we contended were right then, right now, and will be right until the Heavens shall roll together as a scroll and the earth shall [melt] with fervent heat.

Journal of the Thirty-Ninth Annual Encampment, Department of Michigan, Grand Army of the Republic, Held at Battle Creek., June 20, 21, 22 1917 (Lansing: Wynkoop Hallenbeck Crawford Co., State Printers, 1917), 64–65 (source), 73, 77 (quoted material above).

Timeline

1787

July   The Confederation Congress adopts the Northwest Ordinance, creating a framework for government in the national territory north and west of the Ohio River, which included the area that became the state of Michigan. Article VI of the Ordinance declared, "There shall be neither slavery nor involuntary servitude in the said territory."

1795

August   Following its defeat at the Battle of Fallen Timbers, the Western Indian Confederacy cedes to the United States, at the Treaty of Greenville, a narrow strip of land along the Detroit River, Mackinac Island, and portions of the mainland along the Straits of Mackinac.

1796

July   Under the terms of the Jay Treaty, British troops evacuate Detroit, thus bringing the area under the effective control of the United States. In September, British troops evacuate Mackinac Island.

1805

January   The US Congress legislates creation of the Michigan Territory from the Indiana Territory, effective June 30. With Detroit as its capital, the new territory includes the Lower Peninsula and the eastern portion of the Upper Peninsula.

1810

August   The United States census enumerates Michigan Territory's population at 4,762—a figure that does not include Native Americans living beyond federal jurisdiction.

1813

October   Lewis Cass is appointed territorial governor, a position he holds
               until 1831.

1818

December   After Indiana and Illinois gain statehood, the remainder of the Old
               Northwest—present-day Wisconsin, the western Upper Peninsula,
               and northeastern Minnesota—becomes incorporated into Michi-
               gan Territory.   .

1820

August   The United States census enumerates Michigan Territory's popula-
               tion at 8,765, of which nearly 7,500 lived within the boundaries of
               the present-day state. These figures do not include Native Ameri-
               cans living beyond federal jurisdiction.

1825

October   The Erie Canal's completion in New York opens travel and trade
               between Michigan, the northeastern US, and the broader Atlantic
               world and fuels Michigan's population growth, with most settlers
               coming from New England and upstate New York.

1830

August   The United States census enumerates Michigan Territory's popu-
               lation at 31,340, of which approximately 28,000 lived within the
               boundaries of the present day state. These figures do not include
               Native Americans living beyond federal jurisdiction.

1832

October   Quakers in Lenawee County, led by Elizabeth Margaret Chandler
               and Laura Smith Haviland, form the Logan Female Anti-Slavery
               Society, Michigan's first abolitionist organization.

1834

June   The northeast portion of the Louisiana Purchase—present-day
               Iowa, western Minnesota, and the eastern Dakotas—is incorpo-
               rated into Michigan Territory.

1835

May — Delegates assemble in Detroit and draft a constitution for the proposed state of Michigan. Congress delays its vote on Michigan statehood due to a boundary dispute between Michigan and Ohio.

1836

April — With an eye toward Michigan statehood, the US Congress creates the Wisconsin Territory, separating it from Michigan Territory.

November — The Erie and Kalamazoo Rail Road launches a horse-drawn rail service linking Port Lawrence (Toledo) with Adrian. The following year, a steam locomotive services this line.

Anticipating statehood, Michigan voters cast the majority of their ballots for Martin Van Buren, the Democratic nominee for president.

Delegates meet in Ann Arbor to form the Michigan State Anti-Slavery Society.

December — A convention in Ann Arbor accepts a compromise passed by the US Congress that recognizes Ohio's claim to the Toledo Strip (including the mouth of the Maumee River into Lake Erie). Michigan receives, in exchange, the western three-fourths of the Upper Peninsula.

1837

January — President Andrew Jackson signs a bill admitting the state of Michigan into the Union. Stevens T. Mason, elected by voters in October 1835, becomes the state's first governor.

May — After New York banks suspend specie payment, other banks across the country follow suit. The ensuing economic depression continues for a half-dozen years.

1838

February — The Detroit & St. Joseph Railroad is completed between Detroit and Ypsilanti. Eventually this line becomes the Michigan Central Railroad, reaching Kalamazoo by 1846, New Buffalo by 1849, and Chicago by 1852.

1839

September   Seymour B. Treadwell launches the *American Freeman* (soon retitled *Michigan Freeman*), the state's first abolitionist newspaper, in Jackson, where it will continue until 1841.

November   Michigan Whigs win their only governor's race with the election of William Woodbridge as governor.

1840

February   The Michigan State Anti-Slavery Society calls for abolitionists to "form themselves into a systematic and distinct political party." In 1841, this party will begin calling itself the Liberty Party.

August   The United States census enumerates Michigan's population at 212,267—a figure that does not include Native Americans living beyond state jurisdiction.

November   William Henry Harrison is elected President. He wins the majority of Michigan's votes, the only Whig presidential candidate to do so. James G. Birney, the antislavery candidate, receives less than 1 percent of the statewide vote.

December   Michigan's railroad mileage totals 104 miles.

1841

February   In his fourth annual report, state geologist Douglass Houghton describes extensive native copper deposits on the Keweenaw Peninsula, launching a copper rush to the region.

April   The *Signal of Liberty*, Michigan's second newspaper devoted to abolitionism, begins publication in Ann Arbor, where it will continue until 1848.

November   John S. Barry, a Democrat, is elected governor. Jabez S. Fitch, the Liberty Party candidate, receives 3.2 percent of the vote.

1842

October   In the last major Native land cession in Michigan, the Ojibwe sign the Treaty of La Pointe with the United States, ceding the western Upper Peninsula and northern Wisconsin.

1843

November   Democrat John S. Barry is reelected governor. Liberty Party candidate James G. Birney, now a Saginaw resident, receives 7.1 percent of the vote.

1844

November   Embracing a platform of territorial expansion, Democrat James K. Polk is elected president and wins a plurality of Michigan's vote. James G. Birney, the Liberty Party candidate, wins 6.5 percent of Michigan's vote and 3.3 percent of the Northern vote.

1845

March   Days before James Polk's inauguration, President John Tyler signs legislation authorizing Texas annexation. In December, Texas enters the Union as a slaveholding state.

August   Man-je-ki-jik, an Ojibwe, leads S. T. Carr and E. S. Rockwell to a "mountain of solid iron ore" near the present-day city of Negaunee, launching iron mining in the Upper Peninsula.

November   Alpheus Felch, a Democrat, is elected governor. James G. Birney, the Liberty Party candidate, receives 7.6 percent of the vote.

1846

January   After recognizing Texas's dubious claims regarding its southern border, President James Polk orders US troops to the Rio Grande River—land Mexico regards as its sovereign territory.

May   Congress, accepting President Polk's specious claim that the Mexican army had invaded the United States and attacked US troops, declares war on Mexico.

August   US Representative David Wilmot, a Pennsylvania Democrat, introduces the Wilmot Proviso. The Proviso declares that "neither slavery nor involuntary servitude" shall exist in any territory acquired from Mexico. The measure passes the US House but fails in the Senate.

1847

March
Governor William L. Greenly signs a bill to move Michigan's capital from Detroit to Lansing Township in Ingham County. The new capital soon becomes known as Lansing.

November
Epaphroditus Ransom, a Democrat, is elected governor. Chester Gurney, the Liberty Party candidate, receives 5.6 percent of the vote.

Michigan's first telegraph service begins between Detroit and Ypsilanti. By the following April, telegraph lines will connect Detroit with Chicago and New York City.

December
In a letter to Alfred O. P. Nicholson of Tennessee, Senator Lewis Cass of Michigan declares his opposition to the Wilmot Proviso, holding that white settlers, and not the US Congress, should decide on the status of slavery in any territory acquired from Mexico.

Beginning in this year, the majority of the copper mined in the United States comes from Michigan—a position the state will maintain until 1884.

1848

February
Mexico and the United States sign the Treaty of Guadalupe Hidalgo. Mexico surrenders more than half its territory to the United States, including its claims on its former province of Tejas (Texas), all of the modern US states of California, Nevada, and Utah, and large portions of the modern US states of Arizona, New Mexico, Colorado, and Wyoming.

April
Two months after the *Signal of Liberty* ceases publication, the *Michigan Liberty Press,* the state's third antislavery newspaper, begins publishing in Battle Creek, where it will continue until June 1849.

May
Lewis Cass of Michigan receives the Democratic nomination for president at the Democratic National Convention in Baltimore.

August
Desiring to stop the spread of slavery into the territories annexed from Mexico, members of the Liberty Party join with Whig and Democratic dissidents in Buffalo, New York, to form

the Free Soil Party. The Free Soilers nominate former president
Martin Van Buren.

November   Louisiana slaveholder Zachary Taylor, a Whig, wins the presidency.
             Democrat Lewis Cass carries his home state as Free Soiler Martin
             Van Buren wins 16.0 percent of Michigan's vote and 14.4 percent of
             the Northern vote.

1849

January   In his annual address, Governor Epaphroditus Ransom, a Demo-
             crat, asserts that Congress possesses the right to regulate slavery
             in the federal territories, signaling a divide among Michigan
             Democrats.

March   After voting to return Lewis Cass to the US Senate, the Democratic
             Michigan legislature declares that "Congress has the power, and . . .
             duty" to exclude slavery from the federal territories, and instructs
             the state's representatives in Congress to vote for the Wilmot
             Proviso.

1850

June   The United States census enumerates Michigan's population at
             397,654—a figure that does not include Native Americans living
             beyond state jurisdiction.

July   President Zachary Taylor dies suddenly in Washington, DC.

August/   President Millard Fillmore signs into law a series of measures that
September   come to be known, collectively, as the Compromise of 1850. The
             issues raised by the proposed Wilmot Proviso are resolved by Cali-
             fornia's admission to the Union as a free state and by permitting
             the white residents of Utah and New Mexico territories to decide
             whether slavery should exist there. A stronger fugitive slave law
             brings protests across the North.

November   Michigan voters ratify a new state constitution but reject black
             male suffrage, 71.5 percent to 28.5 percent. Democrat Alexander
             Buel, who voted for the Fugitive Slave Act, however, loses his seat
             in the US House of Representatives.

December   Michigan's railroad mileage totals 380 miles.

1852

November   Franklin Pierce, a Democrat, is elected president and easily wins
            Michigan. John P. Hale, the nominee of the Free Democrat Party
            (the new name for the Free Soil Party) receives 8.7 percent of
            Michigan's vote and 6.6 percent of the Northern vote.

1853

June   By a nearly two-to-one margin, Michigan voters approve statewide
            prohibition. Michigan Supreme Court decisions in 1854 will effec-
            tively gut this law. In 1856, the state court also weakens prohibition-
            ist legislation passed in 1855.

1854

January   Senator Stephen Douglas of Illinois introduces the Kansas-
            Nebraska Bill into the Senate, which would permit settlers to de-
            termine the status of slavery in the soon-to-be organized territories
            of Kansas and Nebraska—contrary to a provision of the Missouri
            Compromise (1820) that prohibited slavery from the region.

February   Michiganians begin to hold protest meetings regarding the pro-
            posed Kansas-Nebraska Bill and the expected expansion of slavery
            it would bring.

May   President Franklin Pierce signs the Kansas-Nebraska Act into law.

July   A coalition of Free Democrats, Whigs, and Anti-Nebraska Demo-
            crats convene in Jackson and create a new party, adopting the
            name Republican—the first statewide meeting of a new party that
            spreads across the North during the following years.

November   Michigan's Republicans capture the governorship, both legislative
            chambers, and other statewide offices, ending the Democrats'
            thirteen-year lock on the state government.

1855

January   Kinsley S. Bingham, Michigan's first Republican governor, is
            inaugurated.

February   The legislature passes Michigan's first personal liberty law, thus
            complicating slaveholders' efforts to reclaim escaped fugitives.

Largely composed of former Whigs, however, the Republican legislature devotes relatively little time to antislavery measures.

March   Election for the Kansas territorial legislature occurs with 5,000 voters crossing from Missouri, resulting in a proslavery legislature that does not represent the majority of the territory's settlers. Ultimately Kansas has two rival capitals: a proslavery capital in Lecompton and a free-state capital in Topeka.

June   The completion of the canal and locks at Sault Ste. Marie—the "Soo Locks"—opens navigation between Lake Superior and the lower Great Lakes.

1856

January   President Franklin Pierce declares Kansas's free-state capital in Topeka to be unlawful and refuses to have his administration recognize it.

May   Armed conflict begins between free- and slave-state settlers in Kansas.

August   Abraham Lincoln speaks in Kalamazoo on behalf of Republican nominee John C. Frémont, Lincoln's only Michigan speech.

November   Republican John C. Frémont wins 57 percent of Michigan's vote and a plurality of the Northern vote, and Republicans continue to control Michigan state politics. Democrat James Buchanan of Pennsylvania, however, secures the presidency by winning nearly all the slaveholding states and five nonslaveholding states.

1857

January   Michigan's Republican legislature selects the state's first Republican US senator, Zachariah Chandler, who defeats the Democratic incumbent, Lewis Cass, on a party-line vote.

February   President-elect James Buchanan asks Lewis Cass to serve as his Secretary of State. The aged Cass, confirmed the following month, will play a secondary role to Buchanan, who, as a former secretary of state and diplomat, expects to superintend his administration's foreign policy.

March   In *Dred Scott v. Sandford*, the US Supreme Court rules that Congress
            cannot exclude slavery from the federal territories and that people
            "of the African race" are not US citizens.

September   Bank failures and financial panic spread across the United States,
            particularly in the North, with the economic recession persisting
            for two years.

November   Slave-state settlers in Kansas prepare for statehood by drafting a
            proslavery constitution. Despite opposition from the majority of
            Kansas's residents to this Lecompton Constitution, the Buchanan
            Administration pushes Congress to admit Kansas as a slave state.

                                    1858

April   The US House rejects Kansas statehood under the Lecompton
            Constitution. Despite intense pressure from the Buchanan adminis-
            tration, many Northern Democrats vote against Kansas statehood.
            Kansas remains a territory until 1861.

August–   Abraham Lincoln, a Republican, and Senator Stephen Douglas, a
October   Democrat, hold a series of debates in Illinois. Despite later losing
            the Senate seat to the incumbent Douglas, Lincoln's stature across
            the North benefits from the debates.

November   In response to the Buchanan administration's effort to bring Kansas
            into the Union as a slave state, Democrats suffer huge losses across
            the North in fall congressional elections. Michigan remains solidly
            Republican and elects Moses Wisner governor.

                                    1859

January   Michigan's Republican legislature selects Kinsley Bingham as US
            senator.

October   A multiracial force of twenty-one men, led by abolitionist John
            Brown, attacks a federal arsenal in Harpers Ferry, Virginia, in
            hopes of launching a slave rebellion. Within thirty-six hours, US
            troops capture the wounded Brown, with most of his raiders
            being captured or killed. The state of Virginia executes Brown in
            December.

November   The Grand Trunk Railway begins operating out of Sarnia, Canada
            West (currently Ontario), across the St. Clair River from Port

Huron—effectively linking Michigan to New England by way of Canada.

1860

April-May
The Democratic National Convention meets in Charleston. A division between Northern and Southern factions unable to agree on a nominee leads many Southern delegates to walk out of the convention, and the convention votes to reconvene in Baltimore in June.

May
The Constitutional Union Party, consisting mostly of former members of the Whig and American Parties, convenes in Baltimore and nominates John Bell.

The Republicans hold their national convention in Chicago. Although the Michigan delegation favors William Seward, the convention nominates Abraham Lincoln.

June
The United States census numbers Michigan's population at 749,113—and estimates an additional 7,777 Native Americans, "not enumerated . . . and retaining their tribal character," live in the state.

Democrats reconvene in Baltimore. Unable to resolve their differences with Northern Democrats, most of the Southern delegates exit the convention. The remaining delegates nominate Stephen Douglas, with the departed delegates assembling across town and nominating a separate candidate, John C. Breckinridge.

November
Abraham Lincoln is elected president with only 39.6 percent of the popular vote. His dominance of the free-state vote, however, leads to his winning a clear majority of electoral votes. By giving 57 percent of its vote to Lincoln, Michigan matches its support for Frémont four years earlier.

December
Citing the Republicans' antislavery platform, a state convention votes to have South Carolina secede from the United States.

Michigan's railroad mileage totals 770 miles.

1861

January
In his inaugural address, Governor Austin Blair declares, "Secession is revolution, and revolution, in the overt act, is treason."

Following South Carolina's lead, Mississippi, Florida, Alabama, Georgia, and Louisiana secede from the United States.

February   Delegates from the seceded states meet in Montgomery, Alabama, form the Confederate States of America, and select Jefferson Davis as the Confederacy's president. Later in the month, Texas secedes from the United States and joins the Confederacy.

March   Abraham Lincoln is inaugurated. He continues President James Buchanan's policy of retaining possession of the federal forts in seceded states: Forts Jefferson, Pickens, and Zachary Taylor in Florida; and Fort Sumter in South Carolina.

Recognizing the growing threat of war, the Michigan legislature authorizes Governor Austin Blair to muster regiments of the state militia into federal service "whenever required by the President."

April   South Carolina troops fire on Fort Sumter and force the surrender of the installation's US garrison.

Lincoln issues a proclamation calling on the Union's loyal states to furnish, collectively, 75,000 troops to "suppress" secessionists and to "cause the laws to be duly executed."

Governor Austin Blair authorizes ten companies of Michigan's militia to be mustered into federal service for three months. They form the 1st Michigan Infantry.

May   In an extra session, the Michigan legislature authorizes $1 million in bonds to pay for ten regiments of Michigan infantry.

The Michigan legislature enacts the Soldiers' Relief Law, which authorizes county supervisors to assist families of soldiers in the field.

The 1st Michigan Infantry is mustered into federal service and departs for Washington, where it enlists in the defenses of the national capital.

Arkansas, North Carolina, and Virginia secede from the United States.

June   Tennessee secedes from the United States.

Skirmishes in Virginia—Arlington Mills, Fairfax County, Philippi, and Big Bethel—produce some of the Civil War's earliest casualties.

July	In the first major engagement of the Civil War, Confederate troops defeat US troops at the First Battle of Bill Run (also called First Manassas).
August	To finance the war, Congress passes the first US income tax (3 percent on incomes over $800).
	Following the Union defeat at the First Battle of Bull Run, Congress authorizes an additional 500,000 volunteers.
	Congress enacts the First Confiscation Act.
October	Senator Kinsley Bingham dies.
November	Civilian activists in Detroit, primarily women, form the Detroit Soldiers' Aid Society, later known as the Michigan Soldiers' Aid Society.
	After Winfield Scott's resignation, Abraham Lincoln appoints General George McClellan as general-in-chief of the United States Army.
December	By the end of 1861, over 16,000 soldiers have joined Michigan regiments.

1862

January	Governor Austin Blair convenes an extra session of the legislature and calls for legislation enabling the state to pay the war-tax burden that Congress encumbered upon it.
	In his annual address, Governor Austin Blair calls on the federal government to strike more boldly against slavery.
	The Michigan legislature selects Jacob Howard to fill the US Senate seat made vacant by Kinsley Bingham's death.
February	Troops led by General Ulysses S. Grant capture Forts Henry and Donelson, quickly leading to the surrender of Nashville.
	Congress passes the Legal Tender Act, authorizing the federal government to print paper money for the first time.
March	The Battle of Pea Ridge, Arkansas, closes the Confederate door to Missouri and ensures Union control of northern Arkansas.
	General George McClellan launches the Peninsular Campaign, by which he and 130,000 US troops travel by ships to the Virginia Peninsula with hopes of capturing Richmond.

The Battle of Glorieta Pass repulses the Confederate attack into New Mexico and the Far West.

April   The Battle of Shiloh, Tennessee, the war's bloodiest battle to date, results in almost 24,000 casualties.

The Confederate surrender of Island No. 10, near New Madrid, Missouri, closes the upper Mississippi River to the Confederacy.

Congress abolishes slavery in the District of Columbia.

The capture of Fort Macon concludes a campaign along North Carolina's Outer Banks that closed much of the state's shoreline to Confederate navigation.

Naval forces under USN Flag Officer David Farragut capture New Orleans.

May   Congress passes the Homestead Act, which offers land grants to US citizens who settle on federal public land.

June   Congress abolishes slavery in the federal territories.

June–July   After coming within sight of Richmond, George McClellan's Army of the Potomac retreats from the Virginia Peninsula following the Seven Days battles, which result in 36,000 casualties.

July   Lincoln issues a call for an additional 300,000 troops.

In Detroit, a large rally held to encourage enlistments turns into a shouting match between war supporters and opponents before becoming violent.

Congress enacts the Second Confiscation Act.

Congress passes the Militia Act, authorizing enlistment of all "able-bodied male citizens" regardless of race.

Abraham Lincoln appoints Henry Halleck as general-in-chief of the United States Army.

August   Secretary of War Edwin Stanton orders that 300,000 state militia be called into federal service.

August–   After US troops retreat from the Virginia Peninsula, Confederates led
September   by General Robert E. Lee launch an offensive that takes them into Northern Virginia. At the Second Battle of Bull Run, Confederates

defeat US forces, resulting in over 22,000 casualties, and continue their offensive into Maryland.

September   The Battle of Antietam halts a Confederate invasion of Maryland, results in almost 23,000 casualties, and stands as the Civil War's bloodiest day.

Abraham Lincoln issues the Preliminary Emancipation Proclamation.

Abraham Lincoln meets with Governor Austin Blair and twelve other governors at the Loyal War Governors' Conference in Altoona, Pennsylvania.

October   Union forces repulse a Confederate offensive into Kentucky at the Battle of Perryville, resulting in over 7,600 casualties.

November   Democrats make significant gains in state elections across the North. Republicans continue to control Michigan, with Austin Blair being reelected, albeit with a smaller victory margin and with their massive legislative majorities significantly diminished. Augustus C. Baldwin, a Democrat, wins a seat in the US House, while Republicans control Michigan's other five seats.

Lincoln replaces George McClellan, commander of the Army of the Potomac, with Ambrose E. Burnside.

December   At the Battle of Fredericksburg, Confederates repulse another US offensive toward Richmond, with nearly 18,000 casualties.

1863

January   Lincoln issues the Emancipation Proclamation, freeing enslaved people in the Confederacy and in some US-occupied areas.

The Battle of Stones River, Tennessee, results in 23,000 casualties.

The Michigan legislature reelects Zachariah Chandler to the US Senate.

February   To meet an unfulfilled federal call for troops from the preceding August, Michigan holds its first conscription.

March   Congress passes the Enrollment Act, establishing the conscription system used for the remainder of the war. In contrast, the Confederate Congress enacted its first conscription law in April 1862.

A protest against the recently enacted Enrollment Act turns violent in Detroit when rioters attack the city's African Americans and their property.

The Michigan legislature enacts a law authorizing the state's war bonds to increase from $1 million to $1.25 million.

Governor Blair approves a joint resolution of the legislature that opposes any terms to the Confederates besides unconditional surrender.

May   At the Battle of Chancellorsville, Virginia, Confederates repel another attempted US offensive toward Richmond, resulting in 30,000 casualties.

The War Department launches the Bureau of Colored Troops, opening the door to the active recruitment of African American soldiers.

June   Lincoln issues a call for an additional 100,000 militia.

Confederates commence an offensive against northern Virginia, Maryland, and Pennsylvania, remembered as the Gettysburg Campaign.

July   At the Battle of Gettysburg, US forces turn back the Confederate invasion of south-central Pennsylvania. The three-day battle results in 51,000 casualties.

Confederates surrender Vicksburg, Mississippi, to US forces under General Ulysses S. Grant. With the Confederate surrender of Port Hudson, Louisiana, five days later, the US regains control of the Mississippi River.

Operating under the provisions of the Enrollment Act, the federal government issues its first draft call.

Antidraft riots in New York City result in arson and 120 deaths, with many of the white rioters directing their violence toward the city's African Americans.

Secretary of War Edwin Stanton authorizes Governor Austin Blair "to raise one regiment of infantry to be composed of colored men."

September In the Civil War's second-bloodiest battle, Confederates turn back a Union offensive at Chickamauga, Georgia, resulting in over 34,000 casualties.

October	Lincoln calls for 300,000 additional volunteers for military service; areas not meeting their quota will be subject to the draft. Michigan's quota is set at 11,298.
November	At the dedication of a national cemetery in Pennsylvania, Abraham Lincoln delivers the Gettysburg Address.
	At the Third Battle of Chattanooga (Missionary Ridge), US forces under General Ulysses S. Grant defeat Braxton Bragg's Army of Tennessee, resulting in over 12,000 casualties.
December	Lincoln issues his Proclamation of Amnesty and Reconstruction and looks to Louisiana as an experimental ground for launching this policy.
	John Robertson, Michigan's adjutant general, reports that by the end of 1863, 53,749 Michiganians have entered federal service since the start of the Civil War.

1864

January	Governor Austin Blair again calls an extra session of the legislature to confront the challenges the war has imposed on the state.
February	Lincoln orders that 500,000 men be drafted on March 10, "crediting and deducting therefrom, so many as may have been enlisted or drafted into the service" before March 1.
	Michigan legislature passes the Soldiers' Vote Act, which authorizes Civil War soldiers to vote in elections regardless of whether they are in the state on an election day.
	Members of the 1st Michigan Colored Infantry are mustered into federal service in Detroit.
March	Lincoln calls for 500,000 additional volunteers for military service; areas not meeting their quota will be subject to the draft.
	Lincoln appoints Ulysses S. Grant as general-in-chief of the United States Army.
April	The US Senate passes the Thirteenth Amendment.
May	General Ulysses S. Grant moves the Army of the Potomac south of the Rapidan River, Virginia, and launches the Overland Campaign.

From Chattanooga, Tennessee, General William Tecumseh Sherman launches the Atlanta Campaign.

Iron miners in Marquette, employed by the Cleveland Iron Mining Company, strike for higher wages and shorter hours.

June   At their convention in Baltimore, Republicans renominate Abraham Lincoln and temporarily rename themselves the National Union Party.

After seven weeks, Grant's Overland Campaign ends with US forces laying siege to Petersburg, Virginia. The campaign results in nearly 90,000 casualties.

July   Lincoln calls for 500,000 additional volunteers for military service; areas not meeting their quota will be subject to the draft.

After defeating Union forces in Virginia's Shenandoah Valley, Confederate troops led by General Jubal Early invade Maryland, prevail at the Battle of Monocacy, and reach the northern suburbs of Washington, DC. Reinforced Union defenses of the capital persuade Early to retreat.

August   US forces under Admiral David Farragut close another Confederate port upon capturing Confederate fortifications at Mobile Bay.

At their convention in Chicago, Democrats nominate George McClellan.

September   Sherman's Atlanta Campaign ends with the Confederate surrender of Atlanta.

Confederate agents board the *Philo Parsons* in Detroit and commandeer the ship before jettisoning their plan to capture the USS *Michigan* and then liberate Confederate prisoners on Johnston's Island, Ohio.

October   Mounted Confederates launch an attack on St. Albans, Vermont, from Canada.

At the Battle of Cedar Creek, US troops led by General Philip Sheridan rout General Jubal Early's Confederates, thereby diminishing the Confederate presence in Virginia's Shenandoah Valley and eliminating the Confederate threat to Maryland, Pennsylvania, and Washington, DC.

November   Abraham Lincoln is reelected, winning 55 percent of the Michigan
               vote (counting soldiers' ballots). Republican Henry Crapo is
               elected governor.

               Leaving Atlanta, Sherman launches his March to the Sea.

December   In response to heightened fears stemming from the *Philo Parsons*
               hijacking and the attack on St. Albans, Secretary of State William
               Seward imposes passport controls on the US-Canadian border that
               remain in effect until March 1865.

               US troops under General George Thomas annihilate John
               Bell Hood's Confederate Army of Tennessee at the Battle of
               Nashville.

               Lincoln calls for 300,000 additional volunteers for military service;
               areas not meeting their quota will be subject to the draft.

               Sherman's army reaches Savannah, Georgia.

                                        1865

January   To protect the US against further Confederate incursions from
               Canada, the 30th Michigan Infantry is mustered into federal service
               along the Canadian border—Michigan's only Civil War regiment
               never to leave the state.

               The Michigan legislature votes to return Jacob Howard to the US
               Senate over former governor Austin Blair.

               The Michigan Supreme Court rules the Soldiers' Vote Act (1864)
               unconstitutional, thus invalidating Michigan soldiers' votes from
               the 1864 election. The Republican majorities in the Michigan leg-
               islature and the US House of Representatives, however, choose to
               ignore the court.

               The House of Representatives passes the Thirteenth Amendment
               and sends it to the states for ratification.

February   Michigan ratifies the Thirteenth Amendment.

March   Lincoln delivers his Second Inaugural and begins his second term.

April   After the Confederate defeat at the Battle of Five Forks, the
               Confederate defenses of Petersburg disintegrate, forcing the Con-
               federates to abandon Richmond. Seven days later, Robert E. Lee

surrenders the Army of Northern Virginia to Ulysses S. Grant at
Appomattox Court House, Virginia.

Abraham Lincoln is assassinated; Andrew Johnson becomes
president.

Joseph Johnston surrenders his forces to William Tecumseh Sherman
near Durham, North Carolina.

May On the run for six weeks since fleeing Richmond, Jefferson Davis is
captured by the 4th Michigan Cavalry near Irwinville, Georgia.

General Simon Bolivar Buckner, acting on behalf of General
E. Kirby Smith, surrenders the Confederate Army of the Trans-
Mississippi in New Orleans.

Rather than returning to the state, the Michigan Cavalry Brigade
is ordered to the West, where it establishes a stronger federal presence in the Nebraska, Dakota, and Utah Territories and campaigns
against the Sioux, Arapaho, Cheyenne, and Shoshone.

Andrew Johnson announces his Reconstruction Policy, which
grants amnesty to most former Confederates, except for large
property holders, high-ranking Confederate officials, and individuals who had taken an oath to support the US Constitution before
the war.

June Governor Henry H. Crapo issues a proclamation of welcome and
thanks to the returning Michigan troops.

Confederate General Stand Watie surrenders his forces in the
Indian Territory (present-day Oklahoma).

July Four individuals convicted in June of conspiring with John Wilkes
Booth to assassinate Abraham Lincoln are executed in Washington, DC.

November Mississippi and South Carolina pass their first Black Codes, which
other former Confederate states soon emulate. Black Codes force
freedpeople to stay on plantations and define their freedom to
retain many features of slavery.

December Ratification of the Thirteenth Amendment ends slavery in the
United States. By this time, slavery remains legal only in Delaware
and Kentucky.

1866

April   Andrew Johnson declares the "insurrection to be "at an end" in
            every state except Texas.

            Congress enacts the Civil Rights Act of 1866 over Andrew John-
            son's veto.

June   The 28th Michigan Infantry becomes Michigan's last Civil War unit
            to be discharged from federal service.

            Congress passes the Fourteenth Amendment and sends it to the
            states for ratification.

August   Andrew Johnson declares the "insurrection to be "at an end" in
            Texas.

October   Andrew Johnson personally campaigns against Republicans during
            the fall's congressional elections and makes an unprecedented
            whistle-stop tour through southern Michigan.

November   Voters reject Andrew Johnson's appeals and return Republicans
            to Congress, allowing Republicans to maintain their two-thirds
            supermajority necessary for overriding presidential vetoes.
            Henry H. Crapo is reelected governor, and Republicans win all six
            of Michigan's congressional seats.

1867

January   Michigan ratifies the Fourteenth Amendment.

March   Congress enacts, over Andrew Johnson's veto, the Reconstruc-
            tion Acts of 1867, placing most former Confederate states under
            military rule. States could reenter the Union after establishing
            governments based on universal male suffrage and ratifying the
            Fourteenth Amendment.

1868

February   After President Andrew Johnson violates the Tenure of Office Act,
            and following a lengthy series of battles with congressional Repub-
            licans regarding the course of Reconstruction, the US House of
            Representatives passes a resolution of impeachment for President
            Johnson and issues articles of impeachment the following month.

April	Michigan voters soundly reject a new state constitution.
May	The US Senate falls one vote short of the two-thirds vote necessary to remove President Andrew Johnson from office.
July	After ratification by three-fourths of the states, Secretary of State William Seward issues an official proclamation certifying the Fourteenth Amendment's ratification.
November	Ulysses S. Grant, a Republican, is elected president and wins 57 percent of Michigan's vote. Henry P. Baldwin, also a Republican, is elected governor.

1869

February	Congress passes the Fifteenth Amendment and sends it to the states for ratification.
March	Michigan ratifies the Fifteenth Amendment.

1870

February	The Fifteenth Amendment is ratified, prohibiting states from denying citizens the right to vote "on account of race, color, or previous condition of servitude."
April	For the first time, Michigan's African American voters cast ballots in township elections.
June	The United States census numbers Michigan's population at 1,184,059—a figure that includes, unlike the 1860 census, Native Americans "sustaining tribal relations."
November	Despite the Fifteenth Amendment's ratification in February, Michigan voters only narrowly approve an amendment to the state constitution recognizing African American male suffrage.
December	Michigan's railroad mileage totals 1,739 miles.

1871

April	Congress passes the Ku Klux Klan Act, rendering conspiracies to deprive citizens of their voting and other political rights crimes punishable by federal law.

1872

November | President Ulysses S. Grant is reelected and wins 63 percent of Michigan's vote. Republican John J. Bagley is elected governor.

1873

April | In *Slaughterhouse Cases,* the US Supreme Court narrows the scope of the Privileges or Immunities Clause of the Fourteenth Amendment, thus undermining the ability of the federal government to protect citizens' civil rights against state actions.

September | A financial panic launches an economic depression that persists through the remainder of the decade.

1874

November | Congressional elections favor Democrats, who, the following March, regain control of the US House of Representatives for the first time since 1859. Republicans remain dominant in Michigan, but Democrats make their best showing in two decades by capturing three of the state's nine congressional districts.

1875

January | The Michigan legislature selects Isaac Christiancy as US senator, thus defeating fellow Republican Zachariah Chandler.

March | President Ulysses S. Grant signs into law the Civil Rights Act of 1875, passed in the closing days of the 43rd Congress. The Act outlaws racial discrimination in public accommodations and transportation, and prohibits "race, color, or previous condition of servitude" being used to exclude individuals from federal jury service.

1876

March | In *United States v. Cruikshank,* the US Supreme Court rules that the Fourteenth Amendment provides no federal protections against actions committed by one person against another—including violence intended to prevent people from voting. People whose voting rights have been violated can only file their cases in state courts.

June   A combined force of Lakota, Northern Cheyenne, and Arapaho
              overwhelmingly defeat the 7th US Cavalry, led by Lt. Col. George
              Armstrong Custer, an occasional resident of Monroe, Michigan, at
              the Battle of the Little Bighorn.

November   The initial results of the presidential election show no clear win-
              ner. Democrat Samuel Tilden wins 51 percent of the popular vote
              and 184 electoral votes, with Republican Rutherford B. Hayes
              winning 48 percent of the popular vote and 165 electoral votes.
              Twenty electoral votes from South Carolina, Florida, Louisiana,
              and Oregon, however, remain disputed. Hayes wins 52 percent of
              the Michigan vote.

1877

March   After months of uncertainty, a congressional commission awards
              Hayes the twenty disputed electoral votes and the presidency. To
              secure their rivals' consent, Hayes and Republicans agree to Demo-
              cratic demands, including the restoration of conservative white
              rule in the South.

1879

February   The Michigan legislature votes to return Zachariah Chandler to
              the US Senate following Isaac Christiancy's resignation.

November   After giving a speech denouncing unrepentant Confederates and
              the continued violations of black Southerners' voting rights,
              Zachariah Chandler unexpectedly dies in Chicago.

1880

June   The United States census numbers Michigan's population at
              1,636,937.

December   Michigan becomes the leading iron-mining state in the Union, a
              position it maintains for two decades.

              Michigan's railroad mileage totals 3,823 miles.

1883

October   In *Civil Rights Cases,* the US Supreme Court declares the Civil
              Rights Act of 1875 to be unconstitutional, holding that Congress

lacks authority to ban discrimination in public accommodations and transportation.

1885

May
In response to the Supreme Court's decision in *Civil Rights Cases,* the Michigan legislature enacts a civil rights law designed to "protect all citizens in their civil rights."

1890

June
The United States census numbers Michigan's population at 2,093,890.

December
Michigan's railroad mileage totals 6,957 miles.

1891

January
A bill authorizing the federal government to ensure that congressional elections are conducted fairly—aimed at Southern states that widely violated African Americans' voting rights—fails in the US Senate after passing the House the previous July.

1893

December
At more than 21,000, Michigan's Grand Army of the Republic reaches its peak membership.

1896

May
In *Plessy v. Ferguson,* the US Supreme Court upholds the constitutionality of state racial segregation laws for public facilities.

1898

April
In *Williams v. Mississippi,* the US Supreme Court upholds the constitutionality of a state requiring voters to pass a literacy test and pay poll taxes, opening the door to further disfranchisement of African American and poor white voters across the South.

1900

June
The United States census numbers Michigan's population at 2,420,982.

December   Michigan's railroad mileage totals 7,946 miles (as of 2010, Michigan's railroad mileage had declined to 3,634 miles).

1904

March   The US Commissioner of Pensions issues Order 78, which declares old age an "infirmity" and provides that all Union veterans, aged sixty-two or older, would be eligible to receive a federal pension.

Discussion Questions

CHAPTER 1: MICHIGAN, SLAVERY, AND THE COMING OF THE CIVIL WAR

1. Why did many fugitives from slavery find that the road to freedom led them through Michigan?

2. Why did some white Michiganians oppose slavery? Why did black Michiganians oppose slavery?

3. For whom did Kinsley Bingham believe federal territories were reserved?

4. On what topic(s) did Michigan Republicans focus in their 1854 platform?

5. Would George DeBaptiste's plan have been more effective than John Brown's in overthrowing slavery?

6. Why did Michigan Republicans enact personal liberty laws when they took control of the legislature?

7. Besides their opposition to slavery, what other issues did early Republicans embrace when seeking support from Michigan's voters?

8. Did Stephen Douglas and Michigan Democrats hold proslavery beliefs?

9. How did Michigan's Republicans and Democrats differ as they prepared to vote in 1860?

CHAPTER 2: THE SECESSION CRISIS

1. Why did Michigan's Republicans reject compromise during the secession crisis?

2. How did Michigan Democrats explain the secession crisis?

3. Discuss the role played by Michigan's state government during the secession crisis.

CHAPTER 3: SHIFTING MICHIGAN TO A WAR FOOTING

1. How did Michiganians respond to the firing on Fort Sumter?

2. How did officers in Michigan's regiments receive their commissions? Explain how their method of selection might improve—or diminish—their effectiveness as officers.

3.   Why did the recruitment of soldiers become more difficult in 1862?

CHAPTER 4: THE SOLDIER'S LIFE

1.   How did Civil War soldiers spend their time when they were not engaged in combat?

2.   What did Civil War armies initially do with prisoners of war? Why did this system break down?

3.   Why did some Michiganians discourage men from enlisting?

4.   How did life as a soldier change people?

5.   How did soldiers' experiences affect their perceptions of civilians?

6.   How did the strains of war create tensions between enlisted men and officers?

7.   What role did regimental daughters play in the Civil War? How did responsibilities differ from those of other women near the Civil War battlefront?

8.   How can we account for the willingness of the members of the 1st Michigan Colored Regiment (also known as the 102nd US Colored Regiment) to continue fighting despite being wounded?

CHAPTER 5: CONSCRIPTION, COMMUTATION, AND DISSENT

1.   What incentives did local, state, and federal governments offer to encourage enlistment?

2.   How did Michiganians respond to conscription?

3.   Why did white Detroiters violently riot against the city's black residents in 1863?

4.   What were commutation fees? How did soldiers react to commutation fees?

5.   Why did some Michiganians resist serving in the military? Why did the federal government arrest some civilians during the Civil War?

CHAPTER 6: CIVILIANS CONFRONT THE WAR

1.   How did Michiganians explain the Union army's failure to defeat the Confederate army in 1861?

2.   How could some people financially profit from the Civil War?

3.   What effect did the Civil War have on Michigan's copper mines?

4. How did the Civil War affect Michigan's copper and iron miners?

5. Why were conditions in Civil War hospitals so desperate?

6. What was the United States Sanitary Commission? How did its Michigan auxiliaries advance the Sanitary Commission's work?

7. Did the Civil War foster racism among whites? Or did the Civil War serve to diminish racism?

8. How did Michigan's women demonstrate their support for the war effort? How effective were those actions?

9. Did women's view of the Civil War differ from men's?

10. Discuss the economic circumstances faced by soldiers' families while their fathers and sons were at the war front. How did families make ends meet when their financial providers were in uniform and far away?

11. Discuss the effect that the Civil War had on Michigan's economy.

12. Why were some Michiganians terrified by Canada during the Civil War?

CHAPTER 7: MICHIGAN'S WARTIME POLITICS

1. Did Michigan's Democrats and Republicans regard one another as legitimate adversaries? Or did each party seek the defeat and elimination of the other?

2. Why did Michigan's Republicans allege that many of the state's Democrats embraced treason?

3. How did Civil War–era Michiganians view Abraham Lincoln?

4. How did Michigan's Republicans and Democrats differ as they prepared to vote in 1864?

5. Were Michigan's Civil War Democrats victims of Republicans' aggressive use of patriotism?

CHAPTER 8: THE CIVIL WAR CHANGES MICHIGANIANS' RELATIONSHIP TO SLAVERY

1. Why did some Michiganians welcome emancipation during the Civil War? Who was most likely to favor emancipation?

2. Why did some Michiganians oppose emancipation? Who was most likely to oppose emancipation?

3. What uncertainties did some Michiganians express regarding emancipation? Did these uncertainties always result in outright opposition to emancipation?

4. How did white Michigan soldiers respond to the enlistment of African American soldiers?

5. How did soldiers interpret the differences between the world they knew in Michigan and the world they witnessed in the South?

CHAPTER 9: THE CIVIL WAR'S END AND RECONSTRUCTION

1. How did Michigan soldiers respond to Abraham Lincoln's assassination?

2. What elements of Benjamin Pritchard's report appear in the cartoon depicting Jefferson Davis's capture? What elements of Pritchard's report does the cartoonist omit?

3. How could the 4th Michigan Cavalry convincingly depict themselves as Confederates to Georgians?

4. How did Michigan soldiers respond to continued military service after the Confederacy's surrender? Why did the army require their continued service?

5. To what degree did Republicans and Democrats anticipate the challenges presented by emancipation and Reconstruction?

6. How did Michigan's Democrats and Republicans differ regarding Reconstruction policy?

7. In 1863, Frederick Douglass declared that once an African American man wore a soldier's uniform in defense of his country, "there is no power on earth . . . which can deny that he has earned the right of citizenship in the United States." Did Douglass's assessment in 1863 predict the course of African American rights in Michigan during Reconstruction?

8. How did the passage of time affect the way veterans remembered the Civil War?

9. Who received Civil War pensions? How could a woman receive a Civil War pension?

Notes

PREFACE

1. Ronald P. Formisano, *The Birth of Mass Political Parties: Michigan, 1827–1861* (Princeton: Princeton University Press, 1971), 60–71; Martin J. Hershock, *The Paradox of Progress: Economic Change, Individual Enterprise, and Political Culture in Michigan, 1837–1878* (Athens: Ohio University Press, 2003); Martin J. Hershock, "'Free Commoners by Law': Tradition, Transition, and the Closing of the Range in Antebellum Michigan," *Michigan Historical Review* 29 (Fall 2003): 97–123; John W. Quist, "An Occasionally Dry State Surrounded by Water: Temperance and Prohibition in Antebellum Michigan," in *The History of Michigan Law*, ed. Paul Finkelman and Martin J. Hershock (Athens: Ohio University Press, 2006), 61–82; Willis F. Dunbar and George S. May, *Michigan: A History of the Wolverine State*, rev. ed. (Grand Rapids: William B. Eerdmans, 1980), 281–82.

2. See, for example, Stephen Symonds Foster, *The Brotherhood of Thieves: Or, A True Picture of the American Church and Clergy* (Boston: Anti-Slavery Office, 1844), 8, 39, 69.

INTRODUCTION

1. The 1860 federal census included 6,172 "civilized" Indians in its enumeration of the state population of 749,113. Not included in this total were 7,777 additional Indians "not enumerated in the Eighth Census and retaining their tribal character." By including this second group of indigenous people we can revise the census total upward to 756,890, and count 13,949 Indians living in Michigan in 1860 (or 1.8 percent of the state's population). *Population of the United States in 1860; Compiled from the Original Returns of the Eighth Census* (Washington, DC: Government Printing Office, 1864), 597, 605.

2. Nationwide, 80.2 percent of the 1860 population lived in rural settings, while in the free states, the figure stood at 74.1 percent. *Historical Statistics of the United States: Colonial Times to 1970* (Washington, DC: U.S. Department of Commerce, 1975), 24–37.

3. *Statistics of the United States, (Including Mortality, Property, &c.,) in 1860; Compiled from the Original Returns and Being the Final Exhibit of the Eighth Census* (Washington, DC: Government Printing Office, 1866), 333.

4. Gregory S. Rose, "South Central Michigan Yankees," *Michigan History* 70 (March–April 1986): 32–39; Morris C. Taber, "New England Influence in South Central Michigan," *Michigan History* 45 (December 1961): 305–36.

5. Paul Finkelman, *Slavery and the Founders: Race and Slavery in the Age of Jefferson* (Armonk, NY: M. E. Sharpe, 1996), 34–79; David G. Chardavoyne, "The Northwest Ordinance in Michigan's Territorial Heritage," in *The History of Michigan Law*, ed. Paul Finkelman and Martin J. Hershock (Athens: Ohio University Press, 2006), 19–22; Andrew R. L. Cayton and Peter S. Onuf, *The Midwest and the Nation: Rethinking the History of an American Region* (Bloomington: Indiana University Press, 1990), 15–17.

6. Chardavoyne, "Northwest Ordinance," 19–22; Roy E. Finkenbine, "A Beacon of Liberty on the Great Lakes: Race, Slavery, and the Law in Antebellum Michigan," in Finkelman and Hershock, *History of Michigan Law*, 87. The 1820 federal census enumerated no slaves in the territory. *Abstract of the Returns of the Fifth Census* (Washington, DC: Duff Green, 1832), 42; J. D. B. DeBow, *Statistical View of the United States . . . Being a Compendium of the Seventh Census* (Washington, DC: Beverly Tucker, 1854), 82.

7. Ronald P. Formisano, "The Edge of Caste: Colored Suffrage in Michigan, 1827–1861," *Michigan History* 56 (Spring 1972): 19–41. Formisano notes that black males occasionally cast ballots in some locales, 27, 36.

8. David N. Katzman, *Before the Ghetto: Black Detroit in the Nineteenth Century* (Urbana: University of Illinois Press, 1973), 27–32.

9. Reinhard O. Johnson, *The Liberty Party, 1840–1848: Antislavery Third-Party Politics in the United States* (Baton Rouge: Louisiana State University Press, 2009), 307–12; John W. Quist, "'The Great Majority of Our Subscribers Are Farmers': The Michigan Abolitionist Constituency of the 1840s," *Journal of the Early Republic* 14 (Fall 1994): 325–58.

CHAPTER 1: MICHIGAN, SLAVERY, AND THE
COMING OF THE CIVIL WAR

1. *True Democrat* (Ann Arbor), September 28, 1848.

2. William E. Gienapp, *The Origins of the Republican Party, 1852–1856* (New York: Oxford University Press, 1987); Martin J. Hershock, *The Paradox of Progress: Economic Change, Individual Enterprise, and Political Culture in Michigan, 1837–1878* (Athens: Ohio University Press, 2003); William Stocking, *Under the Oaks: Commemorating the Fiftieth Anniversary of the Founding of the Republican Party, at Jackson, Michigan, July 6, 1854* (Detroit: Detroit Tribune, 1904), 22–56; *Michigan Argus* (Ann Arbor), May 2, 1856.

3. Regarding abolitionism in Michigan, see John W. Quist, "The Great Majority of Our Subscribers Are Farmers," *Journal of the Early Republic* 14 (Fall 1994): 325–58; Quist, *Restless Visionaries: The Social Roots of Antebellum Reform in Alabama and Michigan* (Baton Rouge: Louisiana State University Press, 1998), 354–461.

4. *Detroit Free Press*, January 7, 1860; *Constantine Mercury and St. Joseph County Advertiser*, January 12, 1860; *Acts of the Legislature of the State of Michigan, Passed at the Regular Session of 1859* (Lansing: Hosmer and Kerr, 1859), 526–27. Under the 1859 law's provisions, slaveholders could face ten years in prison and a $1,000 fine for entering the state. See Caleb Cushing's condemnation of the Michigan law in *Liberator* (Boston), April 13, 1860.

5. Seymour B. Treadwell to Nathan M. Thomas, August 21, 1841, Nathan Macy Thomas Papers, Bentley Historical Library, University of Michigan.

6. *Documents Accompanying the Journal of the House of Representatives of the State of Michigan at the Biennial Session of 1861* (Lansing: Hosmer and Kerr, 1861), Document 16; *Journal of the House of Representatives of the State of Michigan, 1861, Part II* (Lansing: Hosmer and Kerr, 1861), 1300–1301.

7. Frederick Douglass may be responsible for historians' ignoring this March 12, 1859, meeting, as he says nothing about it in his autobiography but discusses at length another meeting, five months later, in Chambersburg, Pennsylvania. *Life and Times*

of Frederick Douglass, from 1817 to 1882, Written by Himself (London: Christian Age Office, 1882), 236–81. The Detroit meeting is nonetheless recounted in Richard J. Hinton, *John Brown and His Men* (New York: Funk and Wagnalls, 1894), 227–28; Silas Farmer, *The History of Detroit and Michigan* (Detroit: Silas Farmer, 1884), 347–48; O. B. Curtis, *Of The Twenty-Fourth of The Iron Brigade, Known as Detroit And Wayne County Regiment* (Detroit: Winn & Hammond, 1891), 15–16; Clarence Monroe Burton, William Stocking, and Gordon K. Miller, *The City of Detroit, Michigan, 1701–1922* (Detroit: S. J. Clarke, 1922), 482–84.

8. The correct date for this meeting is March 12, 1859. John Kagi to Charles Plummer Tidd, March 13, 1859, in *Governor's Message and Reports of the Public Officers of the State, of the Boards of Directors, and of the Visitors, Superintendents, and Other Agents of Public Institutions or Interests of Virginia* (Richmond: William F. Ritchie, 1859), 113–14.

9. *Detroit Daily Advertiser,* March 15, 1859, fixed the number of fugitives traveling to Canada at twelve (including the infant John Brown).

10. For a report of Douglass's lecture, see *Detroit Free Press,* March 13, 1859. Brown recorded in his diary that he wrote to Douglass on March 10, 1859, suggesting that the two planned to meet in Detroit. Franklin B. Sanborn, *Life and Letters of John Brown* (Boston: Roberts Brothers, 1891), 519.

11. Responding to reports of his skeptical response to Brown's plan on this occasion, Douglass later informed Richard Hinton "nothing of the sort occurred." Hinton, *John Brown and His Men,* 227–28.

12. A leader among Detroit's African Americans, George DeBaptiste had once worked as a White House steward for President William Henry Harrison and "was an adventurous agent of the underground railroad, and it is alleged that many a former slave owes his freedom to Geo. DeBaptiste's personal efforts" (*Detroit Free Press,* February 23, 1875). In early 1860 Senator James M. Mason of Virginia issued a summons for DeBaptiste to appear before a Senate committee investigating the Harpers Ferry raid. When he learned about DeBaptiste's race, however, Mason instructed the US Marshal in Detroit to withhold the summons, as the Senate committee did not want to interview African Americans and "preferred to ignore any role that blacks might have played" at Harpers Ferry. Benjamin Quarles, *Allies for Freedom: Blacks and John Brown* (1974; repr., Boston: Da Capo, 2001), 157–58.

13. John Brown Jr. returned to Detroit in August 1859 to keep Brown's allies informed of developments, to recruit, and to raise money. John Brown Jr. to John Henry Kagi, August 27, 1859, in *Governor's Message and Reports . . . of Virginia,* 121–23.

14. Osborne P. Anderson, who joined Brown in the Harpers Ferry raid, and survived it, lived in Chatham during the 1850s, but never mentions his recruitment in his memoir, *A Voice from Harper's Ferry: A Narrative of Events at Harper's Ferry; with Incidents Prior and Subsequent to Its Capture by Captain Brown and His Men* (Boston, 1861). The evidence, however, indicates that Anderson enlisted under Brown in Chatham in May 1858. Stephen B. Oates, *To Purge This Land with Blood: A Biography of John Brown,* 2nd ed. (Amherst: University of Massachusetts Press, 1984), 243, 246.

15. "Foster" may be a reference to David J. Gue's decision to inform John B. Floyd, the US Secretary of War, about Brown's plans to attack Harpers Ferry. Oates, *To Purge This Land with Blood,* 284–85.

16. Douglas served as an associate justice on the Illinois Supreme Court from 1841 to 1843. Throughout his subsequent political career, people often referred to him as "Judge Douglas." Robert W. Johannsen, *Stephen A. Douglas* (New York: Oxford University Press, 1973), 111.

17. Regarding two of those speeches, see *Kalamazoo Gazette,* October 19, 1860; *Michigan Argus* (Ann Arbor), October 19, 1860.

18. Organized locally across the North, the "Wide Awakes" were young Republicans, often costumed in quasi-military attire, who assembled for political rallies during the 1860 presidential campaign. In nearby Buchanan, Michigan, one correspondent complained of local Wide Awakes who "go out every night or two, and when passing a democrat's house, late at night," make "groaning and drunken grunts" that were "very annoying to all, and every decent man in town." Jon Grinspan, "'Young Men for War': The Wide Awakes and Lincoln's 1860 Presidential Campaign," *Journal of American History* 96 (September 2009): 357–78; *Niles Republican,* October 6, 1860.

19. William Seward, a New York Republican senator who lost the Republican nomination to Abraham Lincoln but afterward campaigned for Lincoln. Seward later served as Lincoln's secretary of state.

CHAPTER 2: THE SECESSION CRISIS

1. *Acts of the Legislature of the State of Michigan, Passed at the Regular and Extra Sessions of 1861* (Lansing: John A. Kerr, 1861), 545–47.

2. Roy P. Basler, et al., eds., *The Collected Works of Abraham Lincoln* (New Brunswick, NJ: Rutgers University Press, 1953), 4:332; *The War of the Rebellion: A Compilation of the Official Records of the Union and Confederate Armies,* ser. 3, vol. 1 (Washington, DC: Government Printing Office, 1899), 68–69.

3. E. B. Long with Barbara Long, *The Civil War Day by Day: An Almanac, 1861–1865* (New York: Doubleday, 1971), 705–6.

4. *Liberator* (Boston), February 15, 1861; John W. Quist, *Restless Visionaries: The Social Roots of Antebellum Reform in Alabama and Michigan* (Baton Rouge: Louisiana State University Press, 1998), 421–22.

5. *New York Times,* February 8, 1861; Robert Gray Gunderson, *Old Gentleman's Convention: The Washington Peace Conference of 1861* (Madison: University of Wisconsin Press, 1961), ix, 72–74, 90.

6. Gunderson, *Old Gentleman's Convention,* 72–74.

7. Kinsley S. Bingham, Michigan's junior senator in 1861, served as Michigan's governor from 1855 to 1859.

CHAPTER 3: SHIFTING MICHIGAN TO A WAR FOOTING

1. *Wolverine Citizen* (Flint), April 20, 1861; *St. Joseph Traveler,* May 1, 1861.

2. James Fry, *Final Report Made to the Secretary of War, by the Provost Marshal General, of the Operations of the Bureau of the Provost Marshal General of the U.S., from the Commencement of the Business of the Bureau, March 17, 1863, to March 17, 1866* (Washington, DC: Government Printing Office, 1866), 6.

3. J. G. Randall and David Donald, *The Civil War and Reconstruction,* 2nd ed. (Boston: D. C. Heath, 1961), 311–13.

4. *The War of the Rebellion: A Compilation of the Official Records of the Union and Confederate Armies,* ser. 3, vol. 1 (Washington, DC: Government Printing Office, 1899), 68–69; *Acts of the Legislature of the State of Michigan, Passed at the Regular and Extra Sessions of 1861* (Lansing: John A. Kerr, 1861), 545; John Robertson, comp., *Michigan in the War,* rev. ed. (Lansing: W. S. George, 1882), 165.

5. Frank B. Woodford, *Father Abraham's Children: Michigan Episodes in the Civil War* (Detroit: Wayne State University Press, 1961), 18–19.

6. Robertson, *Michigan in the War,* 22.

7. Ibid., 17–21.

8. *Acts of the Legislature of the State of Michigan . . . 1861,* 595, 605–9.

9. *Journal of the House of Representatives of the State of Michigan, 1861, Part II* (Lansing: Hosmer and Kerr, 1861), Joint Doc. No. 1, 7.

10. Robertson, *Michigan in the War,* 740–45. Robertson counts seventeen Michigan companies of infantry and cavalry either offering their services to the states of Missouri, Illinois, New York, or Ohio in 1861 or being recruited into US sharpshooter regiments.

11. Ibid., 23–24, 747–48.

12. The 1st Michigan Infantry Regiment, commanded by Colonel Orlando B. Willcox, secured Alexandria, Virginia, from Confederate troops on May 24, 1861. Contrary to the writer's assertion, though, Willcox allowed Captain Mottrom Dulany Ball of the Confederate army to keep his sword. Robert Garth Scott, ed., *Forgotten Valor: The Memoirs, Journals, and Civil War Letters of Orlando B. Willcox* (Kent, OH: Kent State University Press, 1999), 264–66.

13. William Betts to Irving Metcalf, April 24, 1861, Doris L. King Family Papers, Clarke Historical Library, Central Michigan University; *Record of Service of Michigan Volunteers in the Civil War, 1861–1865,* 46 vols. (Kalamazoo: Ihling Bros. and Everard, 1905), 11: 64. Metcalf's name does not appear in the annals of Michigan's ninety-day regiment (*Record of Service of Michigan Volunteers,* vol. 1).

CHAPTER 4: THE SOLDIER'S LIFE

1. Regarding the numbers who served in the Union army, see E. B. Long with Barbara Long, *The Civil War Day by Day: An Almanac, 1861–65* (Garden City, NY: Doubleday, 1971), 705–6; for those who served in the regular army, see Frederick Phisterer, *Statistical Record of the Armies of the United States* (New York: Charles Scribner's Sons, 1883), 11. Coleman C. Vaughan, *Alphabetical General Index to Public Library Sets of 85,271 Names of Michigan Soldiers and Sailors* (Lansing: Wynkoop Hallenbeck Crawford, 1915), 5, gives the total number of Michiganians who served as 92,220. John Robertson, *Michigan in the War,* rev. ed. (Lansing: W. S. George, 1882), 68–69, calculates the number to be 90,747. Frederick H. Dyer, *A Compendium of the War of the Rebellion* (Des Moines: Dyer, 1908), 11, places Michigan's troop total at 87,364 but presumably did not count the 3,000 to 4,000 Michiganians who served in a federal army unit or in units from other states. See Robertson, *Michigan in the War,* 745; *Record of Service of Michigan Volunteers in the Civil War, 1861–1865,* vol. 45 (Kalamazoo: Ihling Bros. and Everard, 1905).

2. Eventually all males between 18 and 50 were eligible for the Union draft, with sizable numbers of males under 18 enlisting after lying about their age. With the median

age of Union soldiers being 23.5 and with the great majority of men in the military being under 30, though, the figure of 44 percent understates the proportion of Michigan men in the age range that would have been most likely to have served. Regarding the age of eligibility for the Union draft, and the median age of Civil War soldiers, see James W. Geary, *We Need Men: The Union Draft in the Civil War* (DeKalb: Northern Illinois University Press, 1991), 5; James M. McPherson, *For Cause and Comrades: Why Men Fought in the Civil War* (New York: Oxford University Press, 1997), v.

3. Robertson, *Michigan in the War*, 751, puts the number at 14,855. Dyer, *Compendium of the War of the Rebellion*, 11, lists 14,753.

4. *Record of Service of Michigan Volunteers in the Civil War* lists the numbers "discharged for disability" for all of the state's units.

5. Robertson, *Michigan in the War*, 745, reports that 598 Michiganians served in the navy, while Dyer, *Compendium of the War of the Rebellion*, 11, lists 498. *Record of Service of Michigan Volunteers in the Civil War*, 45:315–24, identifies only 144 Michiganians who served in the navy.

6. These thirty-five volunteer infantry regiments included the regiments numbered one through thirty, the Michigan Colored Regiment (later renamed the 102nd U.S. Colored Infantry Regiment), the three-month regiment of 1861 (also sometimes called the Michigan 1st), and the reorganized regiments of the 3rd, 4th, and 11th Michigan regiments. Robertson, *Michigan in the War*, 747–48.

7. Several artillery batteries—L, M, N, and O—had no combat-related deaths.

8. McPherson, *For Cause and Comrades*; Gary W. Gallagher, *The Union War* (Cambridge, MA: Harvard University Press, 2011); Chandra Manning, *What This Cruel War Was Over: Soldiers, Slavery, and the Civil War* (New York: Random House, 2008); Gerald F. Linderman, *Embattled Courage: The Experience of Combat in the American Civil War* (New York: Free Press, 1987); Michael Fellman, Lesley J. Gordon, and Daniel E. Sutherland, *This Terrible War: The Civil War and Its Aftermath* (New York: Longman, 2003), 88, 177–81.

9. James M. McPherson, *Ordeal by Fire: The Civil War and Reconstruction*, 3rd ed. (New York: McGraw Hill, 2001), 181, 187–88.

10. Dyer, *Compendium of the War of the Rebellion*, 582; Robertson, *Michigan in the War*, 995–1001.

11. Brian Matthew Jordan, *Marching Home: Union Veterans and Their Unending Civil War* (New York: W. W. Norton, 2014); Linderman, *Embattled Courage*, 240–97.

12. Robertson, *Michigan in the War*, 747–48.

13. Regarding King's Life, see *Portrait and Biographical Album of St. Joseph County, Michigan* (Chicago: Chapman, 1889), 266–69, and *News Reporter* (Three Rivers), October 15, 1903.

14. Sarah Coleman to David Coleman, August 9, 1863, Jack B. and Barbara Riegel Collection, Archives and Regional History Collection, Western Michigan University.

15. Delos Lake to Calvin Lake, February 12, February 28, 1864, Huntington Library, San Marino, California.

16. Ulysses S. Grant, *Personal Memoirs of U. S. Grant*, vol. 1 (New York: Charles L. Webster, 1885), 368.

17. *Adrian Watchtower*, December 24, 1862; *Record of Service of Michigan Volunteers in the Civil War, 1861–65*, 4:121.

18. Alan T. Nolan, *The Iron Brigade: A Military History,* 4th ed. (Bloomington: Indiana University Press, 1994), 256.

19. Henry Clay Pate led Missouri militia that surrendered to John Brown at the Battle of Black Jack, Kansas Territory, on June 2, 1856. Stephen B. Oates, *To Purge This Land with Blood: A Biography of John Brown,* 2nd ed. (Amherst: University of Massachusetts Press, 1984), 152–54.

20. Historians disagree on whether Huff shot Stuart. Edward G. Longacre, *Custer and His Wolverines: The Michigan Cavalry Brigade, 1861–1865* (Conshohocken, PA: Combined Publishing, 1997), 214; Jeffry D. Wert, *Cavalryman of the Lost Cause: A Biography of J. E. B. Stuart* (New York: Simon and Schuster, 2008), 357.

21. Stephen W. Sears, ed., *For Country, Cause and Leader: The Civil War Journal of Charles B. Haydon* (New York: Ticknor and Fields, 1993), 313; *Constantine Mercury and Advertiser,* April 2, 1863.

22. Gerald F. Linderman, *Embattled Courage: The Experience of Combat in the American Civil War* (New York: Free Press, 1987), 36–37, 229.

23. Regarding Sarah Emma Edmonds, see the modern edition of her narrative, *Memoirs of a Soldier, Nurse, and Spy: A Woman's Adventure in the Union Army,* ed. Elizabeth D. Leonard (DeKalb: Northern Illinois University Press, 1999); Elizabeth D. Leonard, *All the Daring of the Solider: Women of the Civil War Armies* (New York: Norton, 1999), 170–85; Laura Leedy Gansler, *The Mysterious Thompson: The Double Life of Sarah Emma Edmonds, Civil War Soldier* (New York: Free Press, 2005); and Robertson, *Michigan in the War,* 205. Robertson also noted Frank Martin's service (ibid., 461–62). For more on Frank Martin and Annie Lillybridge, see Leonard, *All the Daring,* 211–12, 224.

24. Probably George W. Woodward of Wright, Michigan, who ended the war as a brevet major. Regarding Woodward and the other officers mentioned in this document, see Robertson, *Michigan in the War,* 412.

25. Leonard, *All the Daring of the Soldier,* 113.

26. 18 *Congressional Record,* 49th Congress, 2d Session (1887), 2002.

27. Roy P. Basler, ed., *The Collected Works of Abraham Lincoln* (New Brunswick, NJ: Rutgers University Press, 1953), 6:28–31.

28. James M. McPherson, *The Negro's Civil War: How American Negroes Felt and Acted during the War for the Union* (New York: Pantheon, 1965), 196, 202.

29. John Robertson, *Michigan in the War,* rev. ed. (Lansing: W. S. George, 1882), 488.

30. Regarding the varying figures for the numbers within this regiment, see Michael O. Smith, "Raising a Black Regiment in Michigan: Adversity and Triumph," *Michigan Historical Review* 16 (Fall 1990): 37; *Record First Michigan Colored Infantry Civil War, 1861–1865,* vol. 46 of *Record of Service of Michigan Volunteers in the Civil War, 1861–1865* (Kalamazoo: Ihling Bros. and Everard, 1905), 4; Norman McRae, *Negroes in Michigan during the Civil War* (Lansing: Michigan Civil War Centennial Observance Commission, 1966), 90–122. Analysis of the mustering rolls indicates that over one thousand of the regiment's members were born in the slave states, with many of these individuals living in Canada when the Civil War began. McRae, *Negroes in Michigan,* 47.

31. *Record First Michigan Colored Infantry Civil War, 1861–1865,* 3–4; Smith, "Raising a Black Regiment," 22–41; McRae, *Negroes in Michigan,* 65–76.

32. Laurence M. Hauptman, *Between Two Fires: American Indians in the Civil War* (New York: Free Press, 1995), 126.

33. Ibid., 125–44; Raymond J. Herek, *These Men Have Seen Hard Service: The First Michigan Sharpshooters in the Civil War* (Detroit: Wayne State University Press, 1998), 24–25, 34–37.

CHAPTER 5: CONSCRIPTION, COMMUTATION, AND DISSENT

1. James Fry, *Final Report Made to the Secretary of War, by the Provost Marshal General, of the Operations of the Bureau of the Provost Marshal General of the U.S., from the Commencement of the Business of the Bureau, March 17, 1863, to March 17, 1866* (Washington, DC: Government Printing Office, 1866), 84–87.

2. *Governor's Message to the Legislature of the State of Michigan, in Session, January 7, 1863* (Lansing: John A. Kerr, 1863), 17–18.

3. *Governor's Message to the Legislature of the State of Michigan, in Session, January 19, 1864* (Lansing: John A. Kerr, 1864), 8–9; *Acts of the Legislature of the State of Michigan, Passed at the Regular Session of 1863* (Lansing: John A. Kerr, 1863), 60–61; *Acts of the Legislature of the State of Michigan, Passed at the Extra Session of 1864* (Lansing: John A. Kerr, 1864), 53–61, 64.

4. John Robertson, *Michigan in the War*, rev. ed. (Lansing: W. S. George, 1882), 41–42.

5. *The Statutes at Large, Treaties, and Proclamations of the United States of America from December 5, 1859 to March 3, 1863* (Boston: Little, Brown, 1863), 12:731–37.

6. Fry, *Final Report*, 174–212.

7. James W. Geary, *We Need Men: The Union Draft in the Civil War* (DeKalb: Northern Illinois University Press, 1991), 144–49; Eugene Converse Murdock, *One Million Men: The Civil War Draft in the North* (Madison: State Historical Society of Wisconsin, 1971), 7.

8. Regarding the duties of provost marshals, who reported to the Provost Marshal General, James Fry, in Washington, see *Statutes at Large*, 12:731–37; *The War of the Rebellion: A Compilation of the Official Records of the Union and Confederate Armies*, ser. 3, vol. 3 (Washington, DC: Government Printing Office, 1899), 125–44; Geary, *We Need Men*, 68–77; Eugene Converse Murdock, *Patriotism Limited, 1862–1865: The Civil War Draft and Bounty System* (Kent, OH: Kent State University Press, 1967), 8–15. Michigan had six provost marshals, each of whom administered a distinct enrollment district. Robertson, *Michigan in the War*, 43.

9. Florence McKinnon Gwinn, *Pioneer History of Huron County, Michigan* (Bad Axe, MI: Huron County Pioneer and Historical Society, 1922), 51; Charles Bogue to Bogue Family (in Branch County), March 19, 1863, Anson Bogue to Bogue Family, November 8, 1863, May 15, 1864, October 23, 1864, Anson Bogue to James Bogue, February 12, 1865, Anson and Charles Bogue to Bogue Family, April 28, 1865, May 21, 1865, Bogue Family Papers, Bentley Historical Library, University of Michigan; Robin W. Winks, *Canada and the United States: The Civil War Years*, 4th ed. (Montreal and Kingston: McGill-Queen's University Press, 2002), 202–5; Paul Taylor, *"Old Slow Town": Detroit during the Civil War* (Detroit: Wayne State University Press, 2013), 84–85.

10. Mark E. Neely Jr., *The Fate of Liberty: Abraham Lincoln and Civil Liberties* (New York: Oxford University Press, 1991), 233.

11. John C. Schneider, "Detroit and the Problem of Disorder: The Riot of 1863," *Michigan History* 58 (Spring 1974): 5–24.

12. The federal government postponed this draft, and it did not occur until April 1864. Fry, *Final Report,* 39–42.

13. *Detroit Advertiser and Tribune,* March 25, 1865.

14. Frank L. Klement, "The Hopkins Hoax and Golden Circle Rumors in Michigan: 1861–1862," *Michigan History* 47 (March 1963): 1–14.

CHAPTER 6: CIVILIANS CONFRONT THE WAR

1. Robert Spiro, "History of the Michigan Soldiers' Aid Society, 1861–1865" (PhD diss., University of Michigan, 1959), 39.

2. *Acts of the Legislature of the State of Michigan Passed at the Regular and Extra Sessions of 1861* (Lansing: John A. Kerr, 1861), 602–4.

3. Terry Reynolds, "'Destined to Produce [a] . . . Revolution': Michigan's Iron Ore Industry in the Civil War," *Michigan Historical Review* 39 (Fall 2013): 21–49; *Manufacturers of the United States in 1860; Compiled from the Original Returns of the Eighth Census* (Washington, DC: Government Printing Office, 1865), 275; *Census and Statistics of the State of Michigan, 1864* (Lansing: John A. Kerr, 1865), 615; Martin J. Hershock, *The Paradox of Progress: Economic Change, Individual Enterprise, and the Political Culture in Michigan, 1837–1878* (Athens: Ohio University Press, 2003), 194–96.

4. William B. Gates Jr., *Michigan Copper and Boston Dollars: An Economic History of the Michigan Copper Mining Industry* (Cambridge, MA: Harvard University Press, 1951), 1, 197, 203, 208.

5. Reynolds, "'Destined to Produce.'"

6. Albert A. Blum, "Guns, Grain, and Iron Ore," *Michigan History* 69 (May/June 1985): 13–20.

7. Gates, *Michigan Copper and Boston Dollars;* O. W. Robinson, "Recollections of Civil War Conditions in the Copper Country," *Michigan History* 3 (October 1919): 598–609.

8. John Robertson, *Michigan in the War,* rev. ed. (Lansing: W. S. George, 1882), 22–23.

9. James D. Richardson, ed., *A Compilation of the Messages and Papers of the Presidents, 1789–1897,* 10 vols. (Washington, DC: Government Printing Office, 1898), 2:590.

10. John Strong Newberry, *The U.S. Sanitary Commission in the Valley of the Mississippi during the War of the Rebellion, 1861–1866* (Cleveland: Fairbanks, Benedict, 1871), 113, 243–44.

11. Spiro, "History of the Michigan Soldiers' Aid Society," 323–30.

12. Regarding Lois Bryan Adams, see Evelyn Leasher, ed., *Letter from Washington, 1863–65* (Detroit: Wayne State University Press, 1999); Leasher, "'L' was for Woman," in *Seeking a Voice: Images of Race and Gender in the 19th Century Press,* ed. David B. Sachsman, S. Kittrell Rushing, and Roy Morris Jr. (West Lafayette, IN: Purdue University Press, 2009), 257–65; A. D. P. Van Buren, "Memoir of Lois B. Adams—Poet, Editor and Author," *Michigan Pioneer and Historical Collections* 18 (1892): 312–18.

13. Jane E. Schultz, *Women at the Front: Hospital Workers in Civil War America* (Chapel Hill: University of North Carolina Press, 2004), 185–93; "United States Civil War and Later Pension Index, 1861–1917," Hannah L. Carlisle, March 8, 1893, National Archives and Records Administration, Washington, DC.

14. Richard H. Sewell, "Michigan Farmers and the Civil War," *Michigan History* 44 (December 1960): 353–74; Blum, "Guns, Grain, and Iron Ore."

15. *Acts of the Legislature of the State of Michigan, Passed at the Regular and Extra Sessions of 1861* (Lansing: John A. Kerr, 1861), 602–3.

16. Reynolds, "'Destined to Produce.'"

17. Howard Jones, *Blue and Gray Diplomacy: A History of Union and Confederate Foreign Relations* (Chapel Hill: University of North Carolina Press, 2010).

18. Blair's message of January 2, 1862, in *Joint Documents of the State of Michigan for the Year 1861* (Lansing: John A. Kerr, 1862), 4; *Detroit Free Press,* November 9, 1862. These American fears notwithstanding, the British recognized that Canadian defense of an American invasion would be challenging, if not impossible, given the long and porous Canadian border with the United States.

19. Robin W. Winks, *Canada and the United States: The Civil War Years,* 4th ed. (Montreal: McGill-Queen's University Press, 1998), 178–205, makes clear that, despite the difficult relations between the US and Canadian governments, more Canadians volunteered for the Union army than for the Confederates. Phillip Buckner holds that between "thirty-five and fify thousand British Americans fought in the American Civil War, mainly in the northern forces. Buckner, "British North America and a Continent in Dissolution: The American Civil War in the Making of Canadian Confederation," *Journal of the Civil War Era* 7 (December 2017): 527–28.

20. Martin J. Havran, "Windsor and Detroit Relations during the Civil War," *Michigan History* 38 (December 1954): 371–89.

21. Frank B. Woodford, *Father Abraham's Children: Michigan Episodes in the Civil War* (Detroit: Wayne State University Press, 1961), 137–47, 285–89; Winks, *Canada and the United States,* 287–94; Paul Taylor, *"Old Slow Town": Detroit during the Civil War* (Detroit: Wayne State University Press, 2013), 167–74.

22. *Papers Relating to Foreign Affairs, Accompanying the Annual Message of the President to the First Session, Thirty-Ninth Congress,* Part 1 (Washington, DC: Government Printing Office, 1866), 54; James D. Richardson, *A Compilation of the Messages and Papers of the Presidents, 1789–1897* (Washington, DC: Government Printing Office, 1897), 6:282; *Detroit Free Press,* December 23, 1864, January 1, 4, 5, 10, 18, 22, March 10, 1865; *Detroit Advertiser and Tribune,* December 26, 1864, January 2, 10, 14, 16, 27, 30, 1865; John Robertson, *Michigan in the War,* rev. ed. (Lansing: W. S. George, 1882), 485–87; Winks, *Canada and the United States,* 346.

CHAPTER 7: MICHIGAN'S WARTIME POLITICS

1. Martin J. Hershock, *The Paradox of Progress: Economic Change, Individual Enterprise, and the Political Culture in Michigan, 1837–1878* (Athens: Ohio University Press, 2003), 172–76; Harriette M. Dilla, *The Politics of Michigan, 1865–1878* (New York: Columbia University, 1912), 26–27.

2. Jennifer Weber, *Copperheads: The Rise and Fall of Lincoln's Opponents in the North* (New York: Oxford University Press, 2006).

3. *The People on Relation of Daniel S. Twitchell* v. *Amos C. Blodgett,* 13 Mich. 127–186 (1865). The only out-of-state soldier votes counted from the 1864 election were those from the Michigan Fifth Congressional District, which proved to be the winning margin when the US House of Representatives declared Rowland E. Trowbridge victorious over Augustus C. Baldwin in that highly contested race. Josiah Henry Benton,

Voting in the Field: A Forgotten Chapter of the Civil War (Boston: Privately printed, 1915), 130–31.

4. George A. Prescott, comp., *Michigan Official Directory and Legislative Manual for the Years 1907–1908* (Lansing: Wynkoop, Hallenbeck, Crawford, 1907), 404–5.

5. *Adrian Watchtower,* January 28, 1862.

6. Edward Morton is referencing an 1850 Michigan referendum in which 71.5 percent of Michigan voters rejected suffrage for the state's African American males (mentioned in the introduction), and the US Supreme Court's 1857 decision, *Dred Scott v. John F. A. Sandford,* in which Chief Justice Roger B. Taney wrote that people of African ancestry could not claim US citizenship. Later, the US Constitution's Fourteenth Amendment (1868) overturned the citizenship provisions of the *Dred Scott* decision. Don E. Fehrenbacher, *The Dred Scott Case: Its Significance in American Law and Politics* (New York: Oxford University Press, 1978), 346–54, 580–82.

7. "The Democracy" was a term nineteenth-century Americans often used in reference to the Democratic Party.

8. *Ann Arbor Journal,* November 14, 1860.

9. Ezra C. Seaman, *Commentaries on the Constitutions and Laws, Peoples and History, of the United States—Upon the Great Rebellion and Its Causes* (Ann Arbor: The Journal Office, 1863); see also *Ann Arbor Journal,* June 26, 1861.

10. *Detroit Free Press,* September 11, 1864.

11. John Robertson, *Michigan in the War,* rev. ed. (Lansing: W. S. George, 1882), 82–83; *Twitchell* v. *Blodgett,* 13 Mich. 127–186 (1865).

12. For a similar manifesto from African Americans in Ypsilanti, see *Liberator,* July 24, 1863.

CHAPTER 8: THE CIVIL WAR CHANGES
MICHIGANIANS' RELATIONSHIP TO SLAVERY

1. *Congressional Globe,* 37th Congress, 1st Session, 222–23 (July 22, 1861).

2. George P. Sanger, ed., *The Statutes at Large, Treaties, and Proclamations of the United States of America from December 5, 1859, to March 3, 1863* (Boston: Little, Brown, 1863), 319; James Oakes, *Freedom National: The Destruction of Slavery in the United States, 1861–1865* (New York: W. W. Norton, 2013), 93–144, 224–55, 262–77. Michigan's Senator Zachariah Chandler introduced an earlier version of the First Confiscation Act on July 5, 1861. Silvana R. Siddali, *From Property to Person: Slavery and the Confiscation Acts, 1861–1862* (Baton Rouge: Louisiana State University Press, 2005), 57–69, 76–77.

3. *Joint Documents of the State of Michigan for the Year 1861* (Lansing: John A. Kerr, 1862), 10–11.

4. Michael Vorenberg, *Final Freedom: The Civil War, the Abolition of Slavery, and the Thirteenth Amendment* (New York: Cambridge University Press, 2001).

5. The editor's words to the contrary, the Proclamation immediately freed some 50,000 slaves living under Union control. Eric Foner, *The Fiery Trial: Abraham Lincoln and American Slavery* (New York: W. W. Norton, 2010), 243.

6. Jim Downs, *Sick from Freedom: African-American Illness and Suffering during the Civil War and Reconstruction* (New York: Oxford University Press, 2012).

7. *Detroit Free Press,* February 4, 1865; *Journal of the Senate of the State of Michigan, 1865* (Lansing: John A. Kerr, 1865), 300–303, 366–67, 852–58; *Journal of the House of Representatives of the State of Michigan, 1865* (Lansing: John A. Kerr, 1865), 519–25, 634, 688–89.

CHAPTER 9: THE CIVIL WAR'S END AND RECONSTRUCTION

1. President James Buchanan used the term "reconstruction" in his December 3, 1860, annual message to Congress almost three weeks before South Carolina seceded from the Union. James D. Richardson, *A Compilation of the Messages and Papers of the Presidents,* 10 vols. (Washington, DC: Government Printing Office, 1897), 5:637.

2. Jeremy W. Kilar, "Andrew Johnson 'Swings' through Michigan: Community Response to a Presidential Crusade," *The Old Northwest: A Journal of Regional Life and Letters* 3 (September 1977): 251–73.

3. William Henry Glasson, *Federal Military Pensions in the United States* (New York: Oxford University Press, 1918), 246–47.

4. Harriette M. Dilla, *The Politics of Michigan, 1865–1878* (New York: Columbia University, 1912), 62–64, 92; John Robertson, *Michigan in the War,* rev. ed. (Lansing: W. S. George, 1882), 82–83.

5. Dilla, *Politics of Michigan,* 26–29, 59, 62–66, 72, 132–42, 145–47.

6. *Congressional Globe,* 38th Congress, 2nd Session, 1094 (February 25, 1865); *Congressional Globe,* 39th Congress, 1st Session, 2890 (May 30, 1866); Eric Foner, *Reconstruction: America's Unfinished Revolution* (New York: Harper and Row, 1988), 258, 454–55; Dilla, *Politics of Michigan,* 40–54, 72, 84; Martin J. Hershock, *The Paradox of Progress: Economic Change, Individual Enterprise, and the Political Culture in Michigan, 1837–1878* (Athens: Ohio University Press, 2003), 183–92; *Zachariah Chandler: An Outline Sketch of His Life and Public Services* (Detroit: Post and Tribune Company, 1880), 307–8; Wilmer C. Harris, *Public Life of Zachariah Chandler, 1851–1875* (Lansing: Michigan Historical Commission, 1917), 93; Sister Mary Karl George, *Zachariah Chandler: A Political Biography* (East Lansing: Michigan State University Press, 1969), 138–39, 142–62, 191.

7. Richard H. Abbott, *The Republican Party and the South, 1855–1877* (Chapel Hill: University of North Carolina Press, 1986), 137; Dilla, *Politics of Michigan,* 78–82, 90–92, 105–7, 120–23; Hershock, *Paradox of Progress,* 203–7.

8. Paul Finkelman, "The Promise of Equality and the Limits of Law: From the Civil War to World War II," in *The History of Michigan Law,* ed. Paul Finkelman and Martin J. Hershock (Athens: Ohio University Press, 2006), 191–210; David M. Katzman, *Before the Ghetto: Black Detroit in the Nineteenth Century* (Urbana: University of Illinois Press, 1973), 90–103; *Public Acts and Joint and Concurrent Resolutions of the Legislature of the State of Michigan, Passed at the Regular Session of 1885* (Lansing: W. S. George, 1885), 131–32.

9. Hershock, *Paradox of Progress,* 200–216.

10. George P. Sanger, ed., *The Statutes at Large, Treaties, and Proclamations of the United States of America from December, 1865 to March, 1867,* vol. 14 (Boston: Little, Brown, 1868), 428–30.

11. Mrs. Franc L. Adams, ed., *The Pioneer History of Ingham County* (Lansing: Wynkoop Hallenbeck Crawford, 1923), 140.

12. *The Statutes at Large [of] the United States from December 1873 to March 1875,* vol. 18, part 3 (Washington, DC: Government Printing Office, 1875), 335–37; Civil Rights Cases 109 US 3 (1883).

13. *Journal of the House of Representatives of the State of Michigan, 1885*, vol. 1 (Lansing: W. S. George, 1885), 184, 185, 572, 573, 589, 789, 844, 836, 904.

14. Ibid., 1102–3; *Journal of the Senate of the State of Michigan, 1885*, vol. 2 (Lansing: W. S. George, 1885), 1059; *Public Acts and Joint and Concurrent Resolutions of the Legislature of the State of Michigan, Passed at the Regular Session of 1885* (Lansing: W. S. George, 1885), 131–32; Finkelman, "Promise of Equality," 201–8.

15. David W. Blight, *Race and Reunion: The Civil War in American Memory* (Cambridge, MA: Harvard University Press, 2001), 175.

16. A permanent extension of the foot resulting in only the foot's ball resting on the ground.

17. The "engagement at Blue Ridge" probably refers to the Battle of Blackburn's Ford, a skirmish in which the 2nd Michigan fought on July 18, 1861.

18. Germantown refers to a settlement near Manassas Junction, Virginia. See Stephen W. Sears, ed., *For Country, Cause and Leader: The Civil War Journal of Charles B. Haydon* (New York: Ticknor and Fields, 1993), 51–52.

19. Frank B. Woodford, *Father Abraham's Children: Michigan Episodes in the Civil War* (Detroit: Wayne State University Press, 1961), 245–47. Around the time of LeValley's death, Joseph Clovese, a veteran of the 63rd US Colored Infantry, moved to Michigan from Louisiana, and died in 1951. Ibid., 304–5.

Selected Bibliography

PREFACE AND INTRODUCTION

Atack, Jeremy, and Bateman, Fred. "Yankee Farming and Settlement in the Old Northwest: A Comparative Analysis." In *Essays on the Economy of the Old Northwest,* edited by David C. Klingaman and Richard K. Vedder, 77–102. Athens: Ohio University Press, 1987.

Blackburn, George, and Sherman L. Ricards Jr. "A Demographic History of the West: Manistee County, Michigan, 1860." *Journal of American History* 57 (December 1970): 600–618.

Cayton, Andrew R. L., and Peter S. Onuf. *The Midwest and the Nation: Rethinking the History of an American Region.* Bloomington: Indiana University Press, 1990.

Chardavoyne, David G. "The Northwest Ordinance in Michigan's Territorial Heritage." In *The History of Michigan Law,* edited by Paul Finkelman and Martin J. Hershock, 13–36. Athens: Ohio University Press, 2006.

David, Paul A. "The Mechanization of Reaping in the Antebellum Midwest." In *Industrialization in Two Systems: Essays in Honor of Alexander Gerschenkron,* edited by Henry Rosovsky, 3–39. New York: John Wiley and Sons, 1966.

Dillon, Merton L. "Elizabeth Chandler and the Spread of Antislavery Sentiment to Michigan." *Michigan History* 39 (December 1955): 481–94.

Dunbar, Willis F., and George S. May. *Michigan: A History of the Wolverine State.* 3rd rev. ed. Grand Rapids: William B. Eerdmans, 1995.

Finkelman, Paul. *Slavery and the Founders: Race and Slavery in the Age of Jefferson.* Armonk, NY: M. E. Sharpe, 1996.

Finkenbine, Roy E. "A Beacon of Liberty on the Great Lakes: Race, Slavery, and the Law in Antebellum Michigan." In *The History of Michigan Law,* edited by Paul Finkelman and Martin J. Hershock, 83–107. Athens: Ohio University Press, 2006.

Formisano, Ronald P. "The Edge of Caste: Colored Suffrage in Michigan, 1827–1861." *Michigan History* 56 (Spring 1972): 19–41.

Gray, Susan E. *The Yankee West: Community Life on the Michigan Frontier.* Chapel Hill: University of North Carolina Press, 1996.

Hershock, Martin J. "'Free Commoners by Law': Tradition, Transition, and the Closing of the Range in Antebellum Michigan." *Michigan Historical Review* 29 (Fall 2003): 97–123.

Kooker, Arthur Raymond. "The Antislavery Movement in Michigan, 1796–1840: A Study of Humanitarianism on an American Frontier." PhD dissertation, University of Michigan, 1941.

Michigan Department of Transportation. *Michigan's Railroad History, 1825–2014.* Lansing: Michigan Department of Transportation, 2014.

Quist, John W. "An Occasionally Dry State Surrounded by Water: Temperance and Prohibition in Antebellum Michigan." In *The History of Michigan Law*, edited by Paul Finkelman and Martin J. Hershock, 61–82. Athens: Ohio University Press, 2006.

Rose, Gregory S. "South Central Michigan Yankees." *Michigan History* 70 (March–April 1986): 32–39.

Sinha, Manisha. *The Slave's Cause: A History of Abolition*. New Haven: Yale University Press, 2016.

Taber, Morris C. "New England Influence in South Central Michigan." *Michigan History* 45 (December 1961): 305–36.

CHAPTER 1: MICHIGAN, SLAVERY, AND THE
COMING OF THE CIVIL WAR

Blue, Frederick J. *The Free Soilers: Third Party Politics, 1848–1854*. Urbana: University of Illinois Press, 1973.

Charnley, Jeffrey G. "'Swords into Plowshares,' A Hope Unfulfilled: Michigan Opposition to the Mexican War, 1846–1848." *The Old Northwest: A Journal of Regional Life and Letters* 8 (Fall 1982): 199–222.

Foner, Eric. *Free Soil, Free Labor, Free Men: The Ideology of the Republican Party before the Civil War*. New York: Oxford University Press, 1970.

Formisano, Ronald P. *The Birth of Mass Political Parties: Michigan, 1827–1861*. Princeton, NJ: Princeton University Press, 1971.

Gienapp, William E. *The Origins of the Republican Party, 1852–1856*. New York: Oxford University Press, 1987.

Grinspan, Jon. "'Young Men for War': The Wide Awakes and Lincoln's 1860 Presidential Campaign." *Journal of American History* 96 (September 2009): 357–78.

Holt, Michael F. *The Political Crisis of the 1850s*. New York: John Wiley and Sons, 1978.

———. *The Election of 1860: "A Campaign Fraught with Consequences."* Lawrence: University of Kansas Press, 2017.

Howe, Daniel Walker. "The Evangelical Movement and Political Culture in the North during the Second Party System." *Journal of American History* 78 (March 1991): 1216–39.

———. *What Hath God Wrought: The Transformation of America, 1815–1848*. New York: Oxford University Press, 2007.

Johannsen, Robert W. *Stephen A. Douglas*. New York: Oxford University Press, 1973.

Johnson, Reinhard O. *The Liberty Party, 1840–1848: Antislavery Third-Party Politics in the United States*. Baton Rouge: Louisiana State University Press, 2009.

Klunder, Willard Carl. *Lewis Cass and the Politics of Moderation*. Kent, OH: Kent State University Press, 1996.

McDaid, William. "Kinsley S. Bingham and the Republican Ideology of Antislavery, 1847–1855." *Michigan Historical Review* 16 (Fall 1990): 43–73.

Potter, David M. *The Impending Crisis, 1848–1861*. New York: Harper and Row, 1976.

Quist, John W. "'The Great Majority of Our Subscribers Are Farmers': The Michigan Abolitionist Constituency of the 1840s." *Journal of the Early Republic* 14 (Fall 1994): 325–58.

———. *Restless Visionaries: The Social Roots of Antebellum Reform in Alabama and Michigan*. Baton Rouge: Louisiana State University Press, 1998.

Rosentreter, Roger L. "Michigan and the Compromise of 1850." *The Old Northwest: A Journal of Regional Life and Letters* 6 (Summer 1980): 153–73.

Seavoy, Ronald E. "The Organization of the Republican Party in Michigan, 1846–1854." *The Old Northwest: A Journal of Regional Life and Letters* 6 (Winter 1980–81): 343–76.

Sewell, Richard H. *Ballots for Freedom: Antislavery Politics in the United States, 1837–1860.* New York: Oxford University Press, 1976.

Towers, Frank. "Partisans, New History, and Modernization: The Historiography of the Civil War's Causes, 1861–2011." *Journal of the Civil War Era* 1 (June 2011): 237–64.

Volpe, Vernon L. *Forlorn Hope of Freedom: The Liberty Party in the Old Northwest, 1838–1848.* Kent, OH: Kent State University Press, 1990.

Wilentz, Sean. *The Rise of American Democracy: Jefferson to Lincoln.* New York: W. W. Norton, 2005.

CHAPTER 2: THE SECESSION CRISIS

Abrahamson, James L. *The Men of Secession and the Civil War, 1859–1861.* Wilmington, DE: Scholarly Resources, 2000.

Current, Richard N. *Lincoln and the First Shot.* Philadelphia: J. B. Lippincott, 1963.

Dumond, Dwight L. *The Secession Movement, 1860–1861.* New York: Macmillan, 1931.

Egerton, Douglas R. *Year of Meteors: Stephen Douglas, Abraham Lincoln, and the Election That Brought on the Civil War.* New York: Bloomsbury, 2010.

Freehling, William W. *The Road to Disunion.* Volume 2: *Secessionists Triumphant.* New York: Oxford University Press, 2007.

Gunderson, Robert Gray. *Old Gentleman's Convention: The Washington Peace Conference of 1861.* Madison: University of Wisconsin Press, 1961.

Klein, Maury. *Days of Defiance: Sumter, Secession, and the Coming of the Civil War.* New York: Alfred A. Knopf, 1997.

McClintock, Russell. *Lincoln and the Decision for War: The Northern Response to Secession.* Chapel Hill: University of North Carolina Press, 2008.

Potter, David M. *Lincoln and His Party in the Secession Crisis.* New Haven: Yale University Press, 1942.

Quist, John W., and Michael J. Birkner. *James Buchanan and the Coming of the Civil War.* Gainesville: University Press of Florida, 2013.

Stampp, Kenneth M. *And the War Came: The North and the Secession Crisis, 1860–1861.* Baton Rouge: Louisiana State University Press, 1950.

Thornton, J. Mills III. *Politics and Power in a Slave Society: Alabama, 1800–1860.* Baton Rouge: Louisiana State University Press, 1978.

Williams, Frederick D. "Robert McClelland and the Secession Crisis." *Michigan History* 43 (June 1959): 155–64.

CHAPTER 3: SHIFTING MICHIGAN TO A WAR FOOTING

Bak, Richard. *A Distant Thunder: Michigan in the Civil War.* Ann Arbor: Huron River Press, 2004.

Dempsey, Jack. *Michigan and the Civil War: A Great and Bloody Sacrifice.* Charleston, SC: History Press, 2011.

Destler, Chester McArthur, ed. "The Second Michigan Volunteer Infantry Joins the Army of the Potomac: Letters of Philo H. Gallup." *Michigan History* 41 (December 1957): 385–412.

Long, E. B., with Barbara Long. *The Civil War Day by Day: An Almanac, 1861–1865.* New York: Doubleday, 1971.

Mason, Philip P., and Paul J. Pentecost. *From Bull Run to Appomattox: Michigan's Role in the Civil War.* Detroit: Wayne State University Division of Publications, 1961.

McPherson, James M. *Battle Cry of Freedom: The Civil War Era.* New York: Oxford University Press, 1988.

Robertson, John. *Michigan in the War.* Rev. ed. Lansing: W. S. George, 1882.

Simpson, Brooks D., Stephen W. Sears, and Aaron Sheehan-Dean, eds. *The Civil War: The First Year Told by Those Who Lived It.* New York: Library of America, 2011.

Woodford, Frank B. *Father Abraham's Children: Michigan Episodes in the Civil War.* Detroit: Wayne State University Press, 1961.

CHAPTER 4: THE SOLDIER'S LIFE

Dean, Eric T., Jr. "'A Scene of Surpassing Terror and Awful Grandeur': The Paradoxes of Military Service in the American Civil War." *Michigan Historical Review* 21 (Fall 1995): 37–61.

Egerton, Douglas R. *Thunder at the Gates: The Black Civil War Regiments That Redeemed America.* New York: Basic Books, 2016.

Fellman, Michael, Lesley J. Gordon, and Daniel E. Sutherland. *This Terrible War: The Civil War and Its Aftermath.* New York: Longman, 2003.

Leonard, Elizabeth D. *All the Daring of the Solider: Women of the Civil War Armies.* New York: Norton, 1999.

Linderman, Gerald F. *Embattled Courage: The Experience of Combat in the American Civil War.* New York: Free Press, 1987.

Longacre, Edward G. *Custer and His Wolverines: The Michigan Cavalry Brigade, 1861–1865.* Conshohocken, PA: Combined Publishing, 1997.

Manning, Chandra. *What This Cruel War Was Over: Soldiers, Slavery, and the Civil War.* New York: Random House, 2008.

McPherson, James M. *For Cause and Comrades: Why Men Fought in the Civil War.* New York: Oxford University Press, 1997.

———. *The Negro's Civil War: How American Negroes Felt and Acted during the War for the Union.* New York: Pantheon, 1965.

———. *Ordeal By Fire: The Civil War and Reconstruction.* 3rd ed. New York: McGraw Hill, 2001.

Nolan, Alan T. *The Iron Brigade: A Military History.* 4th ed. Bloomington: Indiana University Press, 1994.

Quaife, Milo M., ed. *From the Cannon's Mouth: The Civil War Letters of General Alpheus S. Williams.* Detroit: Wayne State University Press, 1959.

Rosentreter, Roger L., ed. *Michigan and the Civil War: An Anthology.* Lansing: Michigan Department of State, 1999.

Sears, Stephen W., ed. *For Country, Cause and Leader: The Civil War Journal of Charles B. Haydon.* New York: Ticknor and Fields, 1993.

Williams, Frederick D. *Michigan Soldiers in the Civil War*. Fifth Edition. Lansing: Michigan Department of History, Arts, and Libraries, 2002.

CHAPTER 5: CONSCRIPTION, COMMUTATION, AND DISSENT

Blair, William A. *With Malice toward Some: Treason and Loyalty in the Civil War Era*. Chapel Hill: University of North Carolina Press, 2014.

Geary, James W. *We Need Men: The Union Draft in the Civil War*. DeKalb: Northern Illinois University Press, 1991.

Klement, Frank L. *The Copperheads in the Middle West*. Chicago: University of Chicago Press, 1960.

———. "The Hopkins Hoax and Golden Circle Rumors in Michigan: 1861–1862." *Michigan History* 47 (March 1963): 1–14.

Murdock, Eugene Converse. *One Million Men: The Civil War Draft in the North*. Madison: State Historical Society of Wisconsin, 1971.

———. *Patriotism Limited, 1862–1865: The Civil War Draft and Bounty System*. Kent, OH: Kent State University Press, 1967.

Neely, Mark E., Jr. *The Fate of Liberty: Abraham Lincoln and Civil Liberties*. New York: Oxford University Press, 1991.

Schneider, John C. "Detroit and the Problem of Disorder: The Riot of 1863." *Michigan History* 58 (Spring 1974): 5–24.

Weber, Jennifer. *Copperheads: The Rise and Fall of Lincoln's Opponents in the North*. New York: Oxford University Press, 2006.

White, Jonathan W. *Abraham Lincoln and Treason in the Civil War: The Trials of John Merryman*. Baton Rouge: Louisiana State University Press, 2011.

CHAPTER 6: CIVILIANS CONFRONT THE WAR

Adams, Lois Bryan. *Letter from Washington, 1863–1865*. Edited by Evelyn Leasher. Detroit: Wayne State University Press, 1999.

Blum, Albert A. "Guns, Grain, and Iron Ore." *Michigan History* 69 (May/June 1985): 13–20.

Buckner, Phillip. "British North America and a Continent in Dissolution: The American Civil War in the Making of Canadian Confederation." *Journal of the Civil War Era* 7 (December 2017): 512–40.

Gates, William B., Jr. *Michigan Copper and Boston Dollars: An Economic History of the Michigan Copper Mining Industry*. Cambridge, MA: Harvard University Press, 1951.

Havran, Martin J. "Windsor and Detroit Relations during the Civil War." *Michigan History* 38 (December 1954): 371–89.

Leonard, Elizabeth. *Yankee Women: Gender Battles in the Civil War*. New York: W. W. Norton, 1994.

Paludan, Phillip Shaw. *A People's Contest: The Union and Civil War, 1861–1865*. New York: Harper and Row, 1988.

Reynolds, Terry. "'Destined to Produce [a] . . . Revolution': Michigan's Iron Ore Industry in the Civil War." *Michigan Historical Review* 39 (Fall 2013): 21–49.

Schultz, Jane E. *Women at the Front: Hospital Workers in Civil War America*. Chapel Hill: University of North Carolina Press, 2004.

Sewell, Richard H. "Michigan Farmers and the Civil War." *Michigan History* 44 (December 1960): 353–74.

Spiro, Robert. "History of the Michigan Soldiers' Aid Society, 1861–1865." PhD dissertation, University of Michigan, 1959.

Taylor, Paul. *"Old Slow Town": Detroit during the Civil War.* Detroit: Wayne State University Press, 2013.

Winks, Robin W. *Canada and the United States: The Civil War Years.* 4th ed. Montreal: McGill-Queen's University Press, 1998.

CHAPTER 7: MICHIGAN'S WARTIME POLITICS

Baker, Jean H. *Affairs of Party: The Political Character of Northern Democrats in the Mid-Nineteenth Century.* Ithaca: Cornell University Press, 1983.

Benton, Josiah Henry. *Voting in the Field: A Forgotten Chapter of the Civil War.* Boston: Privately printed, 1915.

Bogue, Allan G. *The Earnest Men: Republicans of the Civil War Senate.* Ithaca, NY: Cornell University Press, 1981.

Fehrenbacher, Don E. *The Dred Scott Case: Its Significance in American Law and Politics.* New York: Oxford University Press, 1978.

Gallagher, Gary W. *The Union War.* Cambridge, MA: Harvard University Press, 2011.

Harris, Robert C. "Austin Blair of Michigan: A Political Biography." PhD dissertation, Michigan State University, 1969.

Hershock, Martin J. *The Paradox of Progress: Economic Change, Individual Enterprise, and Political Culture in Michigan, 1837–1878.* Athens: Ohio University Press, 2003.

Long, David E. *The Jewel of Liberty: Abraham Lincoln's Re-election and the End of Slavery.* Mechanicsburg, PA: Stackpole Books, 1994.

Neely, Mark E., Jr. *Lincoln and the Democrats: The Politics of Opposition in the Civil War.* New York: Cambridge University Press, 2017.

———. *The Union Divided: Party Conflict in the Civil War North.* Cambridge, MA: Harvard University Press, 2002.

Richardson, Heather Cox. *The Greatest Nation of the Earth: Republican Economic Policies during the Civil War.* Cambridge, MA: Harvard University Press, 1997.

Silbey, Joel H. *A Respectable Minority: The Democratic Party in the Civil War Era, 1860–1868.* New York: W. W. Norton, 1977.

White, Jonathan. *Emancipation, the Union Army, and the Reelection of Abraham Lincoln.* Baton Rouge: Louisiana State University Press, 2014.

CHAPTER 8: THE CIVIL WAR CHANGES
MICHIGANIANS' RELATIONSHIP TO SLAVERY

Blackburn, George M., ed. "The Negro as Viewed by a Michigan Civil War Soldier: Letters of John C. Buchanan." *Michigan History* 47 (April 1963): 75–84.

Furman, Jan, ed. *Slavery in the Clover Bottoms: John McCline's Narrative of His Life during Slavery and the Civil War.* Knoxville: University of Tennessee Press, 1998.

Guelzo, Allen C. *Lincoln's Emancipation Proclamation: The End of Slavery in America.* New York: Simon and Schuster, 2004.

Katzman, David N. *Before the Ghetto: Black Detroit in the Nineteenth Century.* Urbana: University of Illinois Press, 1973.

McPherson, James M. *The Struggle for Equality: Abolitionists and the Negro in the Civil War and Reconstruction.* Princeton: Princeton University Press, 1964.

McRae, Norman. *Negroes in Michigan during the Civil War.* Lansing: Michigan Civil War Centennial Observance Commission, 1966.

Oakes, James. *Freedom National: The Destruction of Slavery in the United States, 1861–1865.* New York: W. W. Norton, 2013.

Siddali, Silvana R. *From Property to Person: Slavery and the Confiscation Acts, 1861–1862.* Baton Rouge: Louisiana State University Press, 2005.

Smith, Michael O. "Raising a Black Regiment in Michigan: Adversity and Triumph." *Michigan Historical Review* 16 (Fall 1990): 23–42.

Vorenberg, Michael. *Final Freedom: The Civil War, the Abolition of Slavery, and the Thirteenth Amendment.* New York: Cambridge University Press, 2001.

CHAPTER 9: THE CIVIL WAR'S END AND RECONSTRUCTION

Blackburn, George M. "Michigan: Quickening Government in a Developing State." In *Radical Republicans in the North: State Politics during Reconstruction,* edited by James C. Mohr, 119–43. Baltimore: Johns Hopkins University Press, 1976.

Blight, David W. *Race and Reunion: The Civil War in American Memory.* Cambridge, MA: Harvard University Press, 2001.

Brown, Thomas J., ed. *Reconstructions: New Perspectives in the Postbellum United States.* New York: Oxford University Press, 2006.

Dilla, Harriette M. *The Politics of Michigan, 1865–1878.* New York: Columbia University, 1912.

Dunbar, Willis, and William G. Shade. "The Black Man Gains the Vote: The Centennial of 'Impartial Suffrage' in Michigan." *Michigan History* 56 (Spring 1972): 42–57.

Finkelman, Paul. "The Promise of Equality and the Limits of Law: From the Civil War to World War II." In *The History of Michigan Law,* edited by Paul Finkelman and Martin J. Hershock, 191–210. Athens: Ohio University Press, 2006.

Foner, Eric. *Reconstruction: America's Unfinished Revolution.* New York: Harper and Row, 1988.

George, Sister Mary Karl. *Zachariah Chandler: A Political Biography.* East Lansing: Michigan State University Press, 1969.

Glasson, William Henry. *Federal Military Pensions in the United States.* New York: Oxford University Press, 1918.

Jordan, Brian Matthew. *Marching Home: Union Veterans and Their Unending Civil War.* New York: W.W. Norton, 2014.

Kilar, Jeremy W. "Andrew Johnson 'Swings' through Michigan: Community Response to a Presidential Crusade." *The Old Northwest: A Journal of Regional Life and Letters* 3 (September 1977): 251–73.

McConnell, Stuart. *Glorious Contentment: The Grand Army of the Republic, 1865–1900.* Chapel Hill: University of North Carolina Press, 1992.

Slap, Andrew L. *The Doom of Reconstruction: The Liberal Republicans in the Civil War Era.* New York: Fordham University Press, 2007.

Index

Page numbers in italics denote illustrations.

Richards, John D., 141
Richardson, Israel, 79
Richardson, John H., 91
Richmond, VA, 18, 54, 58, 100, 107, 125, 126, 160, 165, 199, 200, 201, 202, 205, 206
Ridley, Bob, 92
Robertson, John, 38, 102, 203, 221n1, 221n10
Rochester, PA, 47
Rockwell, E. S., 191
Russell, Francis G., 43–44

Saginaw, MI, 1, 90–91, 91, 92, 191
Saginaw County, MI, 123
Sand Beach Township, MI, 93
Sandusky, OH, 118–19
Sanitary Commission, United States, 97, 107–8. *See also* Michigan Soldiers' Aid Society
Sault Ste. Marie, MI, 91–92, 195
Scott, Winfield, 132, 199
Seaman, Ezra C., 136–37
secession crisis, 17, 26–37, 43, 50, 177, 197–98; Democratic reactions, 26, 30–32, 36; Republican reactions, 26–29, 34–35
Seward, William H., 23, 25, 36, 94, 120, 131, 145, 197, 205, 208, 220n
Shenandoah Valley, VA, 54, 160, 204
Sheridan, Philip, 160, 185, 204
Sherman, William Tecumseh, 54, 160, 204, 205, 206
Shiloh, 64–66, 90, 200
Signal of Liberty, 32, 130, 190, 192
Singleton, Benjamin, 88
Slaughterhouse Cases (1873), 209
slavery, 2, 5–24; as a cause of sectional conflict, xvii–xviii, 3, 5–7, 10–24, 27–28, 30–31, 32–33; fugitives from, 7–9, 15, 16–17, 19, 28, 143, 154, 193, 194, 219n
smallpox, 56, 112
Smith, E. Kirby, 206
Smith, Randolph, 96
Soerl, George, 179
soldiers: anger toward unpatriotic civilians, 63, 75; behavior and morals, 57–58, 63; bounties, 59, 60, 62–63, 84–85, 88–89, 90–91, 98, 99, 105; camp life and, 56–58, 63; combat descriptions, 65–73, 81–82; death notifications of, 59; disabled, 47, 52, 78, 161, 181–82, 222n; enlistment and recruitment of, 38, 39–40, 42, 45–47, 52,

53, 54, 55, 59, 60, 61–62, 63–64, 68, 78–79, 81, 83, 84, 85, 86, 88, 89, 90–91, 98, 99, 105, 115, 134, 138, 148, 150, 151, 152, 153, 169, 183, 202, 221n, 221–22n; informal truces, 64, 74; irregular compensation, 76–77; paroling prisoners of war, 58; reenlistment and, 61–63; tensions between officers and enlisted, 77; traveling to the front, 47–48; selecting officers, 44–45
Soldiers' Relief Law, 115, 198
Southerners (white), as fellow Americans, 31–32
Spalding, William, 91
Spaulding, Lilburn A., 70
Spicer, Daniel A., 129
Spotsylvania, 79, 83
Sprague, Thomas S., 92
Stagg, Peter, 73
St. Albans, VT, 120, 204, 205
Stanton, Edwin, 81, 116, 131, 166, 200, 202
St. Clair County, MI, 123
Stephens (Stevens), Ambrose A., 78
Stewart, Duncan, 102–3
St. Johns, MI, 109
St. Joseph, MI, 38
Stones River, Battle of, TN, 90, 201
Storey, Wilbur, 36
Stoughton, William L., 174–76
Stowers, Walter H., 179
strikes (labor stoppages), 99, 101, 102, 116–17, 204
Strong, Rev. A. K., 57–58
Stuart, J. E. B., 72–73, 223n
substitutes. *See* conscription
suffrage, African American male, 3, 24, 141–42, 161, 162, 163, 164, 172, 175, 207, 211, 227n; 1850 Michigan referendum, 3, 128, 193, 227n; proposed 1867 Michigan constitution, 162–63; Fifteenth Amendment, 163; 1870 Michigan referendum, 163, 208
Swineford, Alfred, 101–2

Taney, Roger B., 128, 227
Tappan, Henry, 37
Taylor, John, 173–74
Taylor, Zachary, 11, 193
Texas annexation, 5, 191, 192